KLUWER EUROPEAN LAW COLLECTION – 2

FREE MOVEMENT OF PERSONS IN THE EUROPEAN UNION

Kluwer European Law Collection

LIST OF PUBLICATIONS IN THIS SERIES

EUROPEAN LAW COLLECTION

1. E. Guild: *The Legal Elements of European Identity: EU Citizenship and Migration Law.* 2004. ISBN: 9041123040

Published by:
Kluwer Law International
P.O. Box 316
2400 AH Alphen aan den Rijn
The Netherlands
E-mail: sales@kluwerlaw.com
Website: http://www.kluwerlaw.com

Sold and distributed in North, Central and South America by:
Aspen Publishers, Inc.
7201 Mc Kinney Circle
Frederick, MD 21704
United States of America

Sold and distributed in all other countries by:
Turpin Distribution Services Ltd.
Stratton Business Park
Pegasus Drive, Biggleswade
Bedfordshire SG18 8TQ
United Kingdom

ISBN 9789041124708

KLUWER EUROPEAN LAW COLLECTION – 2

FREE MOVEMENT OF PERSONS IN THE EUROPEAN UNION

Barriers to Movement in their Constitutional Context

By

Dr Eleanor Spaventa

Durham University, Director of the Durham European Law Institute

KLUWER LAW
INTERNATIONAL

Chapter 2. Exploding the Boundaries: The Case Law on the Free Movement of Services in the 1990s and Beyond 35
1. The Free Movement of Goods – the Sunday Trading Saga and the *Keck* Ruling 36
2. Non-discriminatory Barriers to the Provision of Cross-Border Services 42
3. (Un)Lawfully Providing a Service? Challenging the Rules of the State of Establishment 44
4. The Health Care Cases and the Definition of a Service Provided for Remuneration 50
5. A Critical Analysis of the Court's Reasoning 54
6. The Authorization Requirement 58
7. Conclusions 60

Chapter 3. Barriers to the Free Movement of Workers and Establishment Beyond Discrimination 63
1. Non-discriminatory Restrictions to Freedom of Establishment and the Free Movement of Workers 64
2. The Post-*Gebhard* Case Law 68
3. The Case Law on Free Movement of Capital 70
4. The *Gebhard* Test, Tax and Social Security Rules 71
5. Conclusions 73

Chapter 4. Providing a Framework to the Free Movement Provisions: The Narrow Approach 75
1. Discrimination, Double Burden and Mutual Recognition 77
2. The Mutual Recognition Approach 80
3. The Narrow Approach as a Prescriptive Model 84
4. Conclusions 88

Chapter 5. Market Access: A Concept in Search of a Definition 89
1. Market Access as (Almost) a Descriptive Model: The Case Law on Persons 90
2. Market Access: A Concept in Search of a Definition? 93
3. Substantial Hindrances to Market Access: An Intuitive View? 95
4. The *Gebhard* (R)evolution 99
5. Formal Restrictions to Market Access: Not All that Glitters is Gold 102
6. Market Access and the Internal Market 105
   6.1. Formal Barriers and Absolute Bans 105
   6.2. Formal Barriers and Internal Market 106
   6.3. Formal Barriers and Movement 108
7. Conclusions 110

Table of Contents

Foreword ix

Acknowledgements xi

Introduction xiii

Chapter 1. The Rights of Economic Migrants: An Overview 1

1. The Personal Scope of the (Economic) Free Movement Provisions 2
   - 1.1. Article 39 EC and the Definition of 'Worker' 2
     - 1.1.1. Work Seekers 4
     - 1.1.2. When can Article 39 EC be Invoked? 6
   - 1.2. The Personal Scope of Article 43 EC 6
   - 1.3. The Personal Scope of Article 49 EC and the Notion of 'Service' 7
2. The Material Scope of the Free Movement of Persons Provisions: The Rights Granted by the Treaty 11
   - 2.1. The Right to Leave, Enter, Stay and Move 12
     - 2.1.1. The Right of Residence 14
   - 2.2. The Right Not to be Discriminated Against 16
     - 2.2.1. Direct Discrimination 17
     - 2.2.2. Indirect Discrimination 20
3. Examples of Indirect Discrimination in the Context of Free Movement 24
4. Indirect Discrimination and the Free Movement of Services: Mutual Recognition and Double Burden 26
5. The Scope of the Principle of Non-discrimination 27
6. The Family of the Economic Migrant 30
7. Conclusions 32

Chapter 6. Union Citizenship 113
1. From *Sala* to *Baumbast*: The Tortuous Path Towards Union Citizenship 115
2. The Right to Challenge National Rules Falling Within the Scope of the Treaty and Beyond 123
3. Mr Carpenter as a Citizen 126
3.1. The Purely Internal Situation 127
3.2. Giving Effect to Article 17 EC 128
3.3. The Elimination of Reverse Discrimination – Articles 17 and 12 EC 132
4. Conclusions 133

Chapter 7. Mr Gebhard Meets Mr Baumbast: Towards a More Coherent Theory of Free Movement 135
1. Union Citizenship and the Other Free Movement of Persons' Provisions: Creating the 'Fundamental Status' of Union Citizens 137
2. Similarities in Interpretation: The Hermeneutic Technique Adopted by the Court 138
3. Mr Gebhard Meets Mr Baumbast: Towards a Coherent Constitutional Framework 142
3.1. A Right to Exercise an Economic Activity in Another Member State 143
3.2. The *Gebhard* Case Law 146
3.3. The Different Approach Adopted in Relation to Tax Rules 148
4. Seeking Consistency – the Case Law, the Treaty and the Cross-Border Element 149
4.1. The Cross-Border Element 150
5. Conclusions 153

Table of Cases 157

Bibliography 167

Index 177

Foreword

It gives me great pleasure to contribute a foreword to this particular addition to the Kluwer European Law Collection – a series made up of what Andrea Biondi has described as 'state of the art publications focused on specialised areas of EU law'. This book meets that description in full. It addresses the European Court's interpretation of the Treaty provisions on free movement of persons and services and in particular the evolution of the Court's jurisprudence on non discriminatory restrictions on these fundamental freedoms. The case law of the Court holds a wide range of national measures to comprise restrictions on fundamental freedoms requiring justification – from economic regulation of various kinds, to the deportation of the spouse of a service provider resident in his own country of nationality. The writer convincingly argues that the effect of the developing case law is to abolish the distinction between restrictions on cross border economic activity, and restrictions on economic activity *per se*. The seminal cases on Union Citizenship are addressed at length, and it is by reference to the establishment of Union Citizenship that Dr Spaventa explains and relates developments in the rights to freedom of movement of economically active and economically inactive persons. This is an impressive work of scholarship which provides not only detailed and rigorous analysis of an extensive case law, but also a normative justification for that case law and the direction of its evolution in recent years.

Professor Derrick Wyatt QC
Oxford, June 2007

A nonna, mamma e papà
Miei modelli di vita.

Acknowledgments

This book is partially the result of doctoral research started at Oxford, and completed at Cambridge. Whilst engaged in this project I have had the benefit of working in different institutions (Cambridge, Birmingham and Durham) with wonderful and inspirational colleagues, with whom I have had very fruitful discussions on all matters concerning European law and beyond.

My utmost gratitude goes to Professor Bernard Rudden and to Professor Derrick Wyatt. Professor Rudden started me in my doctoral adventure. He taught me self-discipline and, I hope, academic rigour. When Professor Rudden retired, he left me in the very capable hands of Professor Wyatt, whose knowledge and experience are invaluable. Professor Wyatt has been an exceptional academic supervisor. He engaged with me in long academic discussions – much beyond the call of duty – and read my work within hours. He has guided me in all matters academic and working with him, on the doctorate first and on the new edition of Wyatt and Dashwood' EU law later, has enriched me both professionally and personally. I am grateful to Professor Stephen Weatherill and to Professor Takis Tridimas, who examined my doctoral thesis, and provided me with valuable and stimulating comments.

I am thankful to Professor Andrea Biondi, who provided support and advice, and to Catherine Barnard who has been a wonderful colleague at Cambridge, and also provided me with very insightful comments on some parts of this book. And I am grateful to Professor Alan Dashwood and Professor Tony Arnull, who have been kind and intellectually stimulating colleagues.

I am greatly indebted to Michael Dougan. Our endless discussions on European law have enriched me immensely, and his comments have been essential in shaping and refining my arguments. Michael has also been a tireless proof-reader. But most of all, Michael is an exceptional friend, and my dearest ciccio. His support has helped me beyond description, and for his friendship and kindness I will never be grateful enough.

But I am a very lucky person and a number of people have helped me keeping my sanity. My gratitude goes to Neelam Srivastava and Ilaria Esposito, both friends from way back. Neelam and I shared this experience throughout, and I am sure the telephone companies benefited almost as much as I did from our closeness. Ilaria has managed to be present even though she lives in another country, again to the great advantage of telephone companies. But there were many: Guy Kahane and Dorota Ostrowska, patient and valuable friends. My Cambridge supporters – Rosy Thornton, who started as being my boss, to become a dear friend; both Rosy and Mike Gross provided me with excellent food and wine, companionship and support; Zahid and Olivia Kesselring Durrani, who have been always there for me; Pierpaolo Antonello who gave me intellectual respite. Francesca Sicilia and Luca Federici who would change their dining schedule just to suit mine. I am grateful to Luisa whose supply of home made pesto and polpettine helped me survive in the busiest periods and finally, I am grateful to Simon who holds my hand when I need it, and has resisted the temptation to strangle me when I deserved it.

An Italian, by definition, needs family as much as friends, and, Diana and George Abbott, my aunt and uncle, provided me with unqualified support and love, with food and wine, with all that an Italian abroad needs. But my biggest thanks go to my parents without whom all of this would have not happened. My mother, Clare Royce, whose idea it was that I came to Britain, and my father, Luigi Spaventa, who made sure that my mother's idea could be realised. I am grateful for their love, their kindness, their unquestioning support. But most of all I am grateful for all that they taught me and for the example they are to me.

Even an Italian needs more than emotional and academic support, and both Italian and British institutions have been generous in providing me with what friends and family could not provide. I am indebted to the Università La Sapienza in Rome, to the Italian Research Council (CNR), to the British Academy (now AHRC), and to Somerville College Oxford, for providing funding. I am also indebted to New Hall, the Law Faculty at Cambridge University, the School of Law at the University of Birmingham and the Department of Law at Durham University, for providing me with facilities and a stimulating environment.

Finally, I am very grateful to the Kluwer Law International's editorial team, and in particular to Karel van der Linde, Femke Feenstra, Hanneke Verbeek, and John O'Brien for their patience (stretched beyond reasonable limits) and their help.

This book is dedicated to my grandmother, Lydia de Novellis, who saw the start of this project but was not patient enough to see it finished; and to my parents, Luigi and Clare.

Introduction

This book analyzes the scope of the free movement of persons provisions focusing in particular on the notion of barrier to movement. The primary aim of the investigation is to assess whether we can provide a satisfactory conceptual and normative explanation for the broad interpretation given by the Court to those provisions.

The freedom of movement for workers, the freedom of establishment and the freedom to provide services across the Community, together with the free movement of goods and the free movement of capital with which this book is only tangentially concerned, are at the cornerstone of the internal market. Those provisions grant to economically active citizens, i.e., those who are engaged in an economic activity, rights of movement and an extensive right to equal treatment in all matters relating, even indirectly, to their status as economic actors.

The Court has interpreted those freedoms as fundamental Community rights and it has, accordingly, adopted hermeneutic tools typical of rights discourse. Thus, from a very early stage in the integration process, it has adopted a teleological rather than literal interpretation of the Treaty, seeking to maximise the useful effect of the free movement provisions. It has broadly interpreted the rights that economic migrants derive from the Treaty, whilst at the same time interpreting narrowly the possible grounds of derogation that the Member States could invoke to limit those rights. It has given a broad interpretation to the notion of discrimination, including in its scope both direct discrimination (discrimination in law) and indirect discrimination (discrimination in fact). Direct discrimination can be justified only having regard to one of the grounds listed by the Treaty. Indirect discrimination, which has been broadly construed to include any rule which might put nationals of another Member State, or migrants, at a disadvantage, can be justified having regard to broader public interest aims.

Thus, any imperative requirement of public interest, save for those of a purely economic nature, might be relied upon to justify an indirectly discriminatory rule.

However, the Court has imposed upon the Member States significant constraints. In order to be compatible with Community law, the rule pursuing an imperative requirement of public interest must be necessary to achieve the purposed aim, and the restriction that the rule imposes on the free movement right must be proportionate to the achievement of such public interest. Furthermore, the rule restricting a Community freedom must also comply with the general principles of Community law and in particular with fundamental rights.

The imperative requirements doctrine therefore subjects the rules caught by the Treaty to an extensive judicial scrutiny, allowing the national and Community courts a power of review over the *way* a public interest in pursued, as well as imposing a Community standard of fundamental rights protection. Such power of judicial review is not particularly problematic in relation to indirectly discriminatory rules. After all, given the Treaty commitment to the elimination of any discrimination on grounds of nationality, as indicated both in the free movement provisions and in the general prohibition of such discrimination contained in Article 12 EC, it is natural that when a rule places at a disadvantage migrants or nationals from another Member State, then such rule should be justified or should be redrafted so that any discrimination is eliminated. Here, the Treaty rules impinge on national regulatory autonomy only by requiring the abolition of any unjustified discrimination. However, lacking discrimination, the Member State remains entirely free to decide upon the level of market regulation as well as to decide how best to pursue its policy aims.

The situation is more problematic once the scope of the Treaty free movement provisions is broadened to include non-discriminatory restrictions. In the 1990s, the Court changed its interpretation of the notion of barrier to movement so as to include not only directly and indirectly discriminatory restrictions, but also any rule which hinders or otherwise discourages movement between Member States. The expansion of the material scope of the Treaty free movement provisions is sided by other two developments: the relaxation of the intra-Community link required to trigger the Treaty; and the relaxation of the economic nexus necessary for the Treaty free movement of services provisions to apply.

As a result of those developments, an increasing number of national rules might fall within the scope of the Treaty, and be subject to the necessity and proportionality test required by the imperative requirements doctrine. National regulatory autonomy is therefore greatly affected: choices which traditionally pertained to national (and Community) legislatures, are now subject to the possibility of diffuse judicial review. Therefore, the judiciary is called upon to assess whether rules which do not have a specific intra-Community effect strike a reasonable balance between competing interests. Furthermore, since the rule is non-discriminatory in nature, the effect of Community law is to impinge upon the level of regulation chosen by the national regulator since, once the rule is found to be disproportionate, there is no choice but to eliminate it in respect of all economic actors.

The expansion of the scope of the free movement of persons provisions thus gives rise to important (and familiar) constitutional questions. In particular, the problem is whether there is a sufficient normative basis in the Treaty to justify such a pervasive effect of Community law upon national regulatory autonomy. This is the main question that this book seeks to answer. In order to do so, and after having given an overview of the scope of the free movement provisions, we will analyze both the developments of the case law and the two main conceptual frameworks put forward by the scholarship, to argue that the developments occurred in this field should be understood, and explained, in the context of the introduction of Union citizenship.

Taken together, the free movement cases on non discriminatory restrictions point at the emergence of a new constitutional dimension whereby the Member States bear considerable duties towards Union citizens *qua* citizens rather than just *qua* economic actors – a duty not to *interfere* with individual rights (*Gebhard*); a duty to *respect* individual rights (*Carpenter*); a duty to *protect* individual rights (*Peerbooms*). And it is in the context of Union citizenship that these developments are better understood. Thus, it is argued, legitimacy for the Court's extensive interpretation might be more convincingly found in a *joint* teleological interpretation of the free movement and citizenship provisions. As a result of the introduction of Union citizenship, the *telos* justifying the Court's interpretation has shifted from the internal market, to include the protection of individual rights.

Writing in 1931, de Novellis argued that European economic integration would not be achieved in the foreseeable future.[1] This was, of course, before World War II, and things have changed considerably since then. Not only Europe has progressed towards an integrated economy, but the European project has evolved to create a new constitutional dimension which 'puts the individual at the heart of its activities'. The Union citizen is then not merely instrumental to the economic welfare of the Community – rather, she achieves an additional status, and with that, an additional layer of fundamental rights protection.

Synopsis

In the first chapter, I provide an overview of the material and personal scope of the free movement of persons provisions. Many readers will be familiar with the

[1] L. de Novellis *L'unificazione economica dell'Europa* (Fratelli Treves Editori Milano 1931), 203.

cases analyzed in this chapter, which aims simply at providing the background information to understand the developments which form the main focus of analysis in the rest of the book. In particular, it is important to appreciate how the free movement of persons provisions have always been broadly and purposefully interpreted even before the expansion of the scope of the Treaty which has occurred in the 1990s. Thus, both the personal scope (with the inclusion of work-seekers as well as part-timers), and the material scope of the Treaty (with a broad understanding of the concept of discrimination), have been generously construed by the Court. In particular, a refined interpretation of the concept of discrimination has been instrumental to eliminating barriers to integration resulting from the variegated regulatory traditions of the Member States.

In the second and third chapters, we explore the expansion of the Treaty's scope to embrace truly non-discriminatory barriers to movement. Chapter 2 analyzes the expansion of the scope of Article 49 EC. After a brief introduction on the *Sunday Trading* cases and the *Keck* ruling, essential to appreciate both the constitutional implications of the expansion of free movement rights and the terms of the debate as developed in the scholarship, we turn to analyze the case law on Article 49 EC. In particular, we focus on the notion of non-discriminatory barrier; on the relaxation of the intra-Community link required to trigger the Treaty; and on the broadening of the definition of remuneration. The initial expansion of the concept of barrier to movement to embrace all rules imposed by the host-Member State is not in itself particularly problematic, since it ensures the elimination of double regulatory burdens which might truly affect the economic operators' ability to extend their markets beyond the confines of the State of origin. However, matters become more difficult once Article 49 EC can be relied upon also to challenge non-discriminatory barriers imposed by the Member State of establishment. In *Gourmet* the Court allowed the claimant to rely upon the freedom to provide services against its state of establishment, the only regulator, on the grounds that *Gourmet* had potential clients in another Member State. This development, confirmed in later case law, significantly expands the scope of the Treaty by allowing virtually any economic operator to challenge market rules, whether those imposed by the host State, or those imposed by the home State.

The relaxation of the notion of barrier to the cross-border provision of services is accompanied by the relaxation of the economic link necessary to trigger the Treaty. In a series of cases, the Court allowed Article 49 EC to be used to challenge the rules on reimbursement of cross-border medical care. Whilst the Court, in *Watts*, seems to have partially backtracked from a too generous interpretation of Article 49 EC, the health care cases are interesting in that they provide the foundation for a mode of interpretation which will later be applied in defining the parameters of citizenship rights.

In Chapter 3, we look at the concurrent developments which have occurred in the field of freedom of establishment and free movement of workers. Thus, starting with the *Gebhard* ruling, the scope of Article 43 EC is expanded to embrace non-discriminatory barriers to the freedom of establishment. In this way, again, the Court allows economic operators to challenge what might be the only regulator, without the need to establish that the rules at issue have a specific impact on the intra-Community situation. As a result, the dividing line between Articles 49 and 43 EC becomes relevant only at the justification stage, rather than at the definitional stage. A similar development occurs in the field of Article 39 EC. There in the *Bosman* ruling, the scope of Article 39 EC is broadened to embrace non-discriminatory restrictions to the movement of workers. And yet, the development in the field of workers is less marked for two reasons: first of all, the demarcation line, and the market access test, seem more clearly defined in that instance; secondly, the scarcity of cases on non-discriminatory restrictions makes it hard to establish whether the narrower impact of the workers' cases on national regulatory autonomy is simply circumstantial. After having analyzed non-discriminatory barriers to workers and establishment, we turn to a brief analysis of the notion of non-discriminatory barrier to the free movement of capital (especially in the golden share cases, and in *Burtscher*), and then to the case law on tax and social security rules. In the latter, the effect of the *Gebhard* case law is rather limited: were the notion of hindrance/discouragement to movement to be applied in the field of taxation and social security, then high levels of direct taxation and social security contribution would always have to be justified. It is not surprising then that, by and large, in the field of taxation and social security contribution the Court has limited itself to the scrutiny of discriminatory restrictions.

The expansion of the scope of the free movement provisions calls into question the adequacy of the conceptual explanations put forward by the scholarship in order to provide a rationale for the Court's interpretation. The discriminatory/double burden approach, examined in Chapter 4, does not represent an accurate description of the state of the law. Rather, its value is prescriptive, in the sense of indicating what the law *ought to be* or should have been. In this sense, the discrimination theory has the advantage of providing a coherent normative structure for the Treaty free movement provisions.

On the other hand, the market access test, examined in Chapter 5, is better apt at providing a framework which is capable of accommodating most, although not all, of the case law. And indeed the market access rhetoric clearly inspires the Court in its rulings. However, and without subtracting from its merits, the market access test fails to provide a normative explanation capable of providing legitimacy for the Court's interpretation. In this regard, I argue that a more accurate way of describing the Court's case law is to understand the rights granted by the Treaty as a right to pursue an economic activity free of disproportionate market regulation. Whilst this definition is not helpful in drawing the outer boundaries of the free movement provisions, and indeed it does not substantially differ from the market access test, it is useful in highlighting two factors. First of all, the market access test provides no guidance as to what constitutes a barrier to market access or as to why such barriers fall within the scope of the free movement provisions. Secondly, it stresses the fact that the free movement provisions have evolved into a broader 'individual' right which resembles familiar rights known in national constitutional law, and more precisely, the right not to be hindered in the pursuit of one's business without a good reason. Yet, even should we accept that the 'freedom to pursue an economic activity' test provides us with an accurate, or more accurate, descriptive analysis, it still does not shed any light as to the normative justification for such test; and, it does not, in itself, explain all of the case law. In order to address these two problems it is then necessary to take a further step and look at the developments which have occurred in the field of the economic free movement provisions in their constitutional context. This for two related reasons: first of all, it is now impossible to provide an account of the law on the free movement of persons without including an account, however brief, of the way the Court has interpreted the rights of economically inactive citizens. Secondly, and more importantly, the developments in the field of citizenship might help provide a normative explanation for the case law on the economic free movement provisions.

In Chapter 6, we first look at the development of the case law on Article 18 EC, focusing in particular on the hermeneutic techniques adopted by the Court. Here, the Court has adopted a mode of interpretation similar to that used in relation to the health care case law. Faced with secondary legislation which granted residence rights only to those who are economically independent, i.e. those who have sufficient resources and comprehensive health insurance, the Court chose to give effect to Article 18 EC without calling into question the validity of the conditions provided in secondary legislation. Thus, those who do not satisfy the conditions provided in secondary legislation have a right to be treated proportionately (even when the rules of the Member State are not *per se* incompatible with the Treaty) and to see their fundamental rights respected. This diffuse right of judicial scrutiny then resembles the right to judicial review known in national contexts with the fundamental difference that in the latter case such right is usually limited to administrative/executive acts, whilst in the former case it extends to the *way* legislation is applied to the circumstances of the case at issue. After having analyzed the citizenship case law, we turn to assess whether it can provide us with useful tools in relation to the case law on economic migrants. We first analyze the ruling in *Carpenter*, to argue that it should be seen as a citizenship case. In that case, the Court held that the right to provide services of a person established in his own Member State was affected by the deportation of his wife. This rather artificial finding allowed the Court to carry out a fundamental rights review of the legislation at stake, indicating that it constituted a disproportionate interference with the claimant's right to family life. However, seen from the perspective of citizenship, the case can be more convincingly explained. In particular, we advocate the elimination of reverse discrimination by means of the combined effect of Articles 17 and 12 EC. Article 17 EC establishes Union citizenship and does not make such status conditional upon migration; Article 12 EC provides for a prohibition of discrimination on grounds of nationality in all matters falling within the scope of the Treaty and the Court has interpreted such right as comprising also a right not to be discriminated against on grounds of migration. It is argued that there is no hermeneutic nor literal reason why the right not to be discriminated on grounds of nationality and migration should not be extended to static Union citizens when they are in a comparable situation to migrants. Viewed in this light, the approach in *Carpenter* can be more convincingly explained.

In Chapter 7 we turn to the economic free movement case law to argue that it also can be explained having regard to the stance taken by the Court in the citizenship cases. Here a purposive interpretation of the Treaty rights, with the benefit of hindsight derived from the *Baumbast* ruling, allows us to provide a normative justification for the Court's case law. In *Baumbast* the Court held that any limitation to the rights conferred by Article 18 EC must be proportionate and consistent with fundamental rights. If we interpret Articles 39, 43 and 49 EC as granting also a right to exercise an economic activity in another Member State, then any limitation to that right is subject to the proportionality scrutiny, and the *Gebhard* case law can be explained. Any rule regulating an economic activity can be seen as a limitation to the right to pursue an economic activity in another Member State. Here, it is immaterial whether the barrier restricts market access or not. It is the right to pursue an economic activity which is limited by market rules. And it is for this reason that tax and social advantages are scrutinised only insofar as discriminatory or if they are on such a large scale as to totally eliminate the possibility of exercising the economic activity.

Finally, once we redefine the right granted by the Treaty as a right to exercise an economic activity, the case law relating to the challenges to the Member State of establishment, even when it is the only regulator, can also be explained. The Court has always construed the free movement provisions as prohibiting potential barriers to intra-Community trade. Once it is accepted that economic operators can challenge non-discriminatory barriers, and barriers which do not specifically affect movement, then it is clear that any situation has potential intra-Community credentials. After all, the very nature of the internal market, allows for a possible change of ownership or transfer of residence. And the existence of a barrier to the exercise of an economic activity can undoubtedly have a foreclosure effect whereby new entrants do not enter into the market because the existence of the barrier makes entrance economically non-viable.

Chapter 1

The Rights of Economic Migrants: An Overview

As said in the introduction, in approaching the free movement provisions, it is important to understand that, from the very beginning, in fact from the ruling in *Van Gend en Loos*,[1] the Court has interpreted the free movement provisions as *fundamental* Community rights. It is therefore not surprising that in defining the scope of those rights the Court should adopt hermeneutic techniques typical of rights discourse. Thus, the interpretation is teleological rather than literal; it is aimed at achieving the *full effect*, rather than just a formal guarantee, of the rights at stake; it is expansive in nature; the derogations are narrowly construed; and the limitations to those rights are closely scrutinized in order to ensure that the aims are legitimate and consistent with fundamental rights, and that, more importantly, the means are proportionate to those aims. The rights rhetoric permeates then the entire free movement discourse. But those rights serve also another purpose: they are a vehicle for integration, and with time they become a means to shape market regulation along liberal lines. The two purposes rarely clash,[2] rather market integration and individual rights usually go hand in hand, and the expansive interpretation of the Community rights successfully achieves its twofold aim.

In this chapter we are going to examine briefly the scope of the free movement provisions and the rights that Community nationals derive from them. Whilst the rest of the book focuses on the notion of non-discriminatory barrier, a field in which the Court's interpretation continues to develop, posing not insignificant

---

[1] Case 26/62 *Van Gend en Loos* [1963] ECR 1.

[2] But sometimes a clash might arise between non-economic fundamental rights and the free movement provisions, e.g. Case C-112/00 *Schmidberger* [2003] ECR I-5659, where the Court clarified those non-economic fundamental rights might take precedence over the free movement provisions. See also pending case C-438/05 *The International Transport Workers' Federation et al v Viking Line APB et al.*

challenges to scholars attempting to encapsulate such developments in a coherent framework, this chapter aims at providing the reader with the co-ordinates to navigate their way through free movement law. In particular, we are going to examine the personal scope and material scope of the free movement provisions.[3] We will look at who is covered by the Treaty provisions, and the main rights that economic migrants derive from them, focusing in particular on the scope of the right not to be discriminated against on grounds of nationality.

It should always be borne in mind that economic migrants under Community law benefit from far reaching rights: they enjoy access to the employment or service market of all Member States; a right to reside in the host-State; and a right not to be discriminated against in all matters falling within the scope of the Treaty, including the right to receive contributory and non-contributory benefits from the host-State without suffering discrimination.

1. The Personal Scope of the (Economic) Free Movement Provisions

1.1. Article 39 EC and the Definition of 'Worker'

Article 39(1) EC provides that the free movement of workers shall be secured within the Community. The first issue for consideration is therefore who is to be considered as a 'worker' falling within the personal scope of the Treaty. The Court has interpreted the term broadly and, not surprisingly, from the very beginning it has claimed a hermeneutic monopoly over the term. The definition of *worker* depends therefore upon Community and not upon national law, or otherwise it would be easy for the Member States to give a very narrow definition of the term, so as to exclude non-nationals from the domestic employment market and deprive Article 39 EC of any useful effect.[4] Furthermore, if the term *worker* were to be given a national rather than Community interpretation, the scope of application of Article 39 EC would differ from one Member State to another.[5]

For someone to fall within the personal scope of the workers' provisions, two elements must be satisfied: first of all, the worker needs to be in a subordinate relationship, as otherwise him or her would be self-employed and would fall within

---

[3] Throughout the book and unless otherwise specified I will use the expression 'free movement provisions' to indicate the 'economic' free movement of persons provisions, i.e. free movement of workers (Art. 39 EC), freedom of establishment (Art. 43 EC), and freedom to provide services (Art. 49 EC). Of course, Art. 18 EC on citizenship rights also provides for a right to free movement; however, it appeared too cumbersome to specify each time that we are talking about economic migrants. The reader will forgive this slight imprecision, which I hope will benefit the flow of the text. All the provisions have been declared directly effective as soon as the transitional period was over; Case 167/73 *Commission v France* (Code maritime) [1974] ECR 359; Case 2/74 *Reyners* [1974] ECR 631; Case 33/74 *C H M Van Bisbergen* [1974] ECR 1299.

[4] Case 75/63 *Hoekstra* [1964] ECR 1771.

[5] Case 53/81 *Levin* [1982] ECR 1035.

the scope of either Article 43 EC or Article 49 EC. Secondly, there must be an economic element, i.e. the work needs to be remunerated.[6] In order to decide whether a person is actually a 'worker' for Community law purposes, the Court adopts a *substantive* rather than a formalistic approach: thus, the amount earned and the form the compensation takes is immaterial,[7] provided that the activity is 'genuine and effective' and not on such a small scale as to be 'marginal and ancillary'.[8] For this reason, part-time workers are also covered by Article 39 EC, regardless of how many hours they work,[9] and regardless of how much they earn. Thus, a person doing only a few hours work a week and earning below the minimum salary is a 'worker' within the meaning of Article 39 EC, and is therefore entitled to rely on the welfare provision of the host-State in order to supplement her/his earnings.[10]

The reason why the worker is engaged in the economic activity is equally immaterial:[11] thus, the fact that the worker might have moved and sought employment only for the purposes of triggering the Treaty so as to benefit from Community law rights does not, per se, constitute an abuse of rights.[12] However, the reason why the work has been entered into might be relevant to establish whether the activity is genuine and effective, or rather marginal and ancillary;[13] or to establish entitlement to social advantages.[14] Thus, for instance, a person who goes to another Member State and works there for a very short period of time just so as to claim welfare benefits would not be considered a 'worker' for the purposes of Community law.[15] Furthermore, in order for the activity to be 'genuine and effective' it needs to be part of the 'normal labour market'.[16] For this reason, if a person takes advantage of a scheme aimed at giving work to those who would not have access to the labour market under normal conditions, then she or he would not be a 'worker' for Community law purposes since the activity would not be genuine and effective but rather aimed at the rehabilitation and re-integration of the person concerned.[17] In other words, and leaving aside the rights that Union citizens

---

[6] Cp the definition of 'worker' in Case 66/85 *Lawrie-Blum* [1986] ECR 2121, para 17 'The essential feature of an employment relationship (...) is that for a certain period of time a person performs services for and under the direction of another person in return for which he receives remuneration'. Article 39 EC can also be relied upon by employers to challenge their ability to employ a worker from another Member State, Case C-350/96 *Clean Car* [1998] ECR I-2521.

[7] Remuneration does not need to be in the form of monetary compensation but can also be 'in kind'; cp. Case 196/87 *Steymann* [1988] ECR 6159.

[8] Case 53/81 *Levin* [1982] ECR 1035.

[9] Case C-357/89 *Raulin* [1992] ECR I-1027.

[10] E.g. Case 139/85 *Kempf* [1986] ECR 1741.

[11] Case 53/81 *Levin* [1982] ECR 1035.

[12] E.g. Case C-109/01 *Akrich* [2003] ECR I-9607.

[13] Case 344/87 *Bettray* [1989] ECR 1621.

[14] Case 197/86 *Brown* [1988] ECR 3205.

[15] Cp Case C-413/01 *Ninni-Orasche* [2003] ECR I-13187.

[16] Case C-456/02 *Trojani* [2004] ECR I-7573, see also Chapter 6 below.

[17] Case 344/87 *Bettray* [1989] ECR 1621, and more recently Case C-456/02 *Trojani* [2004] ECR I-7573.

might derive from the Treaty citizenship provisions, if the primary aim of the work undertaken is social rather than economic, then it falls outside the scope of the Treaty economic free movement provisions, even when the activity is in fact remunerated. Article 39 EC is equally useless in relation to unpaid voluntary work, since in those cases the economic element is altogether lacking.[18]

1.1.1. Work Seekers

Even though Article 39 EC only refers to 'workers', the Court has extended its scope to cover also work-seekers. The reason for this extensive interpretation is clear: the *effet utile* of the workers' freedom to move would be greatly impaired if individuals were able to exercise their movement rights only *after* having secured a contract of employment.[19] In *Antonissen*, the Court held that Member States have to allow job seekers to enter their territory and stay there for a 'reasonable period of time',[20] and in subsequent case law it found three months to be a reasonable time.[21] After the expiry of a 'reasonable time' the Member States are, at least in theory, allowed to deport the Community national without having to rely on the Treaty derogations, unless the job seeker can demonstrate that she or he has genuine chances of becoming engaged.[22] This case law has now been codified by Directive 2004/38 which provides for a general and unconditional right of residence for *all* Union citizens for a period of three months;[23] and further provides that work-seekers cannot be expelled from the territory of the host-State as long as they provide evidence that they are looking for a job and have genuine chances of being engaged.[24]

The rights of work-seekers are more limited than those of workers: thus, they have a right to enter and stay for the purposes of seeking employment, but they do not have a right to 'reside' as such.[25] Moreover, the Court originally excluded

---

[18] This does not mean, however, that charitable foundations are automatically excluded from the scope of the Treaty; Cf Case C-386/04 *Centro di Musicologia Walter Stauffer v Finanzamt München für Körperschaften*, judgment of 14 September 2006, nyr. See also the Commission's reasoned opinion to the United Kingdom requesting it to end discrimination in relation to its tax rules which exclude foreign charities from tax relief, thus suggesting that even non-profit making activities might come within the scope of the Treaty. See Press Release IP/06/864 of 10 July 2006 (Commission's case reference number 2005/2281).

[19] Case 48/75 *Royer* [1976] ECR 497.

[20] Case C-292/89 ex parte *Antonissen* [1991] ECR-745.

[21] Case C-344/95 *Commission v Belgium* [1997] ECR I-1035.

[22] Case C-344/95 *Commission v Belgium* [1997] ECR I-1035.

[23] Article 6 Directive 2004/38 on the right of citizens of the Union and their family members to move and reside freely within the territory of the Member States amending Regulation (EEC) No 1612/68 and repealing Directives 64/221/EEC, 68/360/EEC, 72/194/EEC, 73/148/EEC, 75/34/EEC, 75/35/EEC, 90/364/EEC, 90/365/EEC and 93/96/EEC, [2004] OJ L 229/35, hereinafter Directive 2004/38.

[24] Article 14(4)(b) Directive 2004/38.

[25] See Case C-138/02 *Collins* [2004] ECR I-2703, para 44. Article 8 Directive 2004/38 provides for the duty to 'register' with the administrative authorities for periods of residence longer than three months. Work seekers have a right to stay in the host-Member State but not a right to have a residence

work-seekers from the right to equal treatment in relation to welfare provision most probably for fear of triggering welfare tourism: the right to equal treatment was then limited to access to employment.[26] However, following the introduction of Union citizenship, the Court has reinterpreted its own case law, and in *Collins*[27] it held that the principle of equal treatment guaranteed by Article 39(2) EC applies now in full also to work-seekers. As a result, a Union citizen work seeker is now in principle entitled to welfare provision, including unemployment benefits, on an equal footing with own nationals. However, the Member State can impose criteria aimed at pursuing legitimate interests in a proportionate way, such as the requirement that the claimant must have spent a given amount of time in the host-State in order to guarantee a genuine link between the claimant and the host labour market.

The ruling in *Collins* is partially at odds with the provisions of Directive 2004/38,[28] Article 24(2) of which allows Member States to exclude from entitlement to social assistance Union citizens (including work-seekers) in their first three months of stay, as well as work-seekers who are prolonging their stay pursuant to Article 14(4)(b), i.e. those who are still looking for a job and have genuine chances of finding one. It is likely that in the first three months of her/his stay the work-seeker would have not established a 'sufficient link' with the host-employment market, and therefore exclusion from welfare benefits could be objectively justified.[29] However, that is not necessarily the case in relation to work-seekers that prolong their stay beyond the initial three months, having shown (where required) that they are still looking for a job and have genuine chances of finding one. In that case it might be more difficult for the Member State to argue that the work-seeker has not established a sufficient link with the host employment market.[30]

---

registration which, as it was the case before the adoption of Directive 2004/38 (see Directive 68/360 on the abolition of restrictions on movement and residence within the Community for workers of Member States and their families [1968(I)] OJ Sp Ed 485, hereinafter Directive 68/360), is dependent upon proof of economic activity.

[26] Case C-292/89 ex parte *Antonissen* [1991] ECR I-745; Case C-278/94 *Commission v Belgium* [1996] ECR I-4307, esp. para 40.

[27] Case C-138/02 *Collins* [2004] ECR I-2703; see below Chapters 6 and 7 for a full discussion of the case.

[28] Directive 2004/38 had not yet been adopted at the time when the *Collins* ruling was delivered. However, that ruling was later confirmed in Case C-258/04 *Ioannidis* [2005] ECR I-8275, decided before the entry into force of the Directive but after its adoption. On this point see Chapter 7 below.

[29] And for the first three months work-seekers have in any event the right to export to the host-country employment benefits to which they are entitled in their home-State; see Regulation 1408/71 on the application of social security schemes to employed persons, to self-employed persons and to members of their families, as amended, Consolidated text in Annex A Regulation 118/97 [1997] OJ L 28/1 (hereinafter Regulation 1408/71); the Regulation will soon be replaced by Regulation 883/2004 on the co-ordination of social security systems [2004] OJ L 166/1, see Commission's Proposal for a Regulation of the European Parliament and the Council laying down the procedure for implementing Regulation (EC) 883/2004 on the co-ordination of social security systems, COM(2006)16 final.

[30] See also A Arnull, A A Dashwood, M Dougan, M Ross, E Spaventa and D Wyatt, *Wyatt and Dashwood's European Union Law* (5th ed. Sweet and Maxwell 2006), at p. 716.

1.1.2. *When can Article 39 EC be Invoked?*

A worker can invoke Article 39 EC whenever there is a cross-border element. This is the case when the worker has moved to another Member State to work there;[31] when the worker resides in one Member State and works in another one (so called frontier workers);[32] when the worker comes back to her or his original Member State, after having exercised her/his free movement right.[33] However, in no case can Article 39 EC be invoked if the situation is purely internal.[34] This, as we shall see further in the book,[35] causes problems of equality between Union citizens (so called reverse discrimination), since in some cases the migrant worker (or self-employed or citizen) benefits from more extensive rights than the national worker.

Article 39 EC can be invoked vertically, i.e. to challenge rules imposed by the State or by a public authority;[36] semi-horizontally, i.e. against rules regulating employment in a collective manner;[37] and horizontally, i.e. against private individuals.[38] In horizontal situations, however, the possibility to invoke Article 39 EC seems to be limited to situations in which the private party is discriminating directly or indirectly against the Community worker.[39] Therefore, the broader notion of barrier to movement which, as we shall see later in the book,[40] encompasses any rule capable of hindering or discouraging movement, is not relevant in relation to horizontal situations: otherwise, any clause of an employment contract regulating the conditions for termination could, for that sole reason, be construed as a restriction to movement caught by Article 39 EC and would have to be justified. If that were the case, either such clauses would almost always be justified, or the expansion of Article 39 EC to include a prohibition of non-discriminatory barriers imposed by private individuals would come at a considerable cost to contractual freedom.

1.2. The Personal Scope of Article 43 EC

Article 43 EC provides for the abolition of restrictions on the freedom of establishment, and it applies to both physical and legal persons (companies). Thus any

[31] E.g. Case 15/69 *Ugliola* [1969] ECR 363.
[32] E.g. Case 152/73 *Sotgiu* [1974] ECR 153.
[33] Case C-370/90 *Singh* [1992] ECR I-4265.
[34] Joined Cases 35 and 36/82 *Morson and Jhanjan* [1982] ECR 3723.
[35] See Chapter 6 below, where we will suggest that the phenomenon of reverse discrimination could and should be remedied by means of a joint application of Articles 17 and 12 EC.
[36] E.g. Case 48/75 *Royer* [1977] ECR 497.
[37] E.g. Case 36/74 *Walrave and Koch* [1974] ECR 1405; Case C-413/93 *Bosman* [1995] ECR I-4921; cp also Article 7(4) Regulation 1612/68 on freedom of movement for workers within the Community OJ Sp. Ed. 1968 L257/2, p.475 (hereinafter Regulation 1612/68).
[38] Case C-281/98 *Angonese* [2000] ECR I-4139; critical of the ruling P Oliver and W H Roth 'The internal market and the four freedoms' (2004) 41 CMLRev 407, at 421 and ff. See also R Lane and N Shuibhne 'Annotation on *Angonese*' (2000) 37 CMLRev 1237.
[39] Case C-281/98 *Angonese* [2000] ECR I-4139.
[40] See esp. Chapter 2 and 3 below.

Community national, or any company based in the Community, can move to another Member State to establish her/him/itself there to pursue an economic activity in a self-employed capacity. Article 43 EC also provides for the right to set up a secondary establishment (branch, agency or subsidiary) in any of the Member States; as well as the right to have more than one establishment.[41]

The main difference between Article 39 EC and Article 43 EC is that the former applies to those in a relationship of subordination, whilst the latter applies to the self-employed.[42] The main difference between Article 43 EC and Article 49 EC is that, whilst both apply to the self-employed, the provisions on the freedom to provide services apply to those who move only temporarily to another Member State to there provide/receive a service. On the other hand, the notion of establishment presupposes some sort of deeper and more 'stable' integration in the host-State's life.[43]

Like in the case of Articles 39 and 49 EC, a cross-border element is necessary to trigger Article 43 EC. This will be the case when the economic activity is exercised in a country different from that of origin or residence,[44] as well as when the migrant is returning to her original Member State after having exercised her right to move.[45] Finally, as in the case of workers, Article 43 EC can be invoked in vertical,[46] semi-horizontal,[47] and horizontal situations.[48]

1.3. The Personal Scope of Article 49 EC and the Notion of 'Service'

Article 49 EC provides for the abolition of restrictions on the freedom to provide services with a cross-border element. As said above, the difference between establishment and services lies on the temporary nature of the latter's relationship with the host-country as opposed to the more 'stable' character of the former.

---

[41] Case 107/83 *Klopp* [1984] ECR 2791.
[42] Cp Case C-268/99 *Jany* [2001] ECRI-8615.
[43] Cp Case C-55/94 *Gebhard* [1995] ECR I-4165, para 25: 'The concept of establishment within the meaning of the Treaty is therefore a very broad one, allowing a Community national to participate, on a stable and continuous basis, in the economic life of a Member State other than his State of origin and to profit therefrom, so contributing to economic and social interpenetration within the Community in the sphere of activities as self-employed persons'. See also Case C-386/04 *Centro di Musicologia Walter Stauffer v Finanzamt München für Körperschaften*, judgment of 14 September 2006, nyr, para 19, for the distinction between Articles 43 and 56 EC.
[44] E.g. Case 2/74 *Reyners* [1974] ECR 631.
[45] Case C-19/92 *Kraus* [1993] ECR I-1663; a company can challenge under Article 43 EC rules which discriminate against its employees, Case 79/85 *Segers* [1986] ECR 2375. As we shall see the need for an intra-Community element has been considerably relaxed. See Chapter 3, below.
[46] E.g. Case 2/74 *Reyners* [1974] ECR 631.
[47] E.g. Case C-319/92 *Haim I* [1994] ECR I-425.
[48] There is no case law on the matter, but the Court's reasoning in Case C-281/98 *Angonese* [2000] ECR I-4139, suggests that it applies to all the free movement of persons provisions.

Article 50 EC provides that in order to be considered a 'service' for the purposes of the Treaty, the service has to be normally provided for remuneration and not be covered by one of the other free movement provisions.[49] The concept of remuneration has been given a purposive interpretation. Thus, the Court found that remuneration does not necessarily need to be monetary, but can also be in the form of a *quid pro quo.*[50] Moreover, in order for a service to fall within the scope of application of the Treaty, the service does not need to be paid for by the recipient. For instance, a television broadcaster that supplies its services free of charge to viewers, but is paid by the advertisers, is clearly providing services for remuneration, even though such remuneration is not paid for by the final user of the service.[51] As long as the service is economic (commercial) in nature, Article 49 EC applies.[52] However, services of a non-economic nature, such as those provided directly by the State free of charge, or for a charge which does not reflect the economic cost of the service, have traditionally been excluded from the scope of application of the Treaty, since in those cases, the services are not provided for 'remuneration', defined as 'consideration for the service in question'. In *Humbel*, the Court relied on two main considerations to exclude general education from the scope of application of Article 49 EC. First of all, the State in providing education was not engaging in a gainful activity but was rather 'fulfilling its duties towards its own population in the social, cultural and educational sphere'; secondly, the service was primarily funded by the public purse, rather than by the service-recipients.[53]

This said, in other cases the nature of the funding proved not to be determinant in assessing whether the non-discrimination obligation applied. The Court has found that European citizens have, in some instances, a right to equal treatment even in cases in which the benefit claimed is entirely paid for by the public purse. These cases did not amend the definition of 'service provided for remuneration'. However, they made clear that the public nature of the funding is not *in itself*

---

[49] It is debatable whether the subsidiary nature of services is still relevant since there are several cases, especially in relation to rules concerning advertisement, in which Article 49 EC was applied alongside another free movement provision; e.g. Case C-34/95 *De Agostini* [1997] ECR I-3843; Case C-405/98 *Gourmet International (GIP)* [2001] ECR I-1795. Given the importance that services have acquired for the economy, this is hardly surprising.

[50] Case 196/86 *Steymann v Staatssecretaris van Justitie* [1988] ECR 2085.

[51] Case 352/85 *Bond van Adverteenders and others v The Netherlands* [1988] ECR 2085, para 16. This reasoning applies also to established persons, Case 300/84 *A J M van Roosmalen v Bestuur van de Bedrijfsvereniging voor de Gezondheid, Geestelijke en Maatschappelijke Belangen* [1986] ECR 3097.

[52] Case 13/76 *G Doná v M Mantero* [1976] ECR 1333, para 12; and AG Slynn's Opinion in Case 293/83 *Gravier v City of Liège* [1985] ECR 379, esp. 603; and in Case 263/86 *Belgium v Humbel and M T Edel* [1988] ECR 5365, esp. 5379.

[53] Case 263/86 *Belgium v Humbel and M T Edel* [1988] ECR 5365, paras 18 and 19. See also Case C-102/92 *Wirth v Landeshauptstadt Hannover* [1993] ECR I-6447. The lack of remuneration was instrumental to avoiding the difficult question on the Irish limitation of information concerning abortion in Case C-159/90 *Society for the Protection of Unborn Children v Grogan* [1991] ECR I-4685.

enough to shelter the benefit from the scope of application of the Treaty free movement of services provisions.[54] In this respect, we can distinguish two different types of cases: those where the Court establishes a connection between the economic service sought and the publicly funded benefit; and the rather anomalous case of *Cowan.* As for the former, in the Spanish *museum admissions* case,[55] the Commission brought proceedings against Spain for maintaining discriminatory conditions for admission to museums. The Commission did not attempt to challenge the definition of remuneration by arguing that publicly funded museums were to be considered as services for the purposes of Community law. Rather, it argued that there was a link between the receipt of (economic) services as tourists and museum admission conditions: the discriminatory condition could then be construed as an indirect barrier affecting the tourists' right to free movement. The Court accepted the Commission's reasoning and found that, since there is a link between the receipt of services as tourists and museum admission conditions, the non-discrimination obligation applied to those advantages.[56]

On the other hand in *Cowan*, the Court seemed to sever the connection between the receipt of services and a scheme entirely financed through the public purse.[57] There, a British tourist, who had been a victim of crime whilst visiting France, claimed a right to equal treatment in relation to a crime compensation scheme. The scheme was reserved to residents, nationals, and nationals of those States which had a reciprocity agreement with France. The French Government relied, *inter alia*, on the fact that the scheme was paid for by the public purse to support its claim that it did not fall within the scope of the Treaty.

The Court found that, notwithstanding the publicly funded nature of the scheme, France could not exclude Community nationals from it. The Court's reasoning, concise as it might be, seems to substantially follow Advocate General Lenz's opinion. The Advocate General found that the crime compensation scheme was an aspect of the State's duty to ensure safety and order in its territory. In establishing a compensation scheme for victims of crime the State was acknowledging its own failure to ensure the individual's safety. Since the State bears this duty towards residents and visitors alike, it could not exclude tourists from the scheme. In the words of the Court, protection from 'harm' is a corollary of the freedom to move, and for this reason a tourist is entitled to protection from the risk

---

[54] Of course social advantages have always been available to Community migrant workers and, where applicable, self-employed.

[55] Case C-45/93 *Commission v Spain* (Museum admission) [1994] ECR I-911; and more recently Case C-388/01 *Commission v Italy* (Italian museums) [2003] ECR I-721; for a critique of the Court's assessment see G Davies '"Any place I hang my hat?" or: residence is the new nationality' (2005) 11 ELJ 43.

[56] The reasoning of the Court in this case mirrors, to a certain extent, existing case law on benefits indirectly related to the provision of services according to which the non-discrimination obligation applies to all that connected, even indirectly, to the ability to pursue the economic activity; e.g. Case 63/86 *Commission v Italy* (Social housing) [1988] ECR I-29. In the field of establishment see Case 197/84 *P Steinhauser v City of Biarritz* [1985] ECR 1819.

[57] Case 186/87 *Cowan v Trésor Public* [1989] ECR 195.

of assault (and compensation when that risk materializes) on equal terms with nationals, regardless of how the scheme is funded.[58]

These cases demonstrate how the fact that a benefit is funded by the public purse is not enough, in itself, for it to be excluded from the reach of Article 49 EC (and/or 12 EC). However, public services which are an expression of social solidarity were excluded from the scope of the Treaty: expressions of solidarity are by definition not 'economic'.[59] Thus, before the developments which have occurred in the late 1990s, we can distinguish two trends: one is to exclude 'public services' from the scope of the Treaty; the second is to extend the scope of application of the Treaty to those benefits, regardless of the way they are funded, which are even remotely connected to the receipt of an economic service and/or to the right to move. This said, and as we shall see in more detail in the next chapter, in the late nineties the Court expanded the definition of what is to be considered a 'service provided for remuneration': as a result, the denial of reimbursement by a health authority or health insurance body of expenses for medical treatment incurred in another Member State is in principle caught by Article 49 EC since it limits the possibility for Union citizens to receive such services in another Member State.[60]

The definition of 'services' for the purposes of the Treaty depends entirely on the economic element: thus it is immaterial whether the service is considered immoral[61] or is illegal in some of the Member States.[62] This said, it is likely

[58] For a detailed conceptual analysis, see M Dougan and E Spaventa '"Wish You Weren't Here . . ." New Models of Social Solidarity in the European Union' in M Dougan and E Spaventa *Social Welfare and EU Law* (Hart publishing 2005), 181, at 207 and ff.

[59] This reasoning applies also in other fields of Community law: see in relation to the applicability of Articles 81 and 82 EC, Joined Cases C-159 and 160/91 *Poucet v Assurances Generales de France (AGF) and Caisse Mutuelle Regionale du Languedoc-Roussillon* and *Pistre v Caisse Autonome Nationale de Compensation de l'Assurance Vieillesse des Artisans* [1993] ECR I-637, and more recently Case C-218/00 *Cisal di Battistello Venanzio & C. Sas v Istituto Nazionale per l'assicurazione contro gli infortuni sul lavoro (INAIL)* [2002] ECR 691; and Joined Cases C-264/01, C-306/01, C-354/01 and C-355/01 *AOK Bundesverband and others v Ichthyol-Gesellschaft Cordes and others*, [2004] ECR I-2493. In relation to Article 43 EC, Case C-70/95 *Sodemare Sa and others v Regione Lombardia* [1997] ECR I-3395.

[60] Case C-158/96 *Kohll* [1998] ECR I-1931; Case C-368/98 *Vanbraekel* [2001] ECR I-5363; Case C-157/99 *Geraets-Smits* and *Peerbooms* [2001] ECR I-5473; Case C-385/99 *Müller Fauré* and *van Riet* [2003] ECR I-4509; Case C-56/01 *Patricia Inizan* [2003] ECR I-12403; Case C-8/04 *Leichtle* [2004] ECR I-2641; Case C-372/04 *Watts* [2006] ECR I-4325. See below p. 50. This case law has not been welcomed by the Member States, see the Employment, Social Policy, Health and Consumer Affairs Council Conclusions *Council Conclusions on Common values and principles in EU Health systems*, Luxembourg 1 and 2 June; and European Parliament Press Release *Services of General Interest: Legal Clarity the Key*, 12 September 2006. See also the exclusion from the scope of Directive 2006/123 on services in the internal market [2006] OJ L 376/36 of health care services.

[61] Case C-159/90 *Grogan* [1991] ECR I-4685.

[62] Case C-275/92 *Schindler* [1994] ECR I-1039. This said, if a service is outlawed in a Member State, it is going to be reasonably easy for that State to justify its rules under either the Treaty derogations or the imperative requirements doctrine.

that a service outlawed throughout the Community might fall altogether outside the scope of the Treaty.[63]

Article 49 EC can be invoked by both the provider and the recipient of a service if there is a cross-border element. This is the case when the provider moves to another Member State to temporarily provide a service;[64] when the recipient moves to another Member State to there receive a service;[65] when both recipient and provider are in a Member State other than that of their residence when the service is provided, even if they reside in the same Member State;[66] and when neither the provider nor the recipient moves, but the service is provided across a border (e.g. via internet, fax, television etc.).[67] As we shall see in more detailed in the next chapters, Article 49 EC can be invoked also against the State of establishment when the service is provided to recipients (even only potential) established in other Member States.[68] This said, Article 49 EC does not apply if there is no cross-border element, i.e. when the situation is purely internal – even though, arguably, the scope of Article 49 EC has grown so much that there is very little margin for purely internal situations.

Again, as in the case of Articles 39 and 43 EC, Article 49 EC can be invoked vertically,[69] semi-vertically,[70] and (at least to a certain extent) horizontally.[71]

2. The Material Scope of the Free Movement of Persons Provisions: The Rights Granted by the Treaty

The free movement provisions grant first and foremost a right to move to any EU country to pursue an economic activity without suffering any discrimination on grounds of nationality.[72] According to the Treaty,[73] the right to move and not to be

---

[63] To the author's knowledge no case has arisen so far in relation to 'illegal services' or 'illegal goods', i.e. services/goods which are illegal throughout the Community. The position of illegal drugs was considered in relation to taxation in Case 240/81 *Senta Einberger v Hauptzollamt Freiburg* [1982] ECR 3699 and Case 294/82 *Senta Einberger v Hauptzollamt Freiburg* [1984] ECR 1177.
[64] Case 33/74 *Van Bisbergen* [1974] ECR 1299.
[65] Joined Cases 286/82 and 26/83 *Luisi and Carbone* [1984] ECR 377. The provider can challenge the rules of the Member State of establishment that impose a restriction on its ability to provide services to persons established in another Member State, Case C-224/97 *Ciola* [1999] ECR I-2517.
[66] Case C-149/89 *Commission v France* (Tourist guides) [1991] ECR I-659.
[67] Case 352/85 *Bond van Adverteerders* [1989] ECR 2085.
[68] E.g. Case C-384/93 *Alpine Investments* [1995] ECR I-114; Case C-405/98 *Gourmet International Products AB (GIP)* [2001] ECR I-1795; Case C-60/00 *Carpenter* [2002] ECR I-6279.
[69] Case 33/74 *Van Binsbergen* [1974] ECR 1299.
[70] Case 36/74 *Walrave and Koch* [1974] ECR 1405.
[71] As in the case of Article 43 EC, there is no explicit case law but Case C-281/98 *Angonese* [2000] ECR I-4139 applies by analogy.
[72] The right to access the labour market of Member States might be suspended for a transitional period following accession of new Member States. See Annexes V to XV of the Treaty concerning the Accession of the Czech Republic, Estonia, Cyprus, Latvia, Lithuania, Hungary, Malta, Poland, Slovenia and Slovakia, [2003] OJ 236/803; and Treaty concerning the accession of the Republic of Bulgaria and Romania to the European Union [2005] OJ L 157/1, Annex VI and VII.
[73] Articles 39 (3) and 46 EC.

discriminated against can be limited only for reasons of public policy, public health and public security; furthermore, the Treaty exempts from the non-discriminatory obligation employment in the public service and activities which entail the exercise of official authority.[74]

In this section we are going to look at the main rights that Union economic migrants derive from the Treaty, to then analyze the most important feature of the free movement provisions, i.e. the right not to be discriminated against on grounds of nationality. We are not going to differentiate between the freedoms unless there is reason to do so. Also, we are not specifically concerned with the free movement of legal persons and we are not going to explore the peculiarities that apply in that field.[75]

2.1. The Right to Leave, Enter, Stay and Move

The rights granted by the free movement provisions would be meaningless if Member States could prevent their nationals from leaving the country, for instance because of a specific skills shortage; or if Member States could protect their domestic market either by preventing other Member States' nationals from entering their territory or by deporting non-nationals at will. The rights to free movement are conferred directly by the Treaty and are detailed in Directive 2004/38 on the right of movement and residence of Union citizens and their family members, which has repealed pre-existing legislation.[76]

Union citizens can move upon production of an identity card and cannot be turned back at the frontier only because they lack the prescribed identity documents. Rather, in that case, the Member State must give the Union citizen (or the citizen's family member) 'every reasonable opportunity' to obtain the necessary documents or to prove that they have a right to move and reside in the Union.[77]

Article 39 (3) EC for workers, and 46 EC for the self-employed, provide that the Member States might derogate from the rights to move and reside granted by the Treaty only for reasons of public policy, public security and public health; those grounds can never be invoked to service economic ends.[78] Furthermore, since those are derogations from fundamental Community rights, they are interpreted narrowly. The public health derogation can be invoked only in relation to diseases

---

[74] Article 39(4) EC and 45 EC respectively.

[75] On corporate actors see A Arnull, A Dashwood, M Dougan, M Ross, E Spaventa and D Wyatt, *Wyatt and Dashwood's European Union Law* (5th ed., Sweet and Maxwell 2006), Chapter 20.

[76] Directive 2004/38; the Directive has amended Regulation 1612/68 and has repealed Directives 64/221, 68/360, 72/194, 73/148, 75/34, 75/35, 90/364, 90/365 and 93/96.

[77] Articles 4 and 5 Directive 2004/38 which, to a certain extent, codified Case C-459/99 *MRAX* [2002] ECR I-6591.

[78] Cp Article 27 Directive 2004/38. Rather peculiarly, given the 'public' nature of those exceptions, the Court has held that they can be invoked also by private organizations/individuals to justify horizontal or semi-horizontal barriers to movement; see Case C-415/93 *Bosman* [1995] ECR I-4921, para 86, and S Weatherill's critical appraisal in 'Annotation on *Bosman*' (1996) 33 CMLRev 991.

with epidemic potential as defined by World Health Organization instruments, and in relation to infectious diseases if protective provisions apply also to own nationals. In any event, the Member State cannot expel a Union citizen on public health grounds if the disease has occurred after three months from arrival.[79]

The public policy derogation can be invoked only in relation to the personal conduct of the individual concerned which must represent a 'genuine, present and sufficiently serious threat affecting one of the fundamental interests of society'.[80] Furthermore, in order to be able to invoke the public policy derogation, the host-State must also impose comparable sanctions on nationals performing the same conduct,[81] and in any event previous criminal convictions cannot in themselves justify the invocation of the public policy derogation.[82] As is the case with any limitation on rights guaranteed by the Treaty, measures taken on grounds of public policy and security have to comply with general principles of Community law, and in particular with the principle of proportionality and with fundamental rights.[83] This means that in deciding whether to deport a Union citizen the public authority must have due regard to her/his personal circumstances, including length of stay, age, family situation etc.[84] In any event, the Court has been generally unwilling to allow the Member States to rely on the Treaty derogations, and only in a very few cases it has accepted that such derogations were necessary.[85]

Thus, for instance, in *Bonsignore*,[86] the Court found that Germany could not invoke the public policy derogation in relation to an Italian national who accidentally shot his brother and was fined for unlawful possession of a firearm: in this case deportation would have been used as a deterrent, i.e. for reasons of a general preventive nature, rather than for reasons connected with the individual's personal conduct. In *Bouchereau*,[87] in relation to a French national who had committed drugs-related offences in the UK, the Court instructed the national court to investigate whether the individual's conduct was a genuine and present threat to one of the fundamental interests of society. In *Adoui and Counouaille*,[88] Belgium tried to rely on the public policy derogation to deport two French citizens who were working as prostitutes. The Court held that no deportation order could be made

---

[79] Article 29 Directive 2004/38.

[80] Case 30/77 *Bouchereau* [1977] ECR 1999; this principle has been codified in Article 27(2) of Directive 2004/38.

[81] Joined Cases 115 and 116/81 *Adoui and Cornuaille* [1982] ECR 1665.

[82] Article 27(2) Directive 2004/38.

[83] This was hinted at in Case 36/75 *Rutili* [1975] ECR 1219, and it was explicitly stated in Case C-260/89 *ERT* [1991] ECR I-2925 in relation to free movement of services; also Case C-60/00 *Carpenter* [2002] ECR I-6279; Joined Cases C-482/01 and 493/01 *Orfanopoulos and Olivieri* [2004] ECR I-5257.

[84] Cf Article 28 Directive 2004/38, and Case C-60/00 *Carpenter* [2002] ECR I-6279.

[85] In Case C-100/01 *Olazabal* [2002] ECR I-10981, the Court allowed a discriminatory territorial restriction on an ETA sympathizer despite having previously found the legislation at issue incompatible with Community law in Case 36/75 *Rutili* [1975] ECR 1219. See discussion below.

[86] Case 67/74 *Bonsignore* [1975] ECR 297.

[87] Case 30/77 *Bouchereau* [1977] ECR 1999; also Case C-348/96 *D Calfa* [1999] ECR I-11.

[88] Joined Cases 115 and 116/81 *Adoui and Cornuaille* [1982] ECR 1665.

unless the same conduct performed by own nationals would have given rise to comparable sanctions. Furthermore, in *Calfa* the Court clarified that exclusion from the territory of a Member State can never be of indefinite duration, since this would clash with the principle according to which the threat to a fundamental interest of society must be a 'present' threat.[89] Consistently, Article 32 Directive 2004/38 provides that after a reasonable period, and in any event after three years, individuals can submit an application for the lifting of the exclusion order.

Individuals have not only a right to enter and reside in any of the Member States, but also a right to move within the territory of the Member State. Thus, Article 22 Directive 2004/38 provides that Member States may impose territorial restrictions on the right of residence only where the same restrictions apply to own nationals. This seems to be a codification of the principle established in *Rutili.*[90] In that case, the Court held that France could not invoke the public policy derogation to justify a restriction on movement and residence imposed on an Italian trade union activist, when a similar restriction could not have been imposed on a French national. However, in *Olazabal*,[91] decided some thirty years later, the Court upheld the compatibility with the Treaty of the same rules which it had found inconsistent with the Treaty in *Rutili.* Here, a territorial restriction was imposed on a convicted Spanish ETA sympathizer, who was banned from the regions bordering with Spain and could not leave the district where he resided without notifying the authorities. Notwithstanding the fact that similar restrictions could have not been imposed on French citizens, the Court found them to be justified on public policy grounds. Following the entry into force of Directive 2004/38, *Olazabal* should not be any longer considered good law.

Directive 2004/38, like its predecessor Directive 64/221, provides for a set of procedural guarantees (right to be notified, minimum time before the decision can be enforced, right to appeal, etc.) in cases in which the Member State refuses to grant the right to free movement.[92]

2.1.1. *The Right of Residence*

Directive 2004/38 provides for an unconditional right of residence for up to three months for Union citizens and their family members in any of the Member States.[93] The short residence right is not dependent upon status, i.e. it applies to economic and non-economic migrants alike, even though Member States are not obliged to confer entitlement to social assistance to non-economic migrants in the first three months of their stay, whilst such right is recognized for economic migrants.[94]

---

[89] Case C-348/96 *D Calfa* [1999] ECR I-11.
[90] Case 36/75 *Rutili* [1975] ECR 1219.
[91] Case C-100/01 *Olazabal* [2002] ECR I-10981.
[92] Article 30 and ff Directive 2004/38.
[93] Article 6 Directive 2004/38.
[94] Article 24(2) Directive 2004/38. We will deal with the rights of non-economic migrants in Chapter 6.

Economic migrants have a right to reside in the host Member State;[95] this right of residence is conditional only upon the Union citizen being engaged in an economic activity, whether as a worker or in a self-employed capacity. Member States might require migrants to register with the competent authorities; in the case of economic migrants the registration certificate must be issued upon production of proof of identity and employment (and for this reason work-seekers have a right to 'stay' rather than a right to reside), or proof of self-employed activity.[96] Directive 73/148,[97] now repealed by Directive 2004/38, specifically provided for the right of residence for service providers and service recipients. According to Article 4(2) of that directive, the right of residence was to be of equal duration with the period during which the services were provided or received. Directive 2004/38 does not contain a similar provision: however, such a right derives directly by Article 49 EC and so also in the case of service recipients, and exception given for recipients of education which are explicitly provided for,[98] the Member States might not impose any conditions (such as sufficient resources and health insurance) upon the recipient's right to entry and stay.

The registration certificate is not constitutive of the right to stay, rather being mere evidence of such right.[99] Thus failure to secure the certificate or to comply with administrative formalities can never be grounds for expulsion, although it might give rise to proportionate and non-discriminatory sanctions.[100]

Economic migrants retain their status, as well as their right to residence, even when they are not exercising an economic activity if this is due to (i) a temporary inability to work due to an illness or accident; (ii) involuntary unemployment, if the migrant had previously worked for at least one year and has registered as a job-seeker; (iii) in the case of involuntary unemployment arising before 12 months of economic activity, the status of economic migrant is retained for at least six months; (iv) the status of economic migrant is also retained when the Union migrant embarks on vocational training relating to her/his activity, or in the case of a person involuntarily unemployed, if she/he embarks in any vocational training.[101]

Furthermore, whilst any Union citizen has the right to become a permanent resident of the host State after five years of lawful residence there,[102] economically

---

[95] Non-economic migrants also have a right to reside in any of the Member States, but such right is conditional upon having comprehensive health insurance and sufficient resources so as not to become an 'unreasonable' burden on the host welfare state. Cp Case C-413/99 *Baumbast and R* [2002] ECR I-7091, and Art. 7 Directive 2004/38. Citizenship rights will be analyzed in detail in Chapter 6 below.

[96] Article 8(3) Directive 2004/38.

[97] Article 4 Directive 73/148 on the abolition of restrictions on movement and residence within the Community for nationals of Member States with regard to establishment and the provision of services [1973] OJ L172/14 (hereinafter Directive 73/148).

[98] Article 7(1)(c) Directive 2004/38, and previously Directive 93/96 on the right of residence for students [1993] OJ L317/59 (hereinafter Directive 93/96).

[99] Case 157/79 *Pieck* [1980] ECR 2171.

[100] Articles 5(5), 8(2) Directive 2004/38.

[101] Article 3 Directive 2004/38.

[102] Article 16 Directive 2004/38.

active migrants might mature such a right earlier, if they retire,[103] have to stop work because of a permanent incapacity to work,[104] or take up employment in another Member State but retain their place of residence in the first Member State.[105]

2.2. The Right Not to be Discriminated Against

The most important and far reaching right conferred upon Union citizens is the right not to be discriminated against on grounds of nationality whenever the Treaty is triggered. Article 39(1) EC provides that 'freedom of movement for workers shall be secured within the Community' and Article 39(2) EC provides that such freedom shall *entail* the 'abolition of any discrimination based on nationality'. Article 43 EC provides for the prohibition of restrictions on the freedom of establishment; and that such freedom shall *include* the right to equal treatment with nationals of the host-State. Article 49 EC provides for the abolition of restrictions on the freedom to provide services; whilst Article 50 EC provides for a right to temporarily pursue an 'activity in the State where the service is provided under the same conditions as are imposed by that State on its own nationals'. Thus, Articles 39, 43 and 49 EC prohibit first and foremost any discrimination based on grounds of nationality. The Treaty free movement provisions are considered a 'specific manifestation' of the general principle of non-discrimination contained in Article 12 EC of the Treaty.[106] Therefore, there is no need to rely on the latter if the case falls within the ambit of the former. According to constant and consistent case law, the prohibition on discrimination encompasses direct as well as indirect discrimination, the latter concept having been broadly construed by the Court.[107] This said, it is of paramount importance to distinguish between the two types of

[103] This is conditional upon three years of residence and 12 months work preceding retirement in the host-State; Article 17(1)(a) Directive 2004/38.

[104] This is conditional upon two years residence in the host-State; Article 17(1)(b) Directive 2004/38.

[105] This is conditional upon three years of continuous employment and residence in the first host-State before taking up the activity in another Member State; Article 17(1)(c) Directive 2004/38.

[106] E.g. Case 2/74 *Reyners* [1974] ECR 631; Case 90/76 *Henry van Ameyde* [1977] ECR 1091. On the principle of equal treatment (also beyond nationality) in EC Law, see K Lenaerts 'L'égalité de traitement en droit communautaire' (1991) 26 CDE 3; G de Búrca 'The Role of Equal Treatment in European Community Law' in A A Dashwood and S O'Leary *The Principle of Equal Treatment in EC Law* (Sweet & Maxwell London 1997), 13; D Martin '«Discriminations», «Entraves» et «Raisons Impérieuses» dans le Traité CE: Trois Concepts en Quête D'Indentité', (1998) 33 CDE 261 and 561; G Davies *Nationality Discrimination in the European Internal Market* (Kluwer Law International The Hague 2003).

[107] E.g. Case 152/73 *Sotgiu* [1974] ECR 153, para 11. It is not crystal clear that this was true also for the early interpretation of Article 43 EC. In Case 182/83 *Fearon & Co.* [1984] ECR 3677, the Court found that a residence requirement was not caught by Article 43 EC since non-discriminatory, thus suggesting that – apart from qualification requirements which needed to be justified from the very beginning – it considered Article 43 EC a protection only against direct discrimination (residence requirements are usually considered inherently indirectly discriminatory). The fact that the prohibition on discrimination contained in the Treaty should be construed as covering also indirect

discrimination since direct discrimination can be justified only on one of the grounds expressly provided for in the Treaty,[108] which are narrowly interpreted and cannot be invoked to serve economic interests, whilst indirect discrimination can be 'justified' by relying on broader public policy grounds. Given the centrality of the principle of non-discrimination for the internal market, we are going to analyze how the notions of direct and indirect discrimination have been construed by the Court.

2.2.1. Direct Discrimination

Discrimination occurs when comparable situations are treated differently or non-comparable situations are treated equally.[109] In the context of free movement law the relevant discrimination is that on grounds of nationality, and there is usually (but not always) a presumption of comparability of situations between nationals and foreigners.[110] Thus, in free movement law, direct discrimination arises when a non-national is treated differently in law. In the case of companies, it is the 'registered office (. . .) that serves as the connecting factor with the legal system of a particular State, like nationality in the case of natural persons'.[111]

Apart from rules which by nature apply only to foreigners, i.e. entry restrictions and deportation, which as we have seen above can be justified on grounds of

---

discrimination had been argued at a very early stage, cf W Van Gerven 'The Right of Establishment and Free Supply of Services within the Common Market' (1965–66) 2 CMLRev 344, 346. It is now consistent case law that a residence requirement amounts to indirect discrimination; e.g. Case C-279/89 *Commission v UK* (Factortame 2) [1992] ECR I-5785.

108 And arguably only by relying on the public authority/service proviso in Articles 39(4) and 45 EC respectively.

109 It is not very often that the Court refers to the latter type of discrimination (i.e. different situations treated equally), but there are sporadic examples of it being relevant, e.g. Case C-148/02 *Garcia Avello* [2003] ECR I-11613; equal treatment of non-comparable situations is considered indirect discrimination. However, equal treatment of different situations does not necessarily lead to a finding of discrimination; cf in the case of goods, Case 13/63 *Italy v Commission* (French duties) [1963] ECR 337, where the Court held 'The different treatment of non-comparable situations does not lead automatically to the conclusion that there is discrimination. An appearance of discrimination in form may therefore correspond in fact to an absence of discrimination in substance. Discrimination in substance would consist of treating either similar situation differently or different situations identically' (360).

110 Such presumption was rebutted in relation to a different regime for spouses of UK nationals and Community nationals in order to obtain indefinite leave to remain, cp. Case C-356/98 *Kaba I* [2000] ECR I-2623. Also such presumption is not present in relation to different treatment of residents and non-residents in relation to tax rules (and especially in relation to how tax is calculated) since the Court considers that residents and non-residents are in principle not in a comparable situation in relation to taxes; this does not mean however that the Court will not investigate whether the situation between residents and non-residents are not *de facto* comparable in the cases it examines; see e.g. recently Case C-169/03 *Wallentin* [2004] ECR I-6443, especially para 16.

111 E.g. Case 270/83 *Commission v France* (Shareholders' tax credits) [1986] ECR 273, para 18; Case C-330/91 ex parte *Commerzbank* [1993] ECR I-4017, para 13.

public policy, public security and public health,[112] directly discriminatory rules can be justified only by invoking the public authority/service exception contained in Articles 39(4) and 45 EC respectively. Those provide that Member States can reserve to own nationals employment in the public service, as well as activities which are connected, even occasionally, with the exercise of official authority. Not surprisingly the Court has narrowly interpreted these provisions,[113] and has refused to allow Member States to rely on these exceptions in relation to *any* job in the public sector/civil service.[114] Member States can exclude foreign nationals from their civil service and other branches of the public sector only to the extent to which the post presupposes a special bond of allegiance to the State and when the post requires the exercise of special public law powers.[115] Furthermore, in order for the exception to be validly invoked, the public law powers must be exercised on a regular basis and must not represent a 'very minor' part of the activities in question.[116] Once foreigners are admitted to a post, the prohibition on discrimination on grounds of nationality applies and they are entitled to equal treatment in relation to working conditions and benefits; this said, it is possible that promotion to the most senior levels, and provided the test is satisfied, could be reserved to own nationals.[117]

Direct discrimination is narrowly construed. This is not surprising given that, as said above, directly discriminatory rules can be justified only by relying on one of the Treaty derogations. For this reason, the Court has adopted a literal rather than a teleological interpretation, and only rules which expressly distinguish on grounds of nationality are considered directly discriminatory.[118] On the other hand, rules which severely affect the freedom granted by the Treaty, either by imposing an absolute barrier to movement or by imposing a condition which is clearly inconsistent with the freedom granted by the Treaty, but which are formally addressed to all economic operators, are not considered as automatically caught by Articles 39, 43 and 49 EC, and can be justified also according to the imperative requirements doctrine.

So, for instance, in the case of free movement of services the Court, usually,[119] accepts that a residence requirement, formally addressed to all economic operators, constitutes indirect discrimination and might thus be justified also having regard

---

[112] Consistent case law; Case 41/74 *Van Duyn* [1974] ECR 1337; Case 67/74 *Bonsignore* [1975] ECR 297; Case 30/77 *Bouchereau* [1977] ECR 1999; Joined Cases 115 and 116/81 *Adoui and Cornuaille* [1982] ECR 1665; Case C-265/88 *Messner* [1989] ECR 4209; Case C-348/96 *Calfa* [1999] ECR I-11. It could be argued that rules which can be imposed only on foreigners are inherently discriminatory much as in sex discrimination law discrimination on grounds of pregnancy is considered to be direct discrimination; Case C-177/88 *Dekker* [1990] ECR I-3941.

[113] Case 2/74 *Reyners* [1974] ECR 631.

[114] E.g. Case 225/85 *Commission v Italy* (CNR) [1987] ECR 2625.

[115] Case C-173/94 *Commission v Belgium* (Employment in the public sector) [1996] ECR I-3265.

[116] Case C-47/02 *Anker and others* [2003] ECR I-10447; see also Case C-405/01 *Colegio de Oficiales de la Marina Mercante Española* [2003] ECR I-10391.

[117] On this point cf A Arnull, A Dashwood, M Dougan, M Ross, E Spaventa and D Wyatt, *Wyatt and Dashwood's European Union Law* (5th ed., Sweet and Maxwell 2006), Chapter 19.

[118] Or rules which are clearly protectionist; *cf* Case C-17/92 *Fedecine* [1993] ECR I-2239.

[119] An establishment requirement was held to be directly discriminatory in Case 352/85 *Bond van Adverteerders* [1988] ECR 2085; Case C-211/91 *Commission v Belgium* (Access to cable television

to the imperative requirements doctrine.[120] However, a residence (or establishment) requirement is the 'very negation of the freedom to provide services'[121] since it determines the inability of the provider to rely on Article 49 EC; an established provider falls in fact within Article 43 EC, not within Article 49 EC.[122] Further, an absolute ban on the possibility of providing a service in a Member State, even though the service is lawfully provided in the State of establishment (i.e. something which in the context of the free movement of goods would be qualified as a quantitative restriction),[123] can be assessed having regard to the imperative requirements doctrine.[124] Rules which distinguish according to the place where the service is received are also considered to be indirectly rather than directly discriminatory: thus in *Van Schaik*, a Dutch rule that imposed a geographical restriction on garages authorized to carry out the mandatory roadworthiness tests, was not considered to be directly discriminatory.[125] Similarly, in the health care cases, which will be more thoroughly examined in Chapter 2 below, rules which distinguished on grounds of the location of the health-care provider have been assessed according to the imperative requirements doctrine.[126] In the case of establishment, rules which limit the number of establishments or which

---

networks) [1992] ECR I-6757. In Case C-484/93 *Svensson and Gustavsson* [1995] ECR I-3955, the Court examined the compatibility with the Treaty of a Luxembourgian provision which limited subsidies on interest rates for loans taken out for housing purposes to loans taken out with institutions established in Luxembourg. The Court held the provision to be discriminatory against credit institutions established elsewhere, and found that such discrimination could be justified *only* having regard to Art. 46 EC. However, since such interpretation partially conflicted with the Court's own interpretation in Case C-204/90 *Bachmann* [1992] ECR I-249, the Court went on to analyze the tax cohesion justification. It seems that in this case the Court interpreted such justification as falling within the public policy derogation contained in Art. 46 EC. More recently see Case C-224/97 *Ciola* [1999] ECR I-2517.

[120] E.g. Case C-360/89 *Commission v Italy* (Award of public works contracts) [1992] ECR I-340; in this case an Italian rule reserving 15 per cent to 30 per cent of public works to undertakings established in a given region was held to be indirectly discriminatory and thus seems to be at odds with Case C-21/88 *Du Pont de Nemours Italiana* [1990] ECR I-889, where a similar rule in relation to goods was found to be directly discriminatory; in Case C-118/96 *Safir* [1998] ECR I-1897, AG Tesauro's call for a clarification on whether an establishment requirement is to be considered directly discriminatory fell into deaf hears. However, since the Court referred to the imperative requirements, it is likely that it considered the residence requirement as indirectly rather than directly discriminatory. On a similar issue, see also Case C-55/98 *Skatteministeriet* [1999] ECR I-7641.

[121] *cf* Case 205/84 *Commission v Germany* (Insurance) [1986] ECR 3755, para 52, and more recently, Case C-493/99 *Commission v Germany* (Restrictions on the construction industry) [2001] ECR I-8163.

[122] Cf, also Case C-398/95 *SETTG v Ypurgos Ergasias* [1997] ECR I-3091, relating to a rule providing that a given service could be provided only in the context of an employment relationship, thus excluding the possibility of providing the service as a *service*.

[123] Case 34/79 *Henn and Darby* [1979] ECR 3795.

[124] Case C-275/92 *Schindler* [1994] ECR I-1039.

[125] Case C-55/93 *Van Schaik* [1994] ECR I-4837; Case C-158/96 *Kohll* [1998] ECR I-1931. See also Case C-39/04 *Laboratoires Fournier SA* [2005] ECR I-2057.

[126] Case C-158/96 *Kholl* [1998] ECR I-1931; Case C-157/99 *Garaets-Smits* and *Peerbooms* [2001] ECR I-5473; Case C-368/98 *Vanbraekel* [2001] ECR I-5363; Case C-385/99 *Müller Fauré* and *van Riet* [2003] ECR I-4509; Case C-8/02 *Leichte* ECR I-2641; Case C-372/04 *Watts* [2006] ECR I-4325.

prescribe a given form of establishment,[127] thus limiting, if not altogether preventing the freedom granted by the Treaty, can also be assessed in relation to the imperative requirements doctrine.

2.2.2. *Indirect Discrimination*[128]

The concept of indirect discrimination, of judicial derivation but then accepted by legislators,[129] acknowledges that discrimination might arise from established patterns of regulatory or private behaviour that, for cultural-historic reasons, work to the disadvantage of a given group. Indirect discrimination occurs when rules, although neutral in their formulation, are likely to bear more heavily on a protected group. Thus, the fact that the rule is likely to affect one category more than the other is a first sign that there might be indirect discrimination. Whilst in the case of directly discriminatory provisions the form alone is relevant and sufficient, in the case of indirectly discriminatory provisions neither the form nor the intention matter, but rather what is relevant is the *effect* of the rule.[130] However, a disparate effect alone is not conclusive. There might be an objective reason which justifies the different impact of the rule, i.e. an aim which is consistent with the values enshrined in a given system, that the rule seeks to pursue, and which cannot be pursued other than through that rule, such that the rule is necessary to achieve the intended aim. Should this be the case, the rule is not considered to be discriminatory,[131] since the fact that the rule affects one category more than the other is but a

---

[127] Case 107/83 *Klopp* [1984] ECR 2971; Case C-106/91 *Ramrath* [1992] ECR I-3351; Case C-101/94 *Commission v Italy* (Dealing in transferable securities) [1996] ECR I-2691.

[128] The explanation below is taken from E Spaventa 'On Discrimination and the Theory of Mandatory Requirements' (2000) 3 CYELS 457.

[129] The concept of indirect discrimination was developed in the context of sex and race discrimination; S Fredman 'Combating Racism with Human Rights: the Right to Equality' in S Fredman (ed) *Discrimination and Human Rights. The Case of Racism* (OUP Oxford 2001) 9, traces the birth of the concept of indirect discrimination to an American case, *Griggs v Duke Power* 401 US 424 (1971). In the EC context the Court first referred to indirect discrimination in Case 152/73 *Sotgiu* [1974] ECR 153 in relation to nationality discrimination. Indirect discrimination in relation to sex equality was codified in Article 2 Directive 76/207 on the implementation of the principle of equal treatment for men and women as regards access to employment, vocational training and promotion and working conditions [1976] OJ L 39/40 (the Directive has been amended by Directive 2002/73 [2002] OJ L 269/15, which however has not amended the original definition of indirect discrimination) and see e.g. Case 97/80 *Jenkins* [1981] ECR 911. Indirect discrimination has also been codified in Article 2 of Directive 2000/43 implementing the principle of equal treatment between persons irrespective of racial and ethnic origin, [2000] OJ L 180/22; and in Article 2 of Directive 2000/78 establishing a general framework for equal treatment in employment and occupation, [2000] OJ L 303/16.

[130] Some authors argue that even in the case of indirect discrimination it is the intention of the legislature which matters, and the objective justifications, which highlight a legitimate aim of the measure, are evidence of absence of discriminatory intent. However, this would mean that discrimination theory cannot be used to correct long standing patterns of legislative behaviour which unintentionally discriminate against a given category.

[131] See also G Davies *Nationality Discrimination in the European Internal Market* (Kluwer Law International The Hague 2003), Chapter 2. Some authors talk about justified discrimination, but it seems more appropriate to say that in the case in which there is an objective justification there is no

'side effect' of a legitimate regulatory choice. On the contrary, if there is no objective justification, then the fact that the rule affects one category more than another brings that rule within the scope of application of the prohibition of discrimination: the rule will then be upheld if, and only if, there is another rule of equal rank allowing such discrimination to occur.

The concept of objective justification should be distinguished, at least as a matter of theory, from the assessment of comparability of situations, which is performed in order to assess whether there is discrimination at all. In the latter case the scrutiny is directed at establishing whether there is an objective difference which brings the rule outside the scope of the prohibition on discrimination which, as said above, occurs when *comparable* situations are treated differently.[132] An example may serve to illustrate the difference: a rule which provides that no woman may play in a men's championship might be non-discriminatory because women and men might be, in this context (sporting activity), in non-comparable situations. If the situations were comparable, the rule would be directly discriminatory and could be justified only if a provision of equal rank so allowed.

On the other hand, a rule which does not distinguish on grounds of sex, but which provides that only people weighing more than 85 kg may perform a given job is, for the sake of argument, likely to affect more women than men. It would then escape the provision prohibiting discrimination only if objectively justified, for instance, because the job is a heavy lifting job and could put smaller people at risk. Admittedly, the distinction between objective differences and objective reasons is more theoretical than real: this is because some indirect discrimination cases may also be solved having regard to an assessment in terms of comparability (in the above example we could say that people weighing less than 85 kg are objectively in a different situation); an objective difference is also an objective reason which explains the different impact of the rule. However, the reverse is not true: in direct discrimination cases, either the situations are comparable, and thus we have discrimination and must have recourse to derogations, or the situations are

---

discrimination although there is a disparate effect. Contrast the view expressed in the text with N. Bernard 'Discrimination and Free movement in EC Law' (1996) 45 ICLQ 82, 101. He believes that the justifications bring the rule out of the scope of discrimination only in an intention-based conception of discrimination (if the intention of the legislator is to achieve a legitimate purpose, its intention is not to discriminate and thus the rule is not discriminatory). In an effect-base conception of discrimination on the other hand, the justification will not change the fact that the effects of the measure are discriminatory and the rule becomes lawfully discriminatory because of values which are given precedence over non-discrimination.

[132] In free movement law comparability between nationals and non-nationals is usually presumed; however sporadically the Court has referred to comparability to exclude the application of the principle of non-discrimination; cf Case C-336/96 *Gilly* [1998] ECR I-2793; Case C-356/98 *Kaba* (No 1) [2000] ECR I-2623; a comparability assessment is crucial in cases relating to discriminatory taxation, see Article 58(1)(a) EC, and e.g. Joined Cases C-430 and 431/99 *Sea-Land Service Inc and Nedlloyd Lijnen BV* [2002] ECR I-5235. On the function of comparability in trade law see G de Búrca 'Unpacking the Concept of Discrimination in EC and International Trade Law' in C Barnard and J Scott (eds) *The Law of the Single European Market. Unpacking the premises.* (Hart Publishing Oxford 2002) 181.

not comparable and there is no discrimination. There is no space in this context for a side effect theory which allows broader public interests to be taken into account.

a) Comparator in Free Movement Law: National or Mover?

In order to assess whether a rule is discriminatory, either directly or indirectly, a comparator is needed. The breadth of the principle will then very much depend on the comparator chosen and on the evidence required in order to plead indirect discrimination. As far as the latter issue is concerned the Court, rather differently from sex discrimination law,[133] is satisfied that in order to plead indirect discrimination need not prove that the rule *actually* affects more foreigners than nationals: the likelihood of a rule to affect one category more than the other, which is to say the *potentiality of the rule* to act to the detriment of foreigners, is enough to bring it within the scope of the prohibition on discrimination.[134]

As for the comparator, the matter is considerably more confused. In other words, is the relevant comparator only a foreigner, or also a non-migrant? The Court has consistently held that the Treaty free movement provisions can be invoked against the State of origin not only in relation to those rules which, by imposing barriers to exit,[135] directly affect the exercise of the right to move, but also in relation to rules imposed on a national who returns to the Member State of origin after having exercised a free movement right.[136] However, there cannot be any discrimination on grounds of nationality if the person relying on the anti-discrimination provision is in fact a member of the allegedly advantaged category. In those cases, the Court avoided this problem by equating the situation of the *returned* national to the situation of a non-national exercising her right to free movement. The Court reasons then as if the national were in fact a non-national and assesses whether there is discrimination on grounds of nationality. Via this legal fiction the Court is then able to grant full protection to those who have exercised their free movement rights. But this remains a legal fiction: it would be more realistic to say that what the Court is comparing – at least in those cases – is the situation of someone who has exercised her/his right to movement with the situation of someone who has not exercised their Community right. It can be argued then that, even before the expansion of the scope of the free movement of persons' provisions to encompass

[133] In sex discrimination law for a rule to be considered indirectly discriminatory it must affect a significantly higher percentage of one of the sexes; the disparate effect must be demonstrated through statistical analysis; e.g. Case C-167/97 *Seymour-Smith* [1999] ECR I-623.
[134] Case C-237/94 *O'Flynn* [1996] ECR I-2617, para 21. However, it seems to be open to the resisting party to demonstrate that the rule does not affect in fact foreigners more than nationals; Case C-18/95 *Terhoeve* [1999] ECR I-345, in which the Court unusually had to resort to the *Bosman* formula in a case relating to social security benefits since it had been demonstrated that the rule affected more nationals than foreigners.
[135] Consistent case law; e.g. Case 286/82 and 26/83 *Luisi and Carbone* [1984] ECR 377, and in the case of companies, Case 81/87 *Daily Mail* [1988] ECR 593.
[136] Consistent case law; e.g. Case 115/78 *Knoors* [1979] ECR 399; Case C-61/89 *Bouchoucha* [1990] ECR I-3551; Case C-370/90 *Singh* [1992] ECR I-4265; Case C-19/92 *Kraus* [1993] ECR I-1663.

non-discriminatory barriers, the Treaty provisions encompassed both a prohibition of discrimination on grounds of nationality and a prohibition of discriminatory treatment of migrants.[137]

This interpretation is consistent with a teleological (and literal) interpretation of the Treaty.[138] If the latter grants a right to movement,[139] it is natural that one should not be penalized for having exercised the right granted therein. The fact that the relevant comparator might be the migrant was openly stated in *O'Flynn*. In this case, Mr O'Flynn, an Irish national who had worked and was still resident in the UK, applied for a funeral payment in respect of expenses for the burial of his son which had taken place in the Republic of Ireland. The benefit was refused on the sole ground that the burial had taken place outside the United Kingdom. The Court found that such rule was indirectly discriminatory, and it held that 'conditions imposed by national law must be regarded as indirectly discriminatory where, although applicable irrespective of nationality, they affect essentially migrant workers (. . .) or the great majority of those affected are migrant workers (. . .), where they are indistinctly applicable but can more easily be satisfied by national workers than by migrant workers (. . .) or where there is a risk that they may operate to the particular detriment of migrant workers'.[140]

This said, in *Singh* the Court actually equated the situation of a national migrant to that of a foreigner in order to extend the Treaty protection to the national's spouse.[141] In that case, a British national returned to the United Kingdom with her husband after having worked in Germany. The United Kingdom applied its own immigration law and refused to grant Mr Singh a right to reside in the UK. Mr Singh argued that he had a right granted by Community law to reside in the UK as the spouse of a Community national: thus, the UK should apply the more favourable Community law regime rather than its own immigration rules. It should be noted that Mr and Mrs Singh were already married before moving to Germany; thus, in coming back to the United Kingdom, they were not in a more disadvantaged position than they were before moving. Any detrimental effect arose because of the application of British immigration rules, not because of the fact that they had moved. This notwithstanding the Court found that: 'A national of a Member State might

---

[137] Cf also AG Fennelly's Opinion in Case C-190/98 *Graf* [2000] ECR I-437, esp. para 21, and the case law, e.g. Case C-224/98 *M N D'Hoop* [2002] ECR I-6191.

[138] In this sense also N Bernard 'Discrimination and Free Movement in EC Law' (1996) 45 ICLQ 82, 89.

[139] Cf the definition of the internal market in Article 3 EC.

[140] Case C-237/94 *O'Flynn* [1996] ECR I-2617, para 18; in social security cases the Court often compares the situation of the migrant against the situation of the non-migrant in order to assess whether there is discrimination; e.g. Case C-165/91 *Van Munster* [1994] ECR I-4661, para 30. However, the Court's reasoning is often confused, e.g. Case C-124/99 *Borawitz* [2000] ECR I-7293, para 25 in which the Court first relies on the *O'Flynn* test, and stresses that the relevant discrimination is that against migrant workers, to then proceed to assess the rule in terms of nationality; cf also Case C-302/98 *Sehrer* [2000] ECR I-4585, esp. para 33 and 34. The Treaty also precludes rules which place at a disadvantage those who want to extend their activities to more than one Member State; cf Case 143/87 *Stanton v INASTI* [1988] ECR 3877.

[141] Case C-370/90 *Singh* [1992] ECR I-4265.

be deterred from leaving his country of origin in order to pursue an activity as an employed or self-employed person as envisaged by the Treaty in the territory of another Member State if, on returning to the Member State of which he is a national in order to pursue an activity there as an employed or self-employed person, the conditions of his entry and residence were not at least equivalent to those which he would enjoy under the Treaty or secondary law in the territory of another Member State'.[142] It therefore held that Mr and Mrs Singh were entitled to rely on Community law in relation to Mr Singh's right to residence. The ruling is badly reasoned; the issue here was not one of 'deterrence' from leaving: the couple did not suffer a detriment because they had migrated to another Member State. Rather, a Union national must have exactly the same right to *move* back to her/his Member State as any other Union migrant: had Mr and Mrs Singh known that Mr Singh would have been subject to harsher immigration rules than those applicable in Germany, they might have not moved back to the United Kingdom. The rules at issue affected the exercise of the right to move (back), and for this reason the Court correctly equated their situation to that of any other Community migrant.[143]

3. Examples of Indirect Discrimination in the Context of Free Movement

Since the scope of the free movement of persons' provisions was limited until the early 1990s to a prohibition on discriminatory rules,[144] the concept of indirect discrimination has been extremely important in order to detect measures which, although neutral in their formulation, would run against the common market objective. It is not surprising then that it is in the context of the persons provisions that the interpretation of indirect discrimination on grounds of nationality finds its most refined application. The underlying principle is that any rule which has a territorial element is likely to be indirectly discriminatory because it is inherently easier to be satisfied by the Member State's own nationals and/or discourage movement.[145] Thus, for instance, a residence requirement is likely to affect non-nationals more severely than nationals since nationals are more likely to be resident in their own Member State, and it has therefore to be justified; and so do rules which link benefits to presence or use within the territory.[146] In the case of

[142] Case C-370/90 *Singh* [1992] ECR I-4265, para 19.
[143] See also the discussion on reverse discrimination in Chapter 6.
[144] The Court explicitly denied the possibility of expanding the scope of Article 43 EC to encompass non-discriminatory restrictions in Case 221/85 *Commission v Belgium* (Clinical biology laboratories) [1987] ECR 719; Case 198/86 *Conradi* [1987] ECR 4469; Case 292/86 *Gullung* [1988] ECR 111.
[145] E.g. the rules in Case C-237/94 *O'Flynn* [1996] ECR I-2617; or the rules in Case C-109/04 *Kranemann* [2005] ECR I-2421, which provided for the reimbursement of trainee lawyers' travel expenses only within Germany; see also Case C-464/02 *Commission v Denmark* [2005] ECR I-7929 on discriminatory taxation for vehicles used for work purposes.
[146] This is now consistent case law; eg 39/75 *Coenen* [1975] ECR 1575; and the cases relating to social security benefits, e.g. Case C-111/91 *Commission v Luxembourg* (childbirth and maternity allowances) [1993] ECR I-817. Social security contributions cannot be imposed if the migrant

rules concerning direct taxation, the assessment of whether the rule is actually discriminatory is slightly more complex, and often requires an assessment on whether residents and non-residents are in a comparable situation.[147] This is not only because direct taxation is inherently territorial, but also because it is normal in international tax law to distinguish according to where the person has her/his primary establishment so as to avoid both double taxation, and double benefits. A resident is taxed over her or his worldwide income, and granted benefits according to her/his personal situation.[148] A non-resident is taxed over the income (source income) earned in the State and no personal situation is taken into account. Thus, the existence of discrimination will depend on whether resident and non-resident are in comparable situations.[149]

Furthermore, rules which impose the possession of a domestic qualification are considered indirectly discriminatory since nationals are more likely to have completed their education or training in the national territory.[150] Whilst the Court has recognized that in theory those requirements are consistent with Community law, since they pursue a public interest worthy of protection, the principles of necessity and proportionality imply that Member States must take into account knowledge and qualifications acquired in another Member State.[151] Similarly,

---

employee or self-employed will not gain any benefit from them; Joined Cases 62 and 63/81 *Seco SA and Desquenne & Giral SA* [1982] ECR 223; Case 143/87 *Stanton v Inasti* [1988] ECR 3877;

[147] E.g. Case C-169/03 *Wallentin* [2004] ECR I-6443, esp. para 16; discriminatory taxation can be challenged also by relying on Articles 18 and 12 EC, e.g. Case C-365/02 *Lindfords* [2004] ECR I-7183; Case C-403/03 *Schempp* [2005] ECR I-6421.

[148] E.g. Case C-391/97 *Gschwind* [1999] ECR I-5451; but the applicability of international conventions or of tax rules cannot lead to no State taking into consideration the entire personal situation of the tax-payer for the purpose of awarding benefits or tax relief, Case C-385/00 *de Groot* [2002] ECR I-4517.

[149] Case C-279/93 *Schumaker* [1995] ECR I-225; Case C-80/94 *Wielockx* [1995] ECR I-2493; Case C-107/94 *Asscher* [1996] ECR I-3089; Case C-87/99 *Zurstrassen* [2000] ECR I-3337; Case C-234/01 *Gerritse* [2003] ECR I-5933. The same approach applies to corporate tax; Case 270/83 *Commission v France* (Shareholders' tax credits) [1986] ECR 273; Case C-330/91 *Commerzbank* [1993] ECR I-4017; Case C-1/93 *Halliburton* [1994] ECR I-1137; Case C-264/91 *ICI v Colmer* [1998] ECR I-4695; Case C-200/98 *X AB, X AC v Riksskatteverket* [1999] ECR I-8261; Case C-307/97 *Compagnie de Saint-Gobain* [1999] ECR I-6161; C-397/98 and C-410/98 *Metallgesellchaft Ltd and Others* [2001] ECR I-1727; Case C-324/00 *Lankhorst-Hohorst GmbH* [2002] ECR I-11779; Case C-446/03 *Marks and Spencer* [2005] ECR I-10837; Case C-170/05 *Denkavit International BV* [2006] ECR I-11949.

[150] Case 11/77 *Patrick* [1977] ECR 1199; when the decision about recognition is final Community law imposes duties to state reasons and a judicial remedy, Case 222/86 *Heylens* [1987] ECR 4097. The cases on recognition of qualifications can also be analyzed within the framework of material discrimination since such requirements amount to equal treatment of different situations (requiring a qualification from a person who already holds a qualification is different from requiring a qualification from a person who holds none); and within the framework of the double burden theory, in that the qualified migrant has already been subject to the rules of the Member State where the qualification was acquired.

[151] Case 71/76 *Thieffry* [1977] ECR 765; and Case C-340/89 *Vlassopoulou* [1991] ECR I-2357. The mutual recognition of qualifications has been the focus of secondary legislation; see e.g. Directive 2005/36 on the recognition of professional qualifications [2005] OJ L 255/22.

Member States have to take into account professional experience acquired in the public sector in other Member States, when seniority in their own public sector is linked to seniority previously acquired in some, or all, branches of the public sector.[152] This applies even when seniority acquired in the domestic private sector is not taken into account,[153] since otherwise non-nationals, less likely to have worked in the public sector of the host country, would be penalized. Finally, it is not only rules which contain a territorial element which might be indirectly discriminatory. For instance a language requirement, easier to be satisfied by nationals than non-nationals,[154] is subject to the necessity and proportionality assessment. But also less favourable employment conditions for foreign language assistants have been considered as indirectly discriminatory since most foreign language teachers are foreigners.[155]

4. Indirect Discrimination and the Free Movement of Services: Mutual Recognition and Double Burden

If the scope of the workers and establishment provisions was limited until the 1990s to a discriminatory assessment, the situation is partially different in the case of services.[156] Even though it is only in 1991 that non-discriminatory restrictions are expressly brought within the scope of the Treaty,[157] the interpretation given to Article 49 EC has always been broader in scope, and the extent to which the host Member State could impose its rules on foreign service providers was more limited than in the case of people who established themselves there. Mandatory compliance with the professional rules of the recipient Member State is likely to bear more heavily on the foreign service provider than on domestic providers. This is the case since the foreign service provider is already subject to the rules of the Member State of establishment. For the host-Member State to impose all of its rules on someone who is already regulated elsewhere, and which might be providing the service only on an occasional basis, might then be seen as indirectly discriminatory

---

[152] Case C-419/92 *Scholz* [1994] ECR I-505, and more recently Case C-278/03 *Commission v Italy* (teaching staff) [2005] ECR I-3747; Member States also have to take into account periods served in another Member State's army, if those are relevant for seniority when served in the national army, Case 15/69 *Ugliola* [1969] ECR 363.

[153] Case C-15/96 *Kalliope Schöning* [1998] ECR I-47; Case C-195/98 *Österreichischer Gewerkschaftsbund* [2000] ECR I-10497; Case C-278/03 *Commission v Italy* [2005] ECR I-3747. In relation to pensionable periods see Case C-443/93 *Ioannis Vougioukas v Idryma Koinonikon Asfalisseon (IKA)* [1995] ECR I-4033.

[154] Case 379/87 *Groener* [1989] ECR 3967; however in Case C-424/97 *Haim I* [2000] ECR I-5123, a language requirement was considered a hindrance rather than a discriminatory restriction. See also Article 3 Regulation 1612/68.

[155] E.g. Case C-33/88 *Allué and Coonan* [1989] ECR I-1591.

[156] After much debate, a political compromise on the services directive has finally been reached; see Directive 2006/123 on services in the internal market [2006] OJ L 376/36.

[157] Case C-288/89 *Gouda* [1991] ECR I-4007; Case C-76/90 *Säger* [1991] ECR I-4221.

since the imposition of the domestic rules bears much more heavily on the foreign provider than on the domestic provider. Furthermore, the imposition of the host-State rules on the foreign provider might also create a double regulatory burden: whilst domestic providers are regulated only by their own Member State, foreign providers would be regulated both by the Member State of establishment and by the host-State and, in any case, the imposition of *all* the rules of the host State might be seen as discriminatory since it amounts to treating two different situations equally.[158]

In order to assess which rules could legitimately be applied by the Member State of the recipient, the Court elaborated, from the very first case,[159] a rule of reason approach: specific requirements having as their scope the application of professional rules *justified* by the general good, binding upon any person providing the service in the Member State, were not to be construed as being incompatible with the Treaty.[160] This 'rule of reason' was extended so as to impose a sort of principle of 'mutual recognition': the recipient Member State cannot impose requirements which the service provider has already satisfied in its country of origin.[161] Therefore, and not withstanding the text of Article 50 EC, not *all* the legislation applicable to nationals of the recipient Member State may be equally applied to foreign service providers. In this regard, even when the requirement imposed by the recipient Member State is justified, evidence and guarantees already given by the provider in the Member State of its establishment must be taken into account.[162]

5. The Scope of the Principle of Non-discrimination

The principle of non-discrimination applies to all rules which fall within the material scope of the relevant Treaty provision; such material scope is interpreted

[158] However only sporadically does the Court rely on this type of reasoning; e.g. Case 427/85 *Commission v Germany* (Restrictions on lawyers) [1988] ECR 1123, para 42.

[159] Case 33/74 *Van Bisbergen* [1974] ECR 1299; U Everling 'Sur la jurisprudence récente de la Cour de Justice en matière de libre prestation des services rendues dans d'autres Etats membres' (1984) 19 CDE 3, 7, at the time judge of the ECJ, argued that *Van Bisbergen* left open the question whether Art. 49 EC restricted only discriminatory provisions or not. After having pointed out that the Treaty drafters' intention was to so limit the scope of the Treaty provisions (he took part in the Treaty negotiations), he argued that the Treaty provisions should not be so limited. However, in subsequent cases, the Court made clear that Article 49 EC was limited to a prohibition on discriminatory restrictions, e.g. Case 90/76 *Henry van Ameyde* [1977] ECR 1091; Case 15/78 *Koestler* [1978] ECR 1971.

[160] And a residence requirement would be justified if necessary to enforce professional rules; operative part of Case 33/74 *Van Bisbergen* [1974] ECR 1299.

[161] Joined cases 110 and 111/78 *van Wesemael* [1979] ECR 35.

[162] Case 279/80 *Webb* [1981] ECR 3305; AG Slynn in his opinion, at 3331, argued that discrimination 'is not an essential or the exclusive element of such a restriction'. It is quite clear that AG Slynn's reasoning draws from the case law pertaining to the free movement of goods; it is interesting to note, however, how the Court, in this case as in Case 52/79 *Debauve* [1980] ECR 833, resists the temptation of broadening the scope of Art. 49 EC, by explicitly including a paragraph mentioning discrimination.

in a generous way. Broadly speaking, we can divide those rules in three categories: rules which, by governing the conditions for the lawful exercise of the economic activity, directly affect the exercise of a Treaty freedom; rules that indirectly affect the exercise of the Treaty freedoms by governing other aspects of social life which might be relevant to the economic operator; and thirdly, rules which are ancillary to the freedom exercised.

Rules which directly affect the exercise of a Treaty freedom are, for instance, rules regulating access and conditions of employment or self-employment. It is in relation to this type of rules that the Court has declared qualification, residence and language requirements to be indirectly discriminatory.[163]

Rules which indirectly affect the exercise of a Treaty freedom are, for instance, those rules regulating access to welfare provision; access to publicly owned property;[164] social housing;[165] taxation;[166] and so on. Here, the basic tenet of post-war welfare societies is that the lawful economic migrant contributes to the economic growth of the State and is therefore entitled to a share of the State's resources.[167] This principle has been transposed in the Community system by Article 7(2) Regulation 1612/68, which provides that migrant Union workers are entitled to the same tax and social advantages as own workers; and this principle was applied to the self-employed despite the previous lack of an explicit provision to guarantee equality of treatment in relation to that category.[168] The breadth of the principle of equal treatment in Community law is, however, particularly ample for two concurrent reasons. First of all, as we have seen before, the notion of 'worker' is very broadly construed, and even those who engage in part time work for a few hours a week would be eligible to social advantages.[169] Secondly, the notion of what constitutes a social advantage has also been broadly construed to include not only those advantages attached to the contract of employment, but also all benefits granted to workers because of their status of workers; those granted by virtue of residence in the national territory; and those which encourage mobility.[170] Furthermore, the non-discrimination principle applies also to social advantages that assist the

---

[163] E.g. Case 33/74 *Van Bisbergen* [1974] ECR 1299; Case 379/87 *Groener* [1989] ECR 3967; Case C-340/89 *Vlassopoulou* [1991] ECR I-2357.
[164] Case 197/84 *Steinhauser* [1985] ECR I-1819.
[165] Case 63/86 *Commission v Italy* (Social housing) [1988] ECR 29. Also Case C-168/91 *Konstantinidis* [1993] ECR I-1191, where the Court found that rules on transliteration of Greek names could, under certain circumstances, affect freedom of establishment.
[166] Article 7(2) Regulation 1612/68 provides for a right not to be discriminated on grounds of nationality in relation to tax and social advantages. See below.
[167] Thus whilst the elimination of discrimination in relation to access to employment is one of the 'revolutionary' elements of the Treaty, the principle of equal treatment in relation to conditions of employment is quite common in relation to all economic migrants.
[168] E.g. Case C-337/97 *Meussen* [1999] ECR I-3289.
[169] But originally not work-seekers, see above.
[170] E.g. interest-free child birth loan, Case 65/81 *Reina* [1982] ECR 33.

Following the amendments introduced by Directive 2004/38, the family members who have a right to reside and work in the host-State[187] (regardless of their nationality) are the spouse; the registered partner when registered partnerships are treated in the host-State as equivalent to marriage; the children under the age of 21 or dependent;[188] and the dependent relatives in the ascending line of both worker and spouse (i.e. their parents).[189] In the case of *Akrich*,[190] the Court clarified that in order to benefit from the right to move and reside provided by Directive 2004/38,[191] the family member must be lawfully present in the territory of the Community. In other words, the provisions of the Directive cannot be used to rectify the illegal status of a migrant and to elude altogether migration controls.[192]

Furthermore, Member States have to 'facilitate' entry and residence of other family members when they are dependent; when they are members of the Union citizen's household; or when they require the personal care of the Union citizen because of serious health grounds. Member States also have to 'facilitate' entry and residence of the partner with whom the Union citizen has a durable relationship duly attested.[193] Member States might impose an entry visa on third country national family members,[194] but cannot deny entrance at the frontier, if the family member can prove the family ties, on the sole ground of the lack of a visa.[195]

The other major omission in the Regulation was the lack of provision of a right to stay for spouses whose marriage had ended through divorce or annulment.[196] The lack of recognition of the right to remain in the host country after the termination of marriage gave rise to serious concerns, especially in relation

---

[187] Articles 2 and 23 Directive 2004/38.

[188] It is immaterial whether the children are born to the non-Union citizen only; Case C-413/99 *Baumbast and R* [2002] ECR I-7091.

[189] Dependency means that the family members need the material support of the Union citizen and/or their spouse in order to meet their basic needs; see Case C-1/05 *Jia*, judgment of 09 January 2007, nyr.

[190] Case C-109/01 *Akrich* [2003] ECR I-9607. The decision in *Akrich* partially overruled Case C-459/99 *MRAX* [2002] ECR I-6591, which allowed migrants' spouses to rely on Regulation 1612/68 regardless of their original migration status. See E Spaventa 'Annotation on *Akrich*' (2005) 42 CMLRev 225 and Chapter 6 below. The Court has clarified that the decision in *Akrich* does not require Member States to make the grant of a residence permit to family members conditional upon their previous lawful residence in another Member State, see Case C-1/05 *Jia*, judgment of 09 January 2007, nyr.

[191] At the time the right provided by Article 10 Regulation 1612/68.

[192] See also AG Geelhoed's opinion in Case C-1/05 *Jia*, opinion delivered 27/04/06, judgment of 09 January 2007.

[193] Article 3 Directive 2004/38.

[194] Rules relating to visas are harmonized for those Member States participating to Title IV EC; Regulation 539/2001 listing the third countries whose nationals must be in possession of visas when crossing the external borders of Member States and those whose nationals are exempt from that requirement [2001] OJ L 81/1 (the UK and Ireland have not opted in). See proposal for a Council Regulation amending Regulation 539/2001 (2006) COM 84 final.

[195] Article 5 Directive 2004/38, cp also Case C-459/99 *MRAX* [2002] ECR I-6591.

[196] But the Court also stated that until when the divorce had been declared, it was immaterial whether the spouses lived together (i.e. separation without divorce would not entail loss of the right to reside), Case 267/83 *Diatta* [1985] ECR 567.

to the possibility that an abused spouse might be left in a position of not terminating the abusive relationship for fear of losing her residence right. Those concerns were fully addressed by Directive 2004/38, which provides for a right to stay upon termination of the marriage provided certain conditions are satisfied; and in any event when the Union citizen's spouse/partner has been the victim of domestic violence.[197]

Finally, Article 12 Regulation 1612/68, which is still in force, provides that the children of a worker have a right to be admitted to education, vocational courses, and apprenticeship under the same conditions as nationals. Not surprisingly, this right to equal treatment has been interpreted broadly by the Court: thus, it extends also to non-dependent children over 21 (so beyond the scope of Article 2(2)(d) Directive 2004/38)[198] and it covers a wide range of courses as well as access to public funding.[199] But also, the right of the Union workers' children to education continues even after the parent has left the country;[200] the employment relationship has terminated;[201] or the family has broken down and the children do not live with the main right-holder.[202]

7. Conclusions

This chapter has provided a brief overview of the rights pertaining to economic migrants. As we have seen, the Court has been generous in interpreting the scope of the free movement provisions. Thus, it included in the definition of worker both part-timers and work seekers; it limited as much as possible the possibility for the Member States to rely on the Treaty derogations, avoiding that a broad reading of what constitutes a legitimate public policy reason, and of what is to be intended as public service/authority, could jeopardize the Treaty rights; it interpreted broadly both the concept of indirect discrimination and the link required to bring a rule within the scope of the Treaty.

We shall see in the rest of the book that the Court's generous interpretation of the Treaty led it to bring within its scope also rules which apply in law and in fact exactly in the same way to nationals and migrants. In this way, the concept of 'barrier to movement', relevant for Community law purposes, is significantly expanded. This generous interpretation however is not without its problems, since the broader the scope of the Treaty free movement provisions, the greater the impact on the Member States' regulatory autonomy. Once a rule falls within the scope of one of the free movement provisions, it has to be assessed in relation not only to its aims, but more importantly in relation to its proportionality.

---

[197] Cp Articles 12 and 13 Directive 2004/38.
[198] Case C-7/94 *Gaal* [1996] ECR I-1031.
[199] Case 76/72 *Michel S* [1973] ECR 457; Case 9/74 *Casagrande* [1974] ECR 773.
[200] Joined Cases 389 and 390/87 *Echternach and Moritz* [1989] ECR 723.
[201] Case C-413/99 *Baumbast and R* [2002] ECR I-7091.
[202] Case C-413/99 *Baumbast and R* [2002] ECR I-7091.

Furthermore, the fact that any justification for a rule which imposes a barrier to movement has to be consistent also with the general principles of Community law, and in particular with fundamental rights, introduces an additional layer of scrutiny. The effect is that of reallocating choices which usually pertain to the legislature in the hands of the judiciary. As a result, the national courts are greatly empowered, since the system results in a diffuse scrutiny of the balancing act between competing interests made by the authorities entrusted with such a task (whether executive, legislative or administrative). Those problems will form the focus of the rest of our investigation. It is now time to turn to the developments of the case law on the free movement of services which have occurred in the 1990s.

Chapter 2

Exploding the Boundaries: The Case Law on the Free Movement of Services in the 1990s and Beyond

We have seen in the previous chapter that the Court had, from the very beginning, adopted a purposive and generous interpretation of the free movement provisions. In particular, the Treaty was stretched to cover as many migrants as possible; the prohibition on indirect discrimination became a useful tool to remove those barriers which arose out of different cultural and legal traditions; the material scope of the Treaty was construed as embracing a wide number of areas, so that a migrant would be entitled to equal treatment in relation to almost all spheres of life. But, however broad the scope of the free movement of persons' provisions, the Court's interpretation was still confined to a discriminatory assessment and thus, in that respect, was much narrower than the interpretation adopted in relation to the free movement of goods during the 1980s. In the 1990s, this state of affairs is reversed. At the same time as the Court, with the *Keck* ruling, contracted the scope of Article 28 EC and defined more clearly the outer boundary of that provision, it expanded the scope of the free movement of persons, so as to include a prohibition on non-discriminatory barriers. In time, the expansion of Articles 39, 43 and 49 EC led to the same problems as those already experienced in relation to the free movement of goods. Thus, it has become increasingly difficult to define the scope of those freedoms; and – much more importantly – this expansion has come at the expense of national regulatory autonomy. More and more rules have to be subjected to judicial scrutiny for their proportionality and compliance with fundamental rights. In this chapter we are going to outline the development of the case law relating to the free movement of services, focusing in particular on the three elements necessary to trigger Article 49 EC: the concept of barrier to the provision of intra-Community services; the intra-Community element; and the notion of remuneration.

Before looking at that case law, however, we are going to recall the problems which arose in the context of the free movement of goods, and the way the Court sought to solve such problems with the *Keck* ruling. This is necessary since the debate about the appropriate scope and test for the free movement of persons provisions cannot be appreciated without reference to the debate in the field of free movement of goods.

1. The Free Movement of Goods – The Sunday Trading Saga and the *Keck* Ruling

The internal market comprises the free movement of goods (and capital) as well as the free movement of persons and indeed it is in the interpretation of Article 28 EC that the Court developed its most important hermeneutic tools. This section is not intended to give a comprehensive account of the scope of free movement of goods, or of the case law and the academic debate surrounding it. It is simply aimed at highlighting some of the problems that arose out of a very broad interpretation of that Treaty provision and the solution achieved by the Court. This is important because the free movement of persons case law is creating challenges not dissimilar from those which arose in the 1980s in respect of the free movement of goods and because, as said above, the debate about any of the individual free movement provisions has to be seen in the wider context of the internal market as a whole.

Article 28 EC provides for the prohibition of quantitative restrictions on imports and measures having equivalent effect to quantitative restrictions. Whilst the Court had no difficulty in defining quantitative restrictions, which are basically quotas and bans on imports, exports, and goods in transit,[1] the concept of measure having equivalent effect was more elusive.[2] The *Dassonville* formula, according to which Article 28 EC caught any trading rule which directly or indirectly, actually or potentially, affected intra-Community trade, did little to provide a precise definition of a measure having equivalent effect.[3] It was clear that rules which discriminated on the origin of the goods were inconsistent with the internal market objective,[4] and the Court made also clear in *Cassis de Dijon* that the existence of different regulatory environments in the Member States gave rise to obstacles to intra-Community trade.[5] For this reason, the Court held, Member

---

[1] Case 2/73 *Geddo* [1973] ECR 865, para 7. For an application of Article 28 to goods in transit, e.g. C-23/99 *Commission v France* (Spare parts for motor vehicles) [2000] ECR I-7653.

[2] See also Commission Directive 70/50/EEC on the abolition of measures which have an effect equivalent to restriction on imports and are not covered by other provisions adopted in pursuance of the EEC Treaty, [1970] OJ Sp Ed I L13/29, p. 17.

[3] Case 8/74 *Procureur du Roi v Dassonville* [1974] ECR 837, para 5.

[4] E.g. Case 113/80 *Commission v Ireland* (Irish souvenirs) [1981] ECR 1625; Case 59/82 *Schutzverband Gegen Unwesen I D Wirtschaft v Weinvertriebs-GMBH* [1983] ECR 1224; Case 229/83 *Association de Centres Distributeurs Edouard Leclerc and others v Sàrl 'Au Blé vert' and Others* [1985] ECR 1.

[5] Case 120/78 *Rewe-Zentrale AG v Bundesmonopolverwaltung für Branntwein* (Cassis de Dijon) [1979] ECR 649.

States should apply their rules to goods which are lawfully marketed in another Member State only to the extent to which that is necessary to protect a mandatory requirement of public interest.

The ruling in *Cassis de Dijon* established two important doctrines: that of mutual recognition, according to which products lawfully marketed in one Member State should be able to be marketed in all other Member States without having to comply with further rules; and the mandatory requirements doctrine, which allowed Member States to impose such further regulation if to do so was necessary to protect a mandatory requirement of public interest and if the restriction imposed by the rule was proportionate to the pursued aim. This said, in the aftermath of the *Cassis* ruling the scholarship was divided as to the scope of Article 28 EC, i.e. as to whether that Article prohibited also non-discriminatory restrictions. Thus, it was argued that, even though the Court neither mentioned discrimination, nor required a discrimination assessment, the scope of Article 28 EC was so limited. That was the case since, to impose rules on how a product should be manufactured (later called product requirements) on goods that had already satisfied the regulatory demands of the Member State of origin, would put those products at a disadvantage in comparison to own goods which needed only to comply with one set of regulatory standards.[6]

Whatever the scope of Article 28 EC after *Cassis*, the combined effect of *Dassonville* and *Cassis* was to establish a twofold test to determine the compatibility of national rules with Article 28 EC. First of all, the rule must be such as to affect directly or indirectly, actually or potentially intra-Community trade, and the application of the importing country's rules on imported products was always deemed to have such an effect. Secondly, the courts need to scrutinize whether the application of the rule on imported products is nonetheless 'justified' on public interest grounds. The ruling in *Cassis* undeniably served a number of purposes, and primarily that of balancing market integration with the regulatory needs of the Member States.[7] However, its very strength, the possibility of taking broader grounds of public interest into account, determined its main shortcoming. The attention of the Court in some cases shifted from defining what was a measure capable of affecting intra-Community trade, to assessing the necessity and proportionality of measures adopted by the Member States. This in time led to considerable problems because an increasing number of national rules had to undergo the proportionality and necessity assessment required by the mandatory requirements doctrine. In other words, the breadth of the *Dassonville* formula determined almost a presumption that *any* trading rule would be capable of affecting intra-Community trade at least indirectly and/or potentially and would therefore need

---

[6] G Marenco 'Pour une interprétation traditionnelle de la notion de mesure d'effet équivalant à une restriction quantitative' (1984) CDE 291, and more recently J Snell *Goods and Services in EC Law* (OUP Oxford 2002). We will come back to this point in Chapter 4.

[7] Cf Communication from the Commission concerning the consequences of the judgement given by the Court of Justice on 20 February in case 120/78 ('Cassis de Dijon'), [1980] OJ C 256/2.

to be justified in relation to a public interest.[8] As a result, in a series of cases starting with the ruling in *Cinéthèque* the Court accepted that national rules which merely regulated trade and, in so doing, caused a reduction in the overall volume of sales, including sales of imported products, fell within the scope of the Treaty.[9]

Cinéthèque concerned a rule which imposed the elapse of a time span between the release of a movie in cinemas and its release on videotapes. The Court held that the existence of disparities in national rules was enough to create a potential barrier to imports and thus needed to be justified.[10] Given the fact that, lacking harmonization, national rules almost always differ, the finding in *Cinéthèque* meant that the application of any rule to a foreign product was a potential barrier in need of justification.

The difficulties of requiring extensive judicial scrutiny of almost any trading rule became clear in the *Sunday Trading* cases.[11] In those cases, retailers attacked the rules on mandatory Sunday closing on the sole grounds that those rules led to a contraction on sale, which meant also a contraction on the sale of imported products. The Court accepted that, in principle, those rules could fall within Article 28 EC and thus needed to be justified according to the mandatory requirements doctrine.[12] The practical problems arising from this wide interpretation were significant: whilst it had been clearly stated by the Court that the objectives pursued by the Sunday trading rules were compatible with Community law, their necessity and proportionality had been left to the national courts' assessment. This led

---

[8] Although the process is not that linear and some non-discriminatory rules which were not intending to regulate intra-Community trade were excluded from the reach of Article 28 EC, e.g. Case 155/80 *Oebel* [1981] ECR 1993; Case 75/81 *JHT Blegsen v Belgium* [1982] ECR 1211; Case C-23/89 *Quietlynn Ltd and B J Richards v Southend Borough Council* [1990] ECR I-3059; Case C-350/89 *Sheptonhurst Ltd v Newnham Borough Council* [1991] ECR I-2387.

[9] The Court had already indicated that a reduction on imports might be enough to trigger the Treaty in Case 286/81 *Criminal Proceedings against Oosthoek's Uitgeversmaatschappij Bv* [1982] ECR 4575.

[10] Joined Cases 60 and 61/84 *Cinéthèque SA and others v Fédération Nationale des Cinéma Français* [1985] ECR 2605; see also Case C-362/88 *GB-INNO-BM v Confédération du Commerce Luxembourgois* [1990] ECR I-667, in which the Court found a rule prescribing that sales offers could not state the duration of the offer or refer to previous prices, not to be justified on consumer protection grounds; and Case C-126/91 *Schutzverband gegen Unwesen in der Wirtschaft e.V. v Yves Rocher GmbH* [1993] ECR I-2361; Case 382/87 *R Buet and Educational Business Services v Ministère Public* [1989] ECR 1235, in which the Court found a ban on canvassing in relation to educational material to be justified on consumer protection grounds; and Case C-239/90 *SCP Boscher, Studer and Fromentin v Sa British Motors Wright and others* [1991] ECR I-2023, where the Court found a rule imposing on the seller a requirement to be registered in the trade register for sale of second hand goods not compatible with Article 28 EC.

[11] Case C-145/88 *Torfaen Borough Council v B & Q plc* [1989] ECR I-3851; Case C-312/89 *Union départementale des syndicats CGT de l'Aisne v SIDEF Conforama and others* [1991] ECR I-997; Case C-332/89 *Criminal Proceedings against A Merchandise et al* [1991] I-1027; Case C-306/88 *Rochdale Borough Council v Steward John Anders* [1992] ECR I-6458; Case C-169/91 *Council of the City of Stoke-on-Trent and Norwich City Council v B & Q plc* [1992] ECR I-6635.

[12] The Court did not actually mention the expression 'mandatory requirements' in the *Sunday trading* cases (nor in *Cinéthèque*) but it still required the measure to be justified. It is striking that the problems raised by the *Sunday trading* cases had already been anticipated by R C Béraud in 'Les mesures d'effet équivalent au sens des articles 30 et suivants du Traité de Rome' (1968) 3 RTDE 265–392, at 285.

different courts to reach different results as to the rules' compatibility with Community law.[13]

The *Sunday Trading* types of rules are by their very nature difficult to assess in terms of necessity and proportionality. As the Court recognized all along, they reflect different cultural traditions and deeply rooted (local) values: the assessment of their necessity and proportionality will then depend on an appraisal of these values.[14] If the courts are willing to assess the rules in their cultural context, recognizing the State's right to impose value choices upon its citizens, the rules will be upheld. On the other hand, a more objective and value-free assessment might lead to a different result: not necessarily a patronizing State, a State which forces some preferences on its citizens as to how to spend their free time, would be seen as acting in a proportionate way in a market-oriented society. The assessment of the rules will then depend upon which values are to be given precedence; yet the Treaty, unlike several national constitutions, is silent as to this choice.

The practical problems raised by the breadth of the *Sunday Trading* interpretation were mirrored by the difficulties in providing a satisfactory conceptual explanation for the scope of, and the appropriate test for, Article 28 EC. As said above, after the *Cassis* ruling, scholars were divided as to the content of Article 28 EC with some authors arguing that Article 28 EC could still be seen as prohibiting only discriminatory restrictions, whilst other authors accepted that the scope of Article 28 EC was broader than a mere prohibition on discrimination. However, the notion of 'obstacle to intra-Community trade' was still deemed central to the interpretation of Article 28 EC. Following the *Sunday Trading* saga, it was clear that, whilst a discriminatory approach did not reflect the state of the law, there was no satisfactory alternative conceptual explanation able to provide an indication as to the boundaries of Article 28 EC. The rules at issue in the *Sunday Trading* cases did not impose a double regulatory burden on the importer, did not require it to change its products, did not prevent it from devising a pan-European marketing strategy, and did not increase its costs. In other words, the disputed national rules merely regulated trade: there was no intra-Community *specificity* to the cases at issue. It is this loss of specificity which renders questionable the fact that the Treaty could be triggered by such rules.

It is not surprising then that the rulings in the *Sunday Trading* cases gave rise to intense academic criticism: several scholars argued that, since the *Sunday Trading* type of rules did not create a *specific* obstacle to intra-Community trade, they should be excluded from the reach of Article 28 EC.[15] However,

---

[13] A Arnull 'What shall we do on Sunday?' (1991) 16 ELRev 112; K Mortelmans 'Article 30 of the EEC Treaty and Legislation Relating to Market Circumstances: Time to Consider a New Definition?' (1991) 28 CMLRev 115.

[14] Case C-145/88 *Torfaen Borough Council v B & Q plc* [1989] ECR 3851.

[15] K Mortelmans 'Article 30 of the EEC Treaty and Legislation Relating to Market Circumstances: Time to Consider a New Definition?' (1991) 28 CMLRev 115; E L White 'In Search of the Limits to Article 30 of the EEC Treaty'(1989) CMLRev 235. Also the Advocates General were not persuaded by the turn taken by the case law; e.g. AG Van Gerven's Opinion in C-145/88 *Torfaen Borough Council v B & Q plc* [1989] ECR I-3851 and in the other Sunday trading cases. In favour of the

having stepped outside a theory based on discrimination, it was not easy to identify clearly which rules should fall within the Treaty, and which should automatically fall outside. During those years, there was then a fertile academic debate as to where to draw the line. In particular, White suggested that in order to delimit the boundaries of Article 28 EC, a distinction should be made according to the type of rules at issue.[16] Rules which regulated the physical characteristics of the products should always be deemed an obstacle to intra-Community trade, since they require the importer to adapt its goods for the host-market and therefore clearly affect trade between Member States. However, in his opinion, rules which merely regulate modalities of sale (selling arrangements) constitute an obstacle to intra-Community trade only to the extent to which they discriminate in law or in fact against imported products. This was the route eventually followed by the Court in its *Keck* ruling.[17]

In *Keck*, the Court distinguished between product requirements, i.e. rules regulating the physical qualities of products such as packaging, content, labelling etc, and selling arrangements, i.e. rules regulating when and how a product should be sold as well as rules regulating advertising. Product requirements should always be caught by the Treaty and always need to be justified according to the mandatory requirements doctrine. However, 'certain' selling arrangements should be caught only if directly or indirectly discriminatory.[18] The Court gave some indication in the *Keck* ruling of why this should be the case. Thus, it held:

> the application of such rules [selling arrangements] to the sale of products from another Member State meeting the requirements laid down by that State is not by nature such as to *prevent their access to the market or to impede access any more than it impedes the access of domestic products.* Such rules therefore fall outside the scope of Article 30 [now 28] of the Treaty (Para 17, emphasis added).

Whilst the *Keck* ruling has not been unanimously welcomed by the scholarship,[19] and whilst it might well have been fine-tuned by the Court in recent

---

application of the *Dassonville* formula to Sunday trading rules L Gormley 'Recent Case Law on the Free Movement of Goods: Some Hot Potatoes' (1990) 27 CMLRev 825; and to a certain extent J Steiner 'Drawing the line: Uses and Abuses of Article 30 EEC' (1992) 29 CMLRev 749; and W P J Wils 'The Search for the rule in Article 30 EEC: much ado about nothing?' (1993) ELRev 475.

[16] E L White 'In Search of the Limits to Article 30 of the EEC Treaty'(1989) CMLRev 235.

[17] Case C-267/91 and C-268/91 *Keck and Mithouard* [1993] ECR I-6097; the Court substantially followed AG Tesauro's opinion in another case raising similar issues, Case C-292/92 *R Hünnermund and others v Landesapothekerkammer Baden-Wurttemberg* [1993] ECR I-6787, which heavily drew from White's suggestions.

[18] The Court failed to clarify which selling arrangements would benefit from the *Keck* presumption and which would not; licence requirements are caught by Article 28 EC and need to be justified regardless of discrimination, see Case C-189/95 *Franzén* [1997] ECR I-5909.

[19] Most notably AG Jacobs in his opinion in Case C-412/93 *Société d'importation Éduard Leclerc-Siplec v TF1 Publicité SA* [1995] ECR I-179, also S Weatherill 'After *Keck*: some thoughts on how to

years,[20] it did solve some considerable problems. By excluding an entire category of rules from the scope of Article 28 EC unless it is demonstrated that such rules discriminate directly or indirectly against imported products, the Court ensured that intra-Community trade-neutral rules were not subject to the necessity and proportionality assessment demanded by the mandatory requirements doctrine. In other words, with the *Keck* ruling the Court recognized that the Member States still have some regulatory autonomy and that, provided there is no discrimination, they can regulate the market place according to their social and political preferences, and indeed, Bernard[21] has interpreted the *Keck* distinction as implying a repartition of regulatory competences: thus, product requirements are in principle regulated by the Member State of production, and further requirements cannot be imposed by the Member State of destination unless that is necessary to pursue a mandatory requirement of public interest. On the other hand, it is for the State where the product is sold to regulate the modalities of sale. For this reason, such rules can be challenged only if they directly or indirectly discriminate against imports. As we shall see in Chapter 4, Bernard's theory is also entirely consistent with the idea that the internal market requires that there is no double regulatory burden (save for when such a double burden is justified by a mandatory requirement of public interest). Thus, the physical characteristics of a product are decided by the State of production alone, whilst the modalities of sale are decided by the importing State alone. Whether this explanation is accepted or not,[22] it is undeniable that, with the *Keck* ruling, the regulatory autonomy of the Member States was reinstated; however, in the very same years, such power was significantly eroded in the field of the free movement of persons, to which we shall now return.

---

clarify the clarification' (1996) 33 CMLRev 885; C Barnard 'Fitting the remaining pieces into the goods and persons jigsaw?' (2001) 26 ELRev 35. See further Chapter 5 below.

[20] Cf P Koutrakos 'On Groceries, Alcohol and Olive Oil: More on the Free Movement of Goods after *Keck*' (2001) 26 ELRev 391; and e.g. Case C-405/98 *Gourmet International (GIP)* [2001] ECR I-1795. On the fact that *Gourmet* (re)introduces a market access test in Article 28 EC, G Straetmans 'Annotation on *Gourmet*' (2002) 39 CMLRev 1407; critical of the Court's timid approach A Biondi 'Advertising alcohol and the free movement principle: the *Gourmet* decision' (2001) 26 ELRev 616.

[21] N Bernard, 'La libre circulation des marchandises, des personnes et des services dans le Traité CE sous l'angle de la compétence' (1998) 33 CDE 11. See also further Chapter 4 below. The idea that the Treaty free movement provisions had effected a reallocation of regulatory competences had been hinted at by AG Mayras as early as in Case 33/74 *J H Van Bisbergen Bestuur van der Berdifsvereniging voor de Metaalnijverheid* [1974] ECR 1299, at 1316 'a fundamental aspect of the difference between, *on the one hand*, mere occasional provision of services, even temporary activities and, *on the other hand*, establishment, is that the person providing services falls outside the competence and control of the country where the service is provided'. (Emphasis in the original).

[22] There are other rules which do not fall within the scope of the product requirements/selling arrangements dichotomy, and that might be caught regardless of discrimination, e.g. licensing rules in Case C-189/95 *H Franzén* [1997] ECR I-5909, or those cases which might trigger State's liability for inaction regardless of discrimination, e.g. Case C-112/00 *Schmidberger* [2003] ECR I-5659. In those cases the double burden/discrimination/regulatory competence test does not seem to provide an entirely satisfactory conceptual framework.

2. Non-discriminatory Barriers to the Provision of Cross-Border Services

We have seen in the previous chapter that Article 49 EC prohibits national rules which discriminate directly or indirectly against service providers/recipients established in another Member State, as well as the imposition of rules similar to those to which a foreign service provider has already been subject in its State of establishment. Thus, the host Member State has to take into account the requirements already satisfied by the provider in its home State, and only if those do not sufficiently protect the pursued aim can it impose further rules. Such interpretation is entirely consistent with both a broad interpretation of indirect discrimination and the double burden theory according to which a migrant should not be subject to two regulatory standards unless those are justified by an imperative reason of public interest.

In the 1990s, the Court went beyond this interpretation, and held that any barrier to the free movement of services, regardless of discrimination, is caught by Article 49 EC and needs to be justified. It is in the two cases of *Gouda* and *Säger* – decided the same day, the former by the full Court, the latter by a chamber – that the Court finally departs explicitly from a discriminatory assessment of Article 49 EC.[23] In *Gouda*[24] a number of Dutch rules on broadcasting were scrutinized and amongst them a ban on Sunday advertisement. After having acknowledged the fact that the national court found the measures to be non-discriminatory, the Court proceeded to assess whether they nonetheless constituted a restriction on the freedom to provide services. In *Säger*,[25] German rules which required that a patent renewal service could be provided only by licensed operators were found to be inconsistent with Community law. The Court held that Article 49 EC required not only the elimination of all discrimination on grounds of nationality, but also:

> the abolition of any restriction, *even if it applies without distinction* to national providers of services and to those of other Member States, when

---

[23] It can be argued that already in Case 205/84 *Commission v Germany* (Insurance) [1986] ECR 3755, paras 25 and ff, noted E Edward 'Establishment and Services: an Analysis of the Insurance Cases' (1987) 12 ELRev 231, the Court had used a non-discriminatory approach to the restrictions under scrutiny. However, even though the language used in the ruling is consistent with this interpretation, the case concerned a residence and registration requirement which can be seen as indirectly discriminatory. AG Tesauro in his Opinion in Cases C-120/95 *Decker* and C-158/96 *Kohll* [1998] ECR I-1834, footnote 63 at I-1859, stated that 'it is clear that the *Gouda, Commission v Netherlands* and *Säger* judgements, far from constituting a new departure, merely clarified the existing approach and provided it with a fuller theoretical analysis'.

[24] Case C-288/89 *Gouda* [1991] ECR I-4007; Y Art 'Legislative Lacunae, the Court of Justice and Freedom to Provide Services' in D Curtin and D O'Keeffe (eds) *Constitutional Adjudication in European Community and National Law* (Butterworths Dublin 1992) 121; and J Feenstra 'Annotation of *Gouda*' (1993) 30 CMLRev 425.

[25] Case C-76/90 *Säger* [1991] ECR I-4221.

> it is liable to *prohibit* or *otherwise impede* the activities of a provider of services established in another Member State where he *lawfully* provides similar services.[26]

The Court then proceeded to acknowledge that, having regard to the particular characteristics of a service, specific requirements imposed on the provider are not incompatible with the Treaty,[27] as long as they are justified by an imperative requirement of public interest, and are necessary and proportionate to the pursued aim. The reasoning of the Court is reminiscent of the *Cassis* mutual recognition principle: once a service is *lawfully* provided in one of the Member States, it should be able to be provided in all the other Member States unless there are imperative requirements of public interest that justify the imposition of further regulation. This step, long awaited by some, is not altogether surprising: after all, to subject a foreign service provider to an additional set of regulations means to impose a double regulatory burden which might be seen as inconsistent with a single market. As in the case of goods, the existence of different regulatory standards might *per se* create obstacles to the establishment of an internal market in services, since it hinders movement by imposing additional costs on economic operators willing to extend their market beyond their Member State of establishment.

This reasoning applies also to rules which, rather than imposing requirements on service providers for the delivery of a given service, altogether prohibit its provision. For instance, in *Schindler*,[28] the Court found that British rules which prohibited lotteries were caught by Article 49 EC even if non-discriminatory. Similarly, in *De Agostini*,[29] Swedish rules which prohibited television advertising aimed at children were found to constitute a barrier to the free movement of services, since broadcasters established in other Member States would be unable to provide such services in Sweden. A similar reasoning applies also to rules which reserve the provision of a given service to a public body. In *Läärä* the Finnish rules under attack restricted gambling activities, such that they could be organized only by a licensed public body.[30] The rules did not impose any discrimination since no undertaking, whether

[26] *Ibid*, para 12, emphasis added. However, in the field of taxation the Court's assessment is limited to a discriminatory one, cf Case C-134/03 *Viacom Outdoor* [2005] ECR I-1167 (although with an obiter in para 38 on the level of taxation that seems to suggest that had the tax been very high it might have been construed as an obstacle falling within the scope of Article 49 EC, see below Chapter 7).

[27] Whilst before the imperative requirements could be conceptualized as objective reasons to assess whether there was indirect discrimination, following *Säger* they become akin to the mandatory requirements, and indeed the different expression does not seem to indicate a conceptual difference.

[28] Case C-275/92 *Schindler* [1994] ECR I-1039. More recently see also Case C-36/02 *Omega* [2004] ECR I-9609.

[29] Case C-34/95 *De Agostini* [1997] ECR I-3843. The rules were justified on consumer protection grounds.

[30] Case C-124/97 *Läärä* [1999] ECR I-6067; see also Case C-67/98 *Zenatti* [1999] ECR I-7289. More recently, Case C-6/01 *Anomar and others* [2003] ECR I-8621; in Case C-243/01 *Gambelli and others* [2003] ECR I-13031, the Court left it to the national court to assess the justification of the rules. As a result of the Court's reticence in indicating clearly whethere the Italian rules on gambling are consistent with the free movement provisions, other Italian courts have felt the need to request a preliminary reference on the same rules, Joined Cases C-338/04, C-359/04 and 360/04 *Placanica*,

established in Finland or not, could engage in such activity; yet the impossibility to provide such services was, as in *Schindler*, construed as a barrier falling within the scope of Article 49 EC which therefore needed to be justified.

In those cases it is easy to conceptualize the existence of a barrier to movement: after all, the service provider – consistently with the internal market rationale – was seeking to extend its market beyond its Member State of establishment by providing the same service that it was lawfully providing in the home State. However, an important development has made it impossible for any mutual recognition type of approach to be of use in conceptualizing the notion of barrier to the provision of services. In recent years the Court has allowed service providers to attack non-discriminatory rules imposed by their Member State of origin, i.e. the main – if not only – regulator. This step challenges the established paradigm, which had been confirmed in the *Säger* formula, according to which the exercise of the freedom granted by the Treaty is conditional upon *lawfully* providing similar services (or marketing the same goods) in the Member State of establishment. It is to this case law that we shall now turn our attention.

3. (Un)Lawfully Providing a Service? Challenging the Rules of the State of Establishment[31]

In the immediate aftermath of *Säger* the Court, consistently with a mutual recognition approach, refused to subject the rules imposed by the Member State of establishment – the main, if not only, regulator – to a non-discriminatory scrutiny. If the recipient Member State was in principle prevented from imposing its rules on services which had already satisfied one set of regulatory standards, the Member State of establishment was free to decide what this regulatory standard should be. Thus, in *Peralta*,[32] the Court clearly stated that the situation of an undertaking in relation to its State of establishment cannot be compared to that of an undertaking established elsewhere. Accordingly, it found rules which imposed an absolute (and extra-territorial) prohibition of the discharge of harmful substances in the sea for Italian vessels, to fall outside the scope of Article 49 EC since those rules were neither discriminatory nor protectionist. As with goods, in the case of rules imposed by the home state, there is no issue of double regulatory burden which might justify departing from a discriminatory assessment.

Palazzese, e Sorrichio, judgment of 6 March 2007, nyr. See also pending reference Case C-466/05 *Damonte*.

[31] This section substantially reproduces some of my findings in 'From *Gebhard* to *Carpenter*: towards a (non-)Economic European Constitution' (2004) 41 CMLRev 743.

[32] Case C-379/92 *Peralta* [1994] ECR I-3453, esp. paras 49 and 50. The proposed reading of the *Peralta* case is not universally shared. See AG Jacobs' Opinion in Case C-384/93 *Alpine Investments* [1995] ECR I-1141, para 58 and ff.

In *Alpine*,[33] however, the Court amended its previous interpretation and ruled that restrictions imposed by the Member State of establishment must undergo the same broad scrutiny as restrictions imposed by the recipient Member State. The facts of the case are well known: Dutch provisions forbade financial service providers from approaching prospective clients by phone (so called 'cold-calling') or in person, unless the prospective client had previously agreed in writing to be contacted. Alpine Investments argued that the prohibition was a restriction on its freedom to provide services, since it hindered its ability to contact potential clients in other Member States. The Dutch Government, on the other hand, relied on the case law on Article 29 EC to argue that its rules should be excluded from the scope of Article 49 EC: as in the case of goods,[34] restrictions imposed by the Member State of establishment to the 'export' of services, should come within the scope of the Treaty only insofar as they were discriminatory. Alternatively, the Dutch Government argued that, in any case, the situation – which concerned rules on 'selling arrangements', i.e. rules disciplining the *way* the service was to be provided – should benefit from the *Keck* exemption. Since the rules at issue were neither directly nor indirectly discriminatory, they should fall outside the purview of Article 49 EC. The Court found the prohibition on cold-calling to be a non-discriminatory restriction on the freedom to provide services, and rejected the analogy with the *Keck*-type selling arrangements, since in this case the rules *directly* affected access to the market in services in other Member States.[35] The rule was then justified by the need to protect the good reputation of the Dutch financial market.[36] The outcome of *Alpine* is not altogether surprising, since the rule was extra-territorial in nature, and thus undeniably imposed a direct hindrance to the provider's ability to supply services abroad, a hindrance which was not faced by providers established in the host Member State. *Alpine* was in fact unable to cold call potential clients abroad, even though that would have been possible under the rules of the Member State where the service was to be provided. It can then be argued that the rules in *Alpine* still bore an intra-Community specificity capable of justifying the Court's scrutiny.

However, subsequent cases relating to home-country rules seem to indicate a much broader construction of the services provisions. In *Sodemare*,[37] the claimant, an Italian subsidiary of a Luxembourg company, attempted to rely on Article 49 EC against Italy, the State of secondary establishment, on the sole ground that it

[33] Case C-384/93 *Alpine Investments* [1995] ECR I-1141.

[34] E.g. Case 15/79 *Groenveld* [1979] ECR 3409; Case 237/82 *Kaas* [1984] ECR 483; Case C-388/95 *Belgium v Spain* (Rioja) [2000] ECR I-3123.

[35] The reference to the *Keck* ruling was seen by some as indicating a 'global approach' to free movement, i.e. the possibility to distinguish between the types of rules, and exclude non-discriminatory selling arrangements from the scope of Article 49 EC. Other authors interpreted *Alpine* as authority to argue that the *Keck* ruling was really about market access rather than discrimination.

[36] The rule could not be justified on consumer protection grounds since Member States cannot adopt measures for the protection of consumers in other Member States; *cf* also C-5/94 *Hedley Lomas* [1996] ECR I-2553.

[37] Case C-70/95 *Sodemare* [1997] ECR I-3395.

provided services to, *inter alia*, foreign recipients. The disputed rule prescribed that only non-profit making bodies could conclude contracts with the local health authority in order to obtain repayment for social insurance services of a health care nature. The company challenged the rule on the grounds that about 2 per cent of its residents were foreigners, and that about 10 per cent of the enquiries were received every year from persons resident in other Member States.[38] The Court, having referred to the general principle according to which a provider might rely on Article 49 EC when providing a service for persons established in another Member State,[39] found that in this case Article 49 EC could not be relied upon, since the recipients would establish their residence in Italy. Thus the situation, from a services viewpoint, was wholly internal. However, the Court failed to curtail or specify the extent to which an established provider may rely on the Treaty just because its recipient *might be* foreign.[40] In other words, was the potentiality of a foreign recipient enough to bring the situation within the scope of the Treaty and challenge the rules of the Member State which might well be the only regulator? Following the ruling in *Gourmet*,[41] the answer to this question seems to be positive.

In *Gourmet*, the claimant, GIP, was a company which published a magazine, Gourmet. GIP was established in Sweden where the magazine was published. Prosecution was brought against GIP since, in one of the issues of the magazine, there were about three pages of advertisement for alcoholic beverages in breach of the almost total ban on alcohol advertising imposed by Swedish legislation. The Swedish court requested a preliminary ruling on the compatibility of the rules prohibiting the advertising of alcoholic beverages with Articles 28 and 49 EC. In relation to the latter, the Court found that the rules restricted 'the right of press undertakings established in the territory of that Member State to offer advertising space in their publications to potential advertisers established in other Member States'.[42] In order to understand the significance of the ruling, it is important to note that the rules were challenged

---

[38] The company challenged the rules also under freedom of establishment; it could be questioned whether the fact that *Sodemare* was in principle allowed to rely both on Article 43 EC and on Article 49 EC in order to challenge the *same* rule, is not inconsistent with the residual nature of the provisions on services provided by Article 50 EC Treaty.

[39] Also Case C-18/93 *Corsica Ferries* [1994] ECR I-1783, esp. para 21; Case C-379/92 *Peralta* [1994] ECR I-3453; Case C-224/97 *Ciola* [1999] ECR 2517; in Case C-384/93 *Alpine Investments* [1995] ECR I-1141, the Court stated that in order to be able to rely on Article 49 EC there is no need for 'the prior existence of an identifiable recipient' (para 19).

[40] In the other cases in which Article 49 EC was relied upon against the Member State of establishment the rules were either indirectly (Case C-18/93 *Corsica Ferries* [1994] ECR I-1783) or directly discriminatory (Case C-224/97 *Ciola* [1999] ECR 2517) and directly affected the providers' freedom to provide the service. On the other hand in Case C-379/92 *Peralta* [1994] ECR I-3453, the claimant could not rely on Article 49 EC against the Member State of establishment since the rule was neither discriminatory nor protectionist. It is a pity that the Court in *Sodemare* failed to notice how preposterous Sodemare's argument was: foreign clients were clearly not affected by the Italian legislation since they were not insured under the Italian system and were therefore not eligible for repayment under Italian rules.

[41] Case C-405/98 *Gourmet International (GIP)* [2001] ECR I-1795.

[42] Case C-405/98 *Gourmet International (GIP)* [2001] ECR I-1795, para 38.

by a company established in the Member State which imposed the rules; the only link with a cross-border element was the fact that some of GIP's clients *might* have been established in another Member State. The approach in *Gourmet* signals a considerable expansion on the scope of Article 49 EC because in this case, *Gourmet* was challenging the very *illegality* of the provision of services in its Member State of establishment, which was also the only regulator. The fact that *Gourmet* could not provide its services to foreign recipients was a purely incidental factor and the specificity of the intra-Community situation was tenuous, if it existed at all. Furthermore, the *Gourmet* approach challenges one of the paradigms of internal market law, according to which goods or services must be lawfully 'produced' before the Treaty provisions can be triggered.

The situation was then different both from that at issue in *Schindler* and from that at issue in *Alpine*.

In *Schindler*, a foreign provider sought to provide a service (lotteries) in a Member State in which that service was unlawful.[43] The restriction amounted thus to a ban on service provision, and the Court found it to be a restriction justified according to imperative requirements of public interest. In *Schindler*, the provider sought to extend its market to another Member State; however, it did *lawfully* provide the service in its Member State of establishment (where it was regulated). In *Gourmet*, the provider could not – in its Member State of establishment – *lawfully* provide the service the ban of which it challenged.

The situation also markedly differed from that at issue in *Alpine*. In *Alpine* the rules at issue directly restricted the possibility of advertisement in *another* Member State. The situation was thus dynamic in nature, the rule was extra-territorial and the barrier to the possibility of 'exporting' services was direct. If *Alpine* was challenging a rule imposed by its Member State of establishment, the rule prohibited something which, although unlawful in the Member State of establishment, was *lawful* in the recipient's Member State *where* the service would be provided. On the other hand, in *Gourmet*, the Swedish rule did not impede domestic producers or service providers from advertising their goods/services *abroad*; nor did it affect the provider's ability to deliver a service in another Member State where the service was lawful.[44] It merely affected the provider's ability to provide the service in the Member State of establishment.

The *Gourmet* approach has to a certain extent been confirmed in the case of *Freskot*,[45] an excellent example of the practical implications of the Court's broad interpretation of the free movement provisions, as well as of the confusion surrounding the field. Here, a Greek company established in Greece challenged a system of compulsory insurance against natural risks for farmers. The insurance was levied on sales and purchases of domestic agricultural products; the amount due was calculated

43 Case C-275/92 *Schindler* [1994] ECR I-1039.

44 The situation was also different from that in Case C-362/88 *GB-INNO-BM* [1990] ECR I-667, where the restriction on advertisement was imposed by the recipients' Member State and directly affected the undertaking's ability to attract clients from that country.

45 Case C-355/00 *Freskot* [2003] ECR I-5263.

as a percentage of the value of agricultural products; the insurance was collected by the tax authorities and the revenue of the tax was entered in the State budget. Freskot attacked the system of compulsory insurance relying on a number of different Community law provisions, amongst them Article 49 EC. In relation to the latter, the Greek Government argued that Article 49 EC was not relevant since the insurance services were not provided for remuneration. The Court accepted that the insurance provider, a private company wholly owned by the State, was not providing a service for remuneration and therefore Articles 49 and 50 EC were not applicable. Despite having so found, the Court then examined the issue from another perspective. It found that the system of compulsory insurance constituted a restriction on the freedom of insurers established in another Member State to offer their insurance services on the Greek market against the risk insured by the State-owned provider. As in *Gourmet*, the Court allowed a person established in one Member State and wholly regulated by that State to challenge its own State's rules on purely hypothetical grounds, i.e. on the grounds that *if* the State had not imposed the compulsory insurance system, then the company *might* have wanted to buy insurance for the same risks, and *might* have chosen an out-of-State provider.[46]

As a result of the *Gourmet* approach it is possible for the service provider to challenge rules imposed by the only regulator, even when those rules do not *specifically* affect the cross-border provision of services. In other words, following the rulings in *Gourmet* and *Freskot*, any service provider/recipient might be able to challenge the rules imposed by its Member State of establishment on the grounds that someone established in another Member State might want to purchase from them, or offer them, that service. Virtually any rule can then be brought within the scope of Article 49 EC and therefore require justification according to the mandatory requirements doctrine.

And indeed this seems to be the outcome arising from the ruling in *Carpenter.*[47] In this case, Mr Carpenter, a UK citizen having a business in the UK which involved some trade with clients established in other Member States, successfully challenged the application to his wife of British immigration rules. According to UK law, Mrs Carpenter, a third country national, was to be deported since she overstayed her entry permit in the UK. Notwithstanding the fact that her marriage was not a sham, British immigration rules provided that she had to return to her country of origin and from there apply for an entry permit. Mr Carpenter argued that his wife's deportation would impact on his freedom to provide services in other Member States since she was the main carer for their children. The UK Government and the Commission considered the situation to be purely internal since Mr Carpenter had not exercised his right of movement. He was thus covered neither by Directive 73/148 according to which the Community national has a right

---

[46] The rules were found to be in principle justified by social policy objectives although the proportionality assessment was left to the national court.

[47] Case C-60/00 *Carpenter* [2002] ECR I-6279. See also AG Geelhoed's Opinion in Case C-109/01 *Akrich* [2003] ECR I-9607.

to bring her spouse into another Member State;[48] nor by the *Singh* ruling, according to which a national of a Member State has the right, upon returning to that Member State after having exercised her right to move, to bring her spouse there (even in those cases in which she was already married when she left her own country).[49] The Court found that Mr Carpenter was a service provider within the meaning of Community law since he provided services for recipients in other Member States. It then found that his separation from his wife would be:

> detrimental to their family life and, therefore, to the conditions under which Mr Carpenter exercises a fundamental freedom. That freedom could not be fully effective if Mr Carpenter were to be *deterred* from exercising it by obstacles raised in his country of origin to the entry and residence of his spouse.[50]

Having found that the situation fell within the scope of Article 49 EC, the Court could then proceed to assess the compatibility of the deportation order with the right to family life, as part of the general principles of Community law.[51] This ruling will be thoroughly analyzed in Chapter 6. For the time being, it is sufficient to note how the causal link between the disputed rule and the relevant barrier to the cross-border provision of services seems in this case to be extremely weak, if one existed at all. After all, if such a rule were to deter Mr Carpenter from taking occasional trips abroad, so might have many other things, the cost of childcare to state the most obvious. It is clear that the real problem with the British immigration rules lay in their compatibility with the right to family life of the Carpenter family, not with a supposed obstacle to intra-Community trade. It is not a coincidence that the Court analyzed more thoroughly the fundamental rights issue than the existence of a barrier to intra-Community movement. Whilst the end result might be welcomed, it is questionable whether it is proper for the Court to use Article 49 EC *only* so as to assess the compatibility of domestic rules with fundamental rights.

The developments in *Sodemare*, *Gourmet*, *Freskot* and *Carpenter*, taken together, suggest the possibility of using the services provisions as a trump card to bring oneself within the scope of the Treaty, and thus demand judicial scrutiny of the proportionality and necessity of the contested rules, together with the assessment of their compatibility (where appropriate) with fundamental rights as general principles of Community law.

---

[48] Directive 73/148 (now repealed and substituted by Directive 2004/38) did not apply since it does not regulate the right of residence of family members of a service provider established in her/his State of origin.

[49] Case C-370/90 *Singh* [1992] ECR I-4265. See above Chapter 1.

[50] Case C-60/00 *Carpenter* [2002] ECR I-6279, para 39.

[51] It is difficult to assess whether this ruling overrules Case C-168/91 *Konstantinidis* [1993] ECR I-1191 (not even mentioned in the Court's ruling), where the Court rejected AG Jacobs' suggestion that whenever one falls within the scope of Community law one should be protected by fundamental rights as general principles of Community law (but only in another Member State), even if the breach of fundamental rights complained of has nothing to do with the free movement right. In that case the Court rejected this submission and ruled that fundamental rights as general principles of Community law would apply only in so far as instrumental to the Treaty freedoms.

The relaxation of the notion of what constitutes a barrier and of the intra-Community element necessary to trigger the Treaty is complemented by another important development, that of the relaxation of the economic element, the 'remuneration' necessary to bring a service within the scope of Article 49 EC. It is to this development that we will now turn our attention.

4. The Health Care Cases and the Definition of a Service Provided for Remuneration[52]

As we have seen in the previous chapter, the Court, although with inconsistencies and qualifications, had until the late 1990s drawn a distinction between public and private services, considering only the latter to be provided for remuneration and thus falling within the scope of the Treaty.[53] Consistently, the Court had found that a rule whereby scholarships were available only for (public) education provided within the national territory was not to be considered a hindrance to the freedom to receive services, since the State in providing general education was not exercising an economic activity but rather fulfilling its duties towards its citizens.[54] Public services which were an expression of social solidarity had therefore been excluded from the scope of the Treaty, as expressions of solidarity are by definition not 'economic'.[55]

This framework has undergone considerable changes as a result of a number of cases brought by patients who had received medical treatment abroad and argued that their health institution's refusal to reimburse them constituted a barrier to the free movement of services.[56] The Court accepted that the requirement of prior

[52] See more thoroughly E Spaventa 'Public Services and European Law: Looking for Boundaries' (2002–3) 5 CYELS 271.
[53] Case 263/86 *Humbel* [1988] ECR 5365, and see above Chapter 1.
[54] Case C-102/92 *Wirth v Landeshauptstadt Hannover* [1993] ECR I-6447; but now see Joined Cases C-11 and 12/06 *Morgan and Bucher*, Opinion delivered 20 March 2007, case still pending at the time of writing.
[55] This reasoning applies also in relation to the applicability of Article 81 and 82 EC, see footnote 59 Chapter 1; in relation to Article 43, Case C-70/95 *Sodemare Sa and others v Regione Lombardia* [1997] ECR I-3395.
[56] Case C-158/96 *Kohll* [1998] ECR I-1931; Case C-368/98 *Abdon Vanbraekel and others v Alliance nationale des mutualités chrétiennes* [2001] ECR I-5363; Case C-157/99 *Geraets-Smits* and *Peerbooms* [2001] ECR I-5473; Case C-385/99 *Müller Fauré* and *van Riet* [2003] ECR I-4509; Case C-56/01 *Patricia Inizan* [2003] ECR I-12403; Case C-8/04 *Leichtle* [2004] ECR I-2641; Case C-372/04 *Watts* [2006] ECR I-4325. The health care cases have been the focus of extensive academic analysis; e.g. P Cabral 'Cross-Border Medical Care in Europe: Bringing Down a First Wall' (1999) 24 ELRev 387; A P Van der Mei 'Cross-border access to medical care in the European Union – some reflections on the judgments in *Decker* and *Kohll*' (1998) 5 MJ 277; M Fuchs 'Free Movement of Services and Social Services: Quo Vadis?' (2002) 8 ELJ 536; E Steyger 'National Health Care Systems Under Fire (but not too heavily)' (1999) 29 LIEI 97; Van der Mei, A.P. 'Cross-border access to medical care in the European Union – some reflections on *Garaets-Smits* and *Peerbooms* and *Vanbraekel*' (2002) 9 MJ 189; G Davies 'Welfare as a Service' (2002) 29 LIEI 27 and V Hatzopoulos 'Killing the National Health Systems but Healing the Patients? The European market for health care after the judgement of the ECJ in *Vanbraekel* and *Peerbooms*' (2002) 39 CMLRev 683; T Hervey 'Mapping the Contours of

authorization for reimbursement by the home-State NHS/health provider in respect of health care services received in other Member States constitutes a barrier to the freedom to receive services and is thus in need of justification.

The first case in which the issue arose is that of *Kohll*;[57] there, the claimant's daughter received orthodontic treatment in another Member State; when Mr Kohll applied for reimbursement from his sickness fund he was denied it on the grounds that he had failed to obtain the required prior authorization. The rules at issue provided for a lump sum reimbursement for medical expenses – rather than treatment in kind – and prior authorization was necessary *only* when the treatment was sought abroad. Thus, Mr Kholl argued that the prior authorization requirement constituted a restriction to his freedom to seek services in another Member State and was therefore caught by Article 49 EC. The Court agreed and held that, since the prior authorization was necessary only when the patient sought treatment abroad, it undeniably deterred patients from approaching providers in other Member States.

In *Kholl*, however, the Court did not thoroughly analyze the issue of remuneration. The fact that the health system in that case provided for reimbursement at a pre-fixed rate, together with the Court's qualification that the treatment had been provided outside any hospital infrastructure, left it unclear whether the Court's reasoning was to affect also health systems which provide for benefits in kind (i.e. which provide for treatment rather than reimbursement), and whether the same principles should apply also to intra-mural care (i.e. treatment provided in hospitals), or whether the ruling was of a more limited application. With the insight of subsequent cases, however, it is clear that *Kohll* signalled the first step towards exposing public health systems, in whatever way organized, to the Treaty rules on the free movement of services.

In *Geraets-Smits* and *Peerbooms*,[58] the claimants challenged the Dutch authorities' refusal to reimburse treatment obtained abroad. Mrs Geraets-Smits requested reimbursement for holistic treatment for Parkinson's disease received in Germany; whilst Mr Peerbooms claimed reimbursement for neuro-stimulation received in Austria, which successfully brought him back from a coma. The authorities refused both requests on the grounds that treatment had not been authorized and the two patients had not met the conditions required before authorization could be granted.

The Dutch health care system is based on providing treatment in kind. Eligible individuals are associated with a sickness fund which enters into agreements with health care providers established in the area where the fund operates.

European Union Health Law and Policy' (2002) 8 EPL 69; A Dawes '"Bonjour Herr Doctor": national health care systems, the internal market and cross-border medical care within the European Union' (2006) 33 LIEI 167; G Davies 'Competition, Free Movement and Consumers of Public Services' (2006) 17 EBL Rev 95.

[57] Case C-158/96 *R Kohll v Union des Caisses de Maladie* [1998] ECR I-1931.

[58] Case C-157/99 *B S M Geraets-Smits v Stichting Ziekenfonds VGZ* and *Peerbooms v Stichting CZ Groep Zorgverzekeringen* [2001] ECR I-5473.

Individuals are then entitled to receive treatment free of charge by one of the providers which have entered into an agreement with their sickness fund. The fund, where necessary, can authorize an insured person to seek treatment in another institution, within or outside the Netherlands, with which the fund has no agreement. The authorization is granted in cases in which treatment is considered 'normal in the professional circles' and is necessary, i.e. not available in a contracted institution without undue delay. It was accepted, for the purpose of the case, that the system was not discriminatory, in that, if it were necessary to have recourse to an external provider (i.e. one with which the fund did not have an agreement) the choice would be made without regard as to whether the provider was established in the Netherlands or elsewhere. Relying on the ruling in *Kohll*, the claimants attacked the prior authorization requirement on the grounds that it constituted a restriction on their ability to receive health services in another Member State.

The first issue for consideration was therefore whether there was a provision of services for remuneration, lacking which, of course, the Treaty could not apply. The Advocate General and the Court disagreed. Advocate General Ruiz-Jarabo Colomer considered that the question was not whether the institutions abroad had provided treatment for remuneration, since the applicants in the main proceedings were not complaining about these institutions' behaviour. Rather, what was relevant was whether the relationship which linked the patients to their sickness funds was to be so considered. The Advocate General found that the relationship between the insured, the sickness funds and the care providers could not be qualified as a provision of services for remuneration. This was the case since, even though a service need not be paid for by its beneficiary,[59] the sickness funds paid fixed sums rather than reimbursed the health care provider for the expenses incurred from time to time. The distinguishing factor in respect of *Kohll* was, in the Advocate General's opinion, that the insurance fund in that latter case provided reimbursement for medical expenses rather than benefits in kind.

The Court considered the relationship both between the patients and the foreign institutions, and between the patients and their sickness funds. Thus, since the patients would have to pay for the treatment received abroad, they received a service provided for remuneration. Furthermore, the Court dismissed the argument that the relationship patient/sickness-funds/hospitals were not one of service provision. The service was paid for by the sickness fund and indeed the hospitals providing the services were exercising an economic activity. The fact that payment to the hospitals occurred through flat rates and the beneficiary was not paying had no bearing on the definition of what is to be considered as a service for remuneration. Consequently, the rules at issue related to services provided for remuneration and fell within the scope of Article 49 EC.[60]

---

[59] Case 352/85 *Bond van Adverteerders and Others v The Netherlands State* [1988] ECR 2085.
[60] Cf Case C-157/99 *Geraets-Smits* and *Peerbooms* [2001] ECR I-5473, paras 53 and ff.

The fact that the Dutch system was organized through contracted institutions left unanswered the question as to whether similar prior authorizations required by systems which directly provide health care without contracting out to external institutions (i.e. NHS-type systems), could also be defined as falling within the scope of Article 49 EC.[61] In *Müller-Fauré*,[62] the Court indicated that that might indeed be the case. The rules under attack were again the Dutch rules on prior authorization. In assessing the existence of a service provided for remuneration, the Court this time merely focused on the fact that the treatment received abroad had been paid for by the patient. Thus, such treatment had been provided for remuneration and fell within the scope of Article 49 EC.[63] There is no mention in this ruling of the relationship between the patient and the sickness fund, nor of the relationship between sickness funds and health care providers, thus suggesting that that case law was of general application.

Indeed, in *Watts*[64] the Court confirmed that this line of cases applies also to national health systems (usually financed through general taxation) which directly, and without the medium of sickness funds, provide for health care. Here, the situation giving rise to the preliminary ruling arose in the UK, where the health care system is publicly funded through taxation and is free at the point of delivery. The claimant, Mrs Watts, went to France for a hip operation despite having been refused authorization from the British authorities on the grounds that the treatment could be provided in England without 'undue' delay. The Court confirmed its previous case law and held that Article 49 EC applied to the authorization requirement. It is interesting to note that the national court referring the case had enquired also as to whether the hospital treatment provided by the NHS was in itself a provision of services within Article 49 EC. This question put the Court in a difficult situation for hermeneutic and practical reasons. For hermeneutic reasons, since Article 50 EC states that in order to fall within the scope of Article 49 EC the service needs to be provided for 'remuneration', which is clearly not the case in relation to public health systems when the treatment is free at the point of delivery. For practical reasons, because if the Court had held that NHS treatment is a service within the scope of Article 49 EC, then Member States would have been in a position of having to justify denial of such service to non-residents. Maybe not surprisingly then, the Court decided that it was not necessary to answer such

---

[61] Some authors had indeed argued that this case law did not apply to NHS-type systems, cf T Hervey 'Mapping the Contours of European Union Health Law and Policy' (2002) 8 EPL 69; and G Davies 'Welfare as a Service' 29 (2002) LIEI 27, both writing before the ruling in *Müller-Fauré*.

[62] Case C-385/99 *Müller-Fauré v Onderlinge Waarborgmaatschappij OZ Zorgverzekeringen UA*, and *van Riet v Onderlinge Waarborgmaatschappi ZAO Zorgverzekeringen* [2003] ECR I-4509.

[63] The ruling in *Müller-Fauré* and *van Riet* is of paramount importance also because the Court held that the requirement of prior authorization for health care received abroad was not justified in the case of out of hospital treatment; see below.

[64] Case C-372/04 *Watts* [2006] ECR I-4325; see also Case C-444/05 *Aikaterini Stamatelaki v Organismos Asfaliseos Eleftheron Epangelmation (O.A.E.E.)*, opinion delivered 11/01/07, case still pending at the time of writing, on whether a sickness insurance fund can limit the reimbursement for treatment received abroad to treatment received in (foreign) public hospitals.

question: rather, as in *Müller-Fauré*, it focused on the relationship between patient and foreign service provider to bring the situation within the scope of Article 49 EC. As we shall see in more detail below, this line of reasoning is less than convincing, and the inadequacy of such an approach is clearly exposed in *Watts*. The British Government, supported by other Member States, pointed out that in England and Wales it is not possible for patients to be treated in private institutions at the expense of the NHS and that patients in England cannot choose when and where to be treated under the NHS. The lack of patients' choice was relevant as it was indicative of the lack of discrimination on grounds of location since no element in the system encouraged the patient to choose a domestic provider rather than a foreign one.

The Court however focused only on the fact that patients could be treated in NHS hospitals without the need of a prior authorization, which was required should they desire treatment in another Member State. For this reason, in the Court's opinion, the authorization requirement for treatment to be undergone in another Member State constituted a restriction on the free movement of services.

5. A Critical Analysis of the Court's Reasoning

The Court's analysis in the above cases is rather superficial and open to criticism. In particular, it is not obvious how the Court could reach its conclusions in *Watts* without having first investigated whether the NHS treatment could be defined as a service falling within the scope of Article 49 EC. If NHS treatment falls outside the scope of the latter provision, then how can it be relevant that the patient can receive such service without authorization? As said above, in order to bring those cases within the scope of the Treaty, the Court focused on the relationship between patient and foreign provider (and between insurance fund and domestic provider) so as to establish an economic link. However, it might be argued that the relevant relationship in determining the existence of a service provided for consideration is that between patient and insurance fund/NHS provider,[65] a relationship that is not economic in nature even in those states which are wholly 'insured based' systems, as Luxembourg in *Kohll*. In relation to this, consider the following two points.

Let's first consider the insured based systems, to then turn to the mixed and NHS-type systems. In some of the Member States (e.g. Luxembourg, France) there is a system of mandatory insurance whereby all residents are insured for health expenditure. When the need for health treatment arises, the insurance fund reimburses the individual for the entire amount; or for a fixed amount; or for a fixed percentage of the expenditure. If the relationship between insured and insurance fund were to be of an economic nature, then contribution to the fund should be made according to an actuarial assessment. Thus, the amount of contribution would

---

[65] Contra P Koutrakos 'Healthcare as an economic service' in M Dougan and E Spaventa (eds) *Social Welfare and EU Law* (Hart Publishing 2005), Ch. 5.

depend on individual risk and not on individual income. The fact that instead contribution is calculated having regard to income, that no individual risk is taken into consideration, and that those who earn below a certain threshold pay nothing, is a rather powerful indication that there is a redistributive element which cannot be reconciled with the idea of an economic service.[66] Furthermore, the insurance fund cannot refuse to insure given risks or given people and indeed insurance coverage is provided also to those who are not able to pay for it. The fact that the relationship between individual and insurance fund/NHS system should not be considered as an economic relationship is entirely consistent with the Court's refusal to consider sickness funds which pursue an exclusively social objective and 'are compelled by law to offer to their members essentially identical obligatory benefits which do not depend on the amount of contributions' as undertakings engaged in an economic activity and subject to competition law.[67]

This is not to say that the relationship between insurance fund and the provider of services is not 'economic in nature', since the fund will 'buy' the services from the provider, and will be subject, when purchasing such services, to the rules of the Treaty. For this reason, the ruling in *Kohll* is a consistent development of existing case law. In the same way as a hospital cannot discriminate on grounds of the origin of the goods when buying medical equipment, or on grounds of nationality when hiring its staff, an insurance fund cannot refuse to reimburse a patient on the sole grounds that the provider is established in another Member State (although it can of course justify such refusal on other grounds). In *Kohll* the fund refused to reimburse Mr Kohll on the sole ground that Mr Kohll bought his medical services outside the national territory without obtaining prior authorization, authorization which would have not been necessary had he bought the orthodontic treatment in Luxembourg. The reimbursement was at a flat rate; and Mr Kohll could choose any dentist provided they had a surgery in Luxembourg. It is clear that the relationship between sickness fund and health provider (as mediated and completed by the patient) is, in that case, of an economic nature and it is that relationship that is relevant for the application of Article 49 EC.

The same is not true, however, for those cases in which the system is organized in a centralized way that leaves little, if any, choice to the patient as to where health

---

[66] It is the combination of income based contribution together with its inherent redistributive element that distinguishes this type of insurance based services from other services of public interest which might well be qualified as economic in nature. Take for instance the case of the postal services where there is some redistributive element in deciding the cost of the service so as to guarantee coverage at the same price also for very remote parts of the territory (which would be clearly anti-economic); those services might well be defined as economic services, since the redistribution is of a different nature and it is not dependant upon the wealth of those who wish to use the service.

[67] Joined Cases C-264/01, C-306/01, C-354/01 and C-355/01 *AOK* [2004] ECR I-2493, para 52; see also Joined Cases C-159 and 160/91 *Poucet v Assurances Generales de France (AGF) and Caisse Mutuelle Regionale du Languedoc-Roussillon* and *Pistre v Caisse Autonome Nationale de Compensation de l'Assurance Vieillesse des Artisans* [1993] ECR I-637, and more recently Case C-218/00 *Cisal di Battistello Venanzio & C. Sas v Istituto Nazionale per l'assicurazione contro gli infortuni sul lavoro (INAIL)* [2002] ECR 691.

services are received, i.e. in those systems where services are provided directly to the patient, regardless of whether this is done through the medium of 'authorized' institutions, or through publicly owned hospitals (NHS-type systems). In these cases, the Court has focused on the fact that the recipient paid for the health services received in another Member State to establish the existence of an economic element capable of triggering Article 49 EC. However, this approach is not very persuasive, as well as being a true revolution in the definition of 'remuneration'.[68] The relevant relationship to establish entitlement to reimbursement for health services obtained abroad is, in this case, that between patient and health provider/social security fund; in this respect the fact that health services abroad have been the subject of an economic transaction is rather immaterial. Here, differently from *Kohll*, the system is not organized in a liberal/market friendly way; the State does not leave any choice to the individual and does not reimburse him/her according to a pre-defined rate. Rather, the State/fund enters into an agreement with health care providers who are guaranteed a certain amount of resources calculated in a complex way, so as to ensure capacity, technological development etc. The patient/individual is not in an economic relationship with either the fund, or the (authorized institution/State) health-care provider, and it is this latter relationship which should be relevant in assessing whether the situation falls within the scope of Article 49 EC.

As always, the NHS provider is bound by the Treaty in relation to all 'economic' transactions that it performs (hiring staff; buying equipment etc). However, there is no economic aspect in the provision of medical services by the NHS since those are not 'bought' by other providers, and are therefore not part of an economic transaction (if, on the other hand, the NHS were to contract out the medical service required then of course it would not be able to impose upon the patient the choice of location of the provider).[69] In providing health care the State is fulfilling one of its primary duties towards its citizens; it is not providing economic services. Thus, not surprisingly an EU citizen could not claim access to medical services in a Member State where he or she is not insured on an equal basis (i.e. for free) with those who are affiliated to that country's social security system. The Court is clearly aware of this problem, and deals with it by adopting a hermeneutic 'trick'. In order to establish the applicability of Article 49 EC, the Court focuses on the relationship between the patient and the foreign health care provider. That is clearly an economic relationship as the foreign provider is providing the service for remuneration. But the fact that the relationship between foreign provider and patient is of an economic nature does not transform the relationship between State of origin health system and patient into one of an economic nature. Consider the case of State

---

[68] The situation is markedly different from that at issue in Case 352/85 *Bond van Adverteerders and Others v The Netherlands State* [1988] ECR 2085. There even though the service was provided free of charge to the recipient (the viewer of television programmes), it was clear that it was 'economic' in nature since dependent upon the revenues of commercial transactions between advertisers and broadcasters.

[69] E.g. Case C-8/02 *Leichtle* [2004] ECR I-2641.

funded education provided free or almost free of charge at point of delivery: if we were to apply the Court's reasoning to education, then pupils (or their parents) would be free to send their children to education establishments in other Member States and then claim reimbursement from the State, at least for that proportion of the cost that the State would incur in directly or indirectly providing education.[70] It is unlikely that this development would occur.[71] The main difference between the two cases is that in the health care cases it is the State itself (and Regulation 1408/71) that recognizes to its citizens/insured persons a right to seek treatment abroad in given circumstances, whilst in the case of education there is usually no such right. The reason for this is obvious: in certain instances, either because of overcrowding or because of technical developments, the only way to ensure effective treatment is to transfer the patient to another Member State. But, it should be remembered, the right to seek treatment abroad is recognized by national social security systems as part of the State's duty to provide effective health care. It is when, for whatever reason, the State cannot 'directly' fulfil its duty towards a patient in need of treatment, that national law provides for an obligation upon the competent institution to meet its duties by alternative means, i.e. by paying for health care in a private institution or in another Member State.[72]

When an individual seeks care outside the State system, she is enforcing her right to receive adequate and effective health care by demanding that the State discharges one of the primary responsibilities it bears towards its citizens. Had the State not accepted an obligation to provide health care in the first place, the citizen would have no claim. In other words, had the State not provided health care, either directly or indirectly, there would be no discussion about the State's duty to reimburse treatment in another Member State.

However, in providing health care, the State is not providing a service for remuneration. Since it is the State's duty to provide health care that vests the right upon individuals to demand reimbursement of expenses incurred for treatment in another Member State, it is conceptually questionable that the Court should dismiss in *Peerbooms*, and not even consider in *Müller-Fauré* and *Watts*, the contention that the service provided by the State was in fact not a service provided

---

[70] And, by analogy with *Müller-Fauré*, the Member States might be under an obligation to set up a system of tariffs to be reimbursed, see Case C-385/99 *Müller-Fauré* and *van Riet* [2003] ECR I-4509, paras 102 to 107.

[71] On the other hand, cases in which Member States grant tax breaks for the cost of private education on condition that such education is undergone within the national territory should fall foul of the Treaty provisions; see Case C-76/05 *Schwarz* and Case C-318/05 *Commission v Germany*, joint opinion delivered 21/09/06, cases still pending at the time of writing.

[72] Of course this right is also recognized by Art 22 Council Regulation (EEC) 1408/71 on the application of social security schemes to employed persons, to self-employed persons ad to members of their families moving within the Community, as amended. Consolidated version [1997] OJ L28/1, and <http://www.europa.eu.int/eur-lex/en/consleg/pdf/1971/en_1971R1408_do_001.pdf> (hereinafter Regulation 1408/71). However, the very recognition of such right in the Regulation is an expression of the State's duty that once a given treatment is covered by its social security system, then such treatment must be effective, i.e. when necessary, the State has to provide for the patient to receive health care abroad.

for consideration but a manifestation of social solidarity.[73] By doing so, and focusing instead on the only economic limb in the relationship, the Court clearly pushes the boundaries of the Treaty a step forward, so as to embrace an area of public services, which was previously excluded.[74] As a result, the State's duties towards its citizens, at least in the field of health care provision, are redefined.[75]

The rulings in *Peerbooms* and *Müller-Fauré* affect the *determination* of the circumstances in which the State *has* to recognize a right to seek health care outside the national health system, rather than just imposing an obligation of non-discrimination between health care providers *once* this right is recognized by national law. As a result, the very *substance* of the right to receive health care is reshaped, and expanded, according to the demands of Community law. In other words, and especially in *Peerbooms*, but also in the case of *Van Riet* (the other claimant in *Müller-Fauré*), the claimants obtained through the medium of Article 49 EC the right to a treatment to which they would have not been entitled to in their own country. The treatment that saved Mr Peerbooms' life was available in the Netherlands but only for those who were below 25 years of age and for this reason he had to go abroad.[76] But even in the other cases, the effect of the Court's interpretation is to redefine the circumstances that give rise to seek treatment in another country.

6. The Authorization Requirement

Having found that treatment provided in another Member State fell in principle within the scope of Article 49 EC, the Court not surprisingly found that the prior authorization requirements at issue in the health cases constituted a barrier to the patients' ability to receive services which therefore needed to be justified according to a mandatory requirement of public interest. In the case of hospital treatment, the Court found that a prior authorization requirement is 'both necessary and reasonable'.

Medical services provided in a hospital take place in an infrastructure which requires planning. However, and consistently with the case law on justifications for barriers to intra-Community movement, the conditions imposed in order to obtain the authorization must be justified by the imperative requirements invoked (i.e. they must be necessary), and must satisfy the requirement of proportionality. What is particularly interesting for our purposes is the intensity of review to which the Court subjects not so much the conditions imposed for the granting of authorization

---

[73] E Spaventa 'Public Services and European Law: Looking for Boundaries' (2002–3) 5 CYELS 271.
[74] But see discussion on public funded benefits in, Chapter 1 above.
[75] On the impact of the health care case law on the English system, see J Montgomery 'Impact of European Union Law on English Healthcare Law' in M Dougan and E Spaventa (eds) *Social Wlefare and EU Law* (Hart Publishing Oxford 2005), Ch. 7.
[76] The same is to a certain extent true for the decision in Case C-145/03 *Keller* [2005] ECR I-2529, even though that case related to Article 22 Regulation 1408/71 and it is hermeneutically defensible.

(i.e. that the treatment should be normal and necessary), but the *way* in which fulfilment of such conditions should be assessed in the specific cases at issue.

Take *Peerbooms.* In this case, the Court stated – consistently with previous case law – that the requirement that the treatment should be considered normal would have to be assessed having regard to objective criteria capable of excluding any discrimination.[77] However, the Court went further, and held that in order to decide whether a given treatment is sufficiently tried and tested for the institution to bear its costs regard must be had also to whether the treatment is covered by the sickness insurance of the Member State where the treatment is received. One cannot but wonder how the fact that another insurance system provides for the treatment has any bearing on the evaluation of a medical practice, given that choices as to which treatments are provided reflect fundamental policy choices which might legitimately differ from one Member State to another. Similarly, the Court's review of the requirement that the treatment be necessary, in that the same or comparable treatment would not be provided without undue delay by one of the care providers contracted by the relevant fund, proved to be rather substantive, instructing the national court that account must be had of the past medical record of the patient requiring the authorization. In *Müller-Fauré*, the Court confirmed this approach, elaborating further on the relevant factors that national authorities have to take into account when deciding whether to authorize treatment abroad. In this context, the Court also made clear that denial of authorization cannot rest only on the existence of waiting lists, i.e. on the fact that there is a queue for the treatment. Such a reason is in fact of a purely economic nature and thus cannot be used to justify a limitation on one of the fundamental Treaty freedoms. In *Watts*, on the other hand, the Court seems more concerned to ensure the procedural propriety of the system: thus the system of prior authorization, in order to be justified, must be based on 'objective, non-discriminatory criteria which are known in advance, in such a way as to circumscribe the exercise of the national authorities' discretion'; the system must be procedurally proper and refusals to grant authorization must be motivated and reviewable. Furthermore, courts or tribunal hearing such cases must be able to seek the advice of 'wholly objective and impartial independent experts'.

If the Court accepts that in the case of medical services provided within hospital structures a system of prior authorization to seek treatment abroad is in principle justified, the same is not true in relation to out of hospital treatment. In *Müller-Fauré* the Court held that in such cases the prior authorization requirement is not justified. The Court admitted that 'removal of the condition that there should be a system of agreements in respect of services supplied abroad adversely affects the ways in which health-care expenditure may be controlled in the Member State of affiliation'.[78] This notwithstanding the Court found that it had not been demonstrated that removal of the authorization requirement would give rise to a considerable afflux of patients to other Member States, given natural barriers to

[77] E.g. Case C-205/99 *Asociación Profesional de Empresas Navieras de Líneas Regulares (Analir) and Others v Administración General del Estado* [2001] ECR I-1271.
[78] Case C-385/99 *Müller-Fauré* and *van Riet* [2003] ECR I-4509, para 95.

movement such as distance, linguistic barriers, costs and lack of information. For this reason, it was unlikely that removal of the prior authorization requirement would have a real impact on the finances of the Dutch social security system.

As a result of the health cases, the Court then expanded the scope of Article 49 EC to impinge on publicly funded health care provision. Admittedly, the impact of the rulings has been somehow re-dimensioned by the *Watts* ruling where the Court brought the interpretation of Article 22 Regulation 1408/71 in line with the interpretation of Article 49 EC.[79] It is thus to be expected that most cases in the future will (in the writer's opinion correctly) be decided under the Regulation. However, Article 49 EC is still relevant for out of hospital care, where no authorization can be imposed on the patient, and in those cases in which the level of reimbursement is higher in the Member State of origin. This said, the cases are still of paramount importance: they signal a considerable expansion in the scope of Article 49 EC, as a result of which another area of national law is brought within the scrutiny of the Court and is subjected to the necessity and proportionality scrutiny. But most of all, the cases are important because, through their hermeneutic inadequacy, they highlight their constitutional significance and demonstrate a shift in the Court's perception of its own role to which we shall return in Chapter 7.

7. Conclusions

Starting in the 1990s, we see a progressive expansion in the interpretation of Article 49 EC:[80] thus, its scope is broadened to cover non-discriminatory restrictions; the need for an intra-Community element is considerably weakened and the remuneration requirement relaxed.

The step to bring within the scope of the free movement of services non-discriminatory restrictions is not in itself particularly problematic when it applies to the host State, the State where the service is provided. In this case, as in the case of goods, the mere difference in regulatory standards in the Member States might give rise to obstacles. If the provider had to satisfy different sets of rules each time it wishes to provide the service abroad, the usefulness of the Treaty freedom, and the possibility of achieving an internal market lacking harmonization, would be considerably reduced.[81] However, the extension of the scope of Article 49 EC to cover also non-discriminatory rules imposed by the Member State of establishment

---

[79] Cf also Case C-56/01 *Patricia Inizan* [2003] ECR I-12403.

[80] For an interestig perspective see A Biondi 'Recurring Cycles in the Internal Market: Some Reflections on the Free Movement of Services' in A Arnull, P Eeckhout and T Tridimas *Liber Amicorum Jacobs* (Oxford, OUP, forthcoming).

[81] Directive 2006/123 on services in the internal market [2006] OJ L 376/36 has fallen short of expressly codifying the home-State principle; however, it arguably did so 'silently' and went even beyond the existig case law by restricting the legitimate reasons that can be invoked by the host State to justify the imposition of its rules to a foreign service provider to public poliy, public security, public health and environemntal protection (see Article 16(1); Article 16(3) allows the Member States to apply their own rules in relation to employment conditions).

is more problematic. This is especially the case where the specificity of the intra-Community situation seems to be lacking, and a potential, and purely hypothetic, client or provider in another Member State is sufficient to bring the situation within the scope of the Treaty. In such cases, the link between the contested national rule and the alleged obstacle to intra-Community trade is extremely weak.

The expansion of the notion of barrier is sided by an expansion of what is to be understood as relevant 'remuneration' for the purposes of bringing a service within the scope of Article 49 EC. This, once more, signifies that complex policy and budgetary choices are attracted within the orbit of the Court's proportionality and necessity assessment, which lie within the Court's hermeneutic monopoly. This might have practical implications: if the Member States have to foot the bill of those who seek health care abroad (more likely to be the educated middle-class), less resources are available for solving the structural problems which led people to seek health care in another Member State in the first place. The fact that such case law might have important budgetary effects is implicitly recognized by the Court itself when, in *Müller Fauré*, relies on the fact that it is unlikely that many people will exploit its own case law liberalizing out of hospital care.

The constitutional impact of this case law is significant: the expansion of the notion of barrier and of the notion of remuneration subject the regulatory power of the Member States to a diffuse judicial scrutiny in terms of proportionality and necessity. Whilst this might in itself not be such a bad thing, the question is whether it is justified by the Treaty. We shall now turn to the case law on the free movement of workers and establishment, to then analyze the theoretical problems and the possible solutions arising from the Court's broad interpretation of the free movement of persons' provisions.

Chapter 3

Barriers to the Free Movement of Workers and Establishment Beyond Discrimination

In the previous chapter we saw that in the 1990s the Court expanded its interpretation of Article 49 EC to truly non-discriminatory barriers even when imposed by the Member State of establishment; and that it relaxed the notion of 'economic element' necessary to trigger the Treaty. The developments which took place in the services case law were soon mirrored in the workers and establishment case law. Thus, the notion of barrier to the free movement of workers and the freedom of establishment was broadened to include also non-discriminatory barriers, and, indeed, in the *Gebhard* case,[1] the Court adopts a common test for all of the free movement of persons' provisions.

When assessing this case law, the difference between the provision of services on the one hand, and establishment and workers on the other, should be borne in mind. In the case of the former, the relationship between provider and host-State is more tenuous; the provider is established in another Member State and is fully subject to the rules of that State. In the case of establishment, the self-employed moves and establishes him/herself in the host-country. For all intents and purposes the economic migrant is fully assimilated in the host-State; she/he is regulated by the host-country in relation to most issues and especially in relation to professional and market rules. The same can be said in relation to employed people. Even frontier workers/self-employed have a more durable link with the host-country, since, even taking into account the peculiarity of their situation, in their professional life they are regulated only or mainly by the host-State. For this reason, whilst, as seen in the previous chapter, the expansion of the scope of Article 49 EC to cover non-discriminatory barriers is not in itself particularly

---

[1] Case C-55/94 *Gebhard* [1995] ECR I-4165.

surprising,[2] the expansion of the scope of Articles 39 and 43 EC impacts on the very nature, and on our understanding of the demands, of the internal market.

In this chapter we are going to provide the reader with a brief overview of those developments in the case law which will form part of detailed investigation in Chapters 5 and 7.

1. Non-discriminatory Barriers to the Freedom of Establishment and the Free Movement of Workers

As said in the first chapter, the Court's interpretation of Articles 39 and 43 EC was for a long time limited to a discriminatory assessment. It is only in 1993 (*Kraus*),[3] and more explicitly in 1995 (*Gebhard* and *Bosman*),[4] that the scope of these provisions is broadened so as to encompass non-discriminatory restrictions.

In *Kraus*, the Court held that Articles 39 and 43 EC precluded a national measure which – even though applicable without discrimination – was 'liable to hamper or render less attractive' the exercise of the freedoms granted by the Treaty. The rule at issue, an authorization and fee requirement in order to be able to use a foreign academic title in Germany, could have been easily assessed having regard to the existing case law on indirectly discriminatory restrictions, since non-German nationals are more likely to hold a foreign academic title.[5] The fact that, this notwithstanding, the Court analyzed the issue in terms of *discouragement* is thus significant.

In *Gebhard*, this choice is made clearer. Mr Gebhard was a German lawyer working in Italy, who used the title *avvocato* without having previously enrolled at the local bar, as required by Italian law. When other lawyers complained about the improper use of the title, Mr Gebhard argued that the Italian rule was incompatible with Article 43 EC and/or Article 49 EC. Having instructed the national court as to the criteria to assess whether a person is established in a Member State, or rather just providing services there, the Court went on to analyze the compatibility of the enrolment requirement with Community law. It is important to stress that, for the purposes of the case, there was no issue of mutual recognition of qualifications. The issue was not whether Italy had a duty to recognize experience and qualifications acquired elsewhere (which it obviously had). Rather, it was whether Italy

---

[2] Although, as we have seen in the previous chapter and as we shall see later in the book, the case law on services is problematic because of the potential client/provider doctrine.

[3] Case C-19/92 *Kraus* [1993] ECR I-1663. It should be noted that a first indication of the fact that the Court might follow the non-discriminatory restrictions path was already given in Case C-340/89 *Vlassopoulou* [1991] ECR I-2357, esp. para 15, where the Court examining a qualification requirement reasons in terms of hindrance. There is however hardly any doubt that rules on qualifications may comfortably sit in the indirect discrimination category since inherently less likely to be satisfied by nationals than non-nationals. W H Roth 'Annotation of *Kraus*' (1993) 30 CMLRev 1251, argued that the step towards a non-discrimination assessment significantly predated *Kraus*.

[4] Case C-55/94 *Gebhard* [1995] ECR I-4165; and Case C-415/93 *Bosman* [1995] ECR I-4921.

[5] Cf AG Van Gerven's Opinion in Case C-19/92 *Kraus* [1993] ECR I-1663.

could impose a formal requirement for the exercise of a profession (registration at the local bar) on a foreigner who was taking advantage of his freedom of establishment under Article 43 EC. The rule was non-discriminatory since it applied, exactly in the same way, to Italian citizens wishing to use the title *avvocato*. The Court found that citizens wishing to establish themselves in another Member State must in principle comply with the professional requirements imposed by that State. It then continued:

> It follows, however, from the Court's case-law that national measures liable to *hinder or make less attractive* the exercise of fundamental freedoms guaranteed by the Treaty *must fulfil four conditions*: they must be applied in a non-discriminatory manner; they must be justified by imperative requirements in the general interest; they must be suitable for securing the attainment of the objective which they pursue; and they must not go beyond what is necessary in order to attain it.[6]

It should be noticed that the *Gebhard* formula does not distinguish between freedoms; rather, it seems to indicate that the extent to which host-State rules are subject to the assessment required by the imperative requirements doctrine is unaffected by the type of relationship that the migrant has with the host country. Thus, as far as the scope of the Treaty is concerned, it is immaterial whether the migrant is participating on a 'stable and continuous basis' in the economic life of the host-State or whether she/he is just participating, if at all, on a temporary basis. Even though the three free movement of persons' freedoms are mutually exclusive, after *Gebhard*, the test for assessing the existence of a barrier to movement becomes the same. In this way the conceptual difference between the three freedoms is significantly eroded, and non-discriminatory rules imposed by the Member State of establishment, which might be the sole regulator, have to be assessed having regard to the imperative requirements doctrine.[7] And indeed the ruling in *Gebhard* has been confirmed in later case law, where, as we shall see, the Court found non-discriminatory professional requirements to fall in principle within the scope of Article 43 EC.[8]

As a result of this case law, the situation of a person established in another Member State is not conceptually different from the situation of a person merely providing a service there: both might demand that the professional rules imposed

---

[6] Case C-55/94 *Gebhard* [1995] ECR I-4165, para 37 emphasis added; AG Legèr in his Opinion did not question the fact that should Mr Gebhard's situation be regarded as falling within the rules on freedom of establishment, it was for national law to regulate it.

[7] J Lombay 'Annotation on *Gebhard*' (1996) 33 CMLRev 1073, praises the deregulatory effects of *Gebhard*; L Goffin 'Liberté d'établissement et égalité de traitement ou un avocat peut-il 's'établir' sans être inscrit à l'ordre professionnel? (A propos de l'arrêt *Gebhard*)' (1996) 31 CDE 723 is more critical, pointing out the fact that such an approach might give raise to problems in that it would require different treatment of foreigners and thus produce significant reverse-discrimination effects; also critical L Daniele 'Non-discriminatory restrictions to the free movement of persons' (1997) 22 ELRev 191.

[8] E.g. Case C-108/96 *Mc Quen* [2001] ECR I-837; Case C-294/00 *Gräbner* [2002] I-6515; Case C-79/01 *Payroll Data Services (Italy) et al* [2002] ECR I-8923; Case C-442/02 *Caixa-Bank* [2004] ECR I-8961.

by the host State be assessed having regard to the imperative requirements doctrine. This is not to say, however, that the end result will be the same: it is more likely that the imposition of professional rules on established people will meet the proportionality and necessity threshold, than the imposition of the same rules on service providers, who are already regulated somewhere else in the Community.[9] But also, the *Gebhard* formula provides very little guidance as to which rules (if any) should be excluded from the reach of Article 43 EC. After all, any rule disciplining an economic activity might be seen as hindering or discouraging the exercise of that activity, and consequently as hindering or discouraging Community citizens from moving in order to exercise that activity.[10]

The ruling in *Bosman*, could then be seen as partially qualifying the *Gebhard* approach.[11] There, Mr Bosman challenged, *inter alia*, a rule imposed by the football association which provided that a club wishing to employ a footballer who had previously been employed by another football club was liable to pay a transfer fee to the latter. This rule applied even in cases in which the football club which previously employed the footballer did not want to renew his contract. Mr Bosman found himself in a limbo: his previous club did not wish to renew his contract, but the club where he wanted to move did not want (or could not afford) to pay his transfer fee. Relying on the fact that the clubs were situated in different Member States, and on the fact that rules imposed by sporting associations are fully subjected to the free movement rules,[12] he argued that the system constituted an unjustified barrier to take up employment in another Member State, and was thus incompatible with Community law. The rules were truly non-discriminatory since they applied in the same way to transfers between clubs established in one Member State, and transfers between clubs established in different Member States. Indeed, the rules were the same for all European clubs since they were imposed by the Football Association (UEFA). The latter argued, *inter alia*, that the rules should not be caught at all by Article 39 EC since they were comparable to selling arrangements (as defined in *Keck*) and should therefore fall outside the scope of the Treaty unless directly or indirectly discriminatory. The Court found that the rules were caught regardless of discrimination since they:

> *directly affect*[ed] players' *access* to the employment market in other Member States and are thus capable of impeding freedom of movement for workers. They cannot, thus, be deemed comparable to the rules on selling arrangements for goods which in *Keck and Mithouard* were held to fall outside the ambit of Article [28] of the Treaty.[13]

---

[9] And cf Case C-58/98 *Corsten* [2000] ECR I-7919, paras 44 and ff.

[10] The Court has been urged to curtail the *Gebhard* formula in several cases. See for instance the Commission's and Member States' pleadings in Case C-190/98 *Graf* [2000] ECR I-437; Case C-176/96 *Lehtonen* [2000] ECR I-2681. Also Case C-255/97 *Pfeiffer* [1999] ECR I-2835.

[11] Case C-415/93 *Bosman* [1995] ECR I-4921.

[12] Consistent case law; Case 36/74 *Walrave and Koch* [1974] ECR 1405; Case 13/76 *Doná v Mantero* [1976] ECR 1333.

[13] Case C-415/93 *Bosman* [1995] ECR I-4921, para 103, emphasis added.

In some respects, the *Bosman* ruling is less surprising than it might seem at first sight. If it is true that the fee was to be paid regardless of whether the prospective football club was a domestic or a foreign one, the rule did impose a direct barrier to cross-border movement. Mr Bosman was in fact prevented from taking up employment in another Member State. This said, the ruling does represent a considerable expansion of the scope of Article 39 EC. Even if the reference to market access might be providing some guidance as to the issue,[14] the broad approach to the free movement of persons' provisions creates the usual definitional problems as to which rules,[15] if any, should fall outside the reach of the Treaty and not be subject to the necessity and proportionality assessment demanded by Community law. Indeed in *Graf*,[16] an imaginative claimant tried to exploit this lack of a clear demarcation between what lies within and what lies outside the boundaries of the free movement provisions in order to claim compensation from his employer. Mr Graf argued that German employment rules which provided for compensation for dismissal, but not for voluntary resignation, constituted a barrier to the free movement of workers. In Mr Graf's opinion, a worker could be deterred from moving to take up employment in another Member State by the fear of losing the right to compensation for dismissal. The Court, consistently with *Bosman*, held that for non-discriminatory rules to be considered an obstacle for the purposes of Article 39 EC, they 'must affect access of workers to the labour market'.[17] It then added that the rules under scrutiny were not such as to preclude or deter a worker from resigning to take a job in another Member State, since the right to compensation would accrue only in case of a future and hypothetical event, i.e. dismissal by the employer. Such event was 'too uncertain and indirect' for the rules to be regarded as capable of hindering free movement.[18]

In two subsequent cases, *Deliège*[19] and *Lehtonen,*[20] the Court's reasoning is much more confusing (albeit the result is hardly surprising) and the difficulties of delimiting the scope of the free movement provisions clearer. In the former case, Ms Deliège argued that the fact that she had not been selected by the competent sporting association to participate in a number of international judo championships constituted a restriction on her freedom to provide services. The application of the selection rules in fact determined her inability to take part in the competitions in question. In order to exclude the selection rules from the scope of Article 49 EC – so as not to have to assess their proportionality and necessity – the Court relied both on the fact that the rules at issue did not govern access to the labour market by

---

[14] The role of the market access test will form part of detailed analysis in Chapter 5 below.
[15] Cp in the case of goods the Sunday Trading cases; see Chapter 2 above.
[16] Case C-190/98 *Graf* [2000] ECR I-437.
[17] *Ibid.*, para 23.
[18] *Ibid.*, paras 23 to 25.
[19] Joined Cases C-51/96 and C-191/97 *Deliège* [2000] ECR I-2549.
[20] Case C-176/96 *Lehtonen* [2000] ECR I-2681.

professional sportsmen,[21] and that in any case those rules were 'inherent' in the organization of sporting competition.[22] The operative part of the ruling focuses on this latter aspect, by stating that selection rules are not caught by Article 49 EC 'so long as' they derive from 'a need inherent in the organization' of sporting competitions.

On the other hand, in *Lehtonen*,[23] the Court found that transfer deadlines imposed on teams in order to field players during the ongoing championship could constitute an obstacle to freedom of movement for workers: 'a rule which restricts (...) participation [in matches] *obviously* also restricts the chances of employment of the player concerned'.[24] It cannot be doubted, however, that selection rules, by impeding Ms Deliège from competing in international tournaments, had a more severe effect than the transfer deadlines in *Lehtonen*. If we have to take the ruling at face value, the two cases seem thus difficult to reconcile.[25] More importantly, however, the rather unorthodox reasoning in *Deliège* shows the difficulties incurred by the Court in delimiting the effect of the broad approach to the free movement provisions espoused by the Court. Thus, whilst in *Graf* the Court resorts to both lack of hindrance to market access and to the remoteness doctrine in order to exclude the application of the Treaty, in *Deliège* it introduces a new type of rule to be excluded from the reach of the free movement provisions, i.e. those rules which are *inherent* in the organization of the sporting (and perhaps other types of economic) activity.

2. The Post-*Gebhard* Case Law

The *Gebhard* approach is now established case law.[26] In *Mc Quen*,[27] a rule which reserved eye examinations to qualified ophthalmologists was found to fall within the scope of application of Article 43 EC. As in *Gebhard*, the issue was not one of

---

[21] Joined Cases C-51/96 and C-191/97*Deliège* [2000] ECR I-2549, para 61. It is debatable whether this statement really reflects the factual situation since one would think that the selection rules are aimed exactly at governing access to the 'market'. S Van Den Bogaert 'The Court of Justice on the Tatami: Ippon, Waza-Ari or Koka' (2000) 25 ELRev 554, points out the confusion stemming from the ruling since the Court then proceeds to find that the limitation of the number of participants is inherent in the conduct of international high level sports events, thus suggesting a justificatory approach which is hardly reconcilable with the statement that it does not affect market access.

[22] Joined Cases C-51/96 and C-191/97 *Deliège* [2000] ECR I-2549, para 64.

[23] Case C-176/96 *Lehtonen* [2000] ECR I-2681.

[24] *Ibid.*, para 50, emphasis added.

[25] This said, the outcome of *Lehtonen* was clearly influenced by the fact that players in non-European teams benefited from a different and more extensive deadline.

[26] We are concerned only with those cases which cannot be explained having regards to double burden/discrimination. Of course there are many more cases in which the ruling in *Gebhard* has been referred to by the Court. See e.g. Case C-424/97 *S Haim v Kassenzahnärztliche Vereinigung Nordrhein* [2000] ECR I-5123, in relation to a language requirement. We are not including Case C-255/97 *Pfeiffer Großhandel GmbH v Löwa Warenhandel GmbH* [1999] ECR I-2835 in the cases decided according to the *Gebhard* rationale since the Court's reasoning, confused if not flawed, relies on the fact that the rules at issue, an order restraining an undertaking from using a given name already

mutual recognition of qualifications or of taking into account experience acquired elsewhere, but rather it was whether a Member State could subject the exercise of a profession to a qualification requirement. Consistently with *Gebhard*, the Court found that such a rule had to be scrutinized according to the imperative requirements doctrine. In *Gräbner*[28] the same reasoning applied to an Austrian rule which prevented people not holding a degree in medicine from acting as *Heilpraktiker* (naturo-therapist). In *Payroll*,[29] the claimants attacked Italian legislation reserving the calculation and printing of payslips for undertakings with less than 250 employees to data-processing centres established and staffed exclusively by persons registered as labour consultants, lawyers, professional accountants, and other regulated professions.[30] Once again, the Court confirmed the *Gebhard* ruling and found that, even though aimed at the protection of employees, the Italian legislation was unnecessary and thus inconsistent with the freedom of establishment.[31]

Furthermore, the *Gebhard* approach extends beyond the rules aimed at regulating access to an economic activity. In *Caixa-Bank*,[32] a subsidiary of a Spanish bank (Caixa-Bank) having its secondary establishment in France successfully challenged French rules that prohibited remuneration of sight (i.e. current) accounts. The rule was non-discriminatory since it applied to both foreign and domestic undertakings; and it did not *prevent* market access, since it just regulated one aspect of banking activities. Advocate General Tizzano warned the Court about the dangers of a blanket application of the hindrance/discouragement to movement test, and especially about the danger that such a broad definition of 'obstacle' might lead to qualify *any* rule regulating an economic activity as an obstacle. If that were the case, he argued, then the internal market could be used to achieve a market without rules rather than a market where operators can move freely. He thus suggested that the Court should narrow down the scope of Article 43 EC to encompass only discriminatory restrictions and those rules which directly restrict access to the market, by directly impeding the taking up of an economic activity. Advocate General Tizzano then left it to the national court to determine whether the rules at issue were factually discriminatory. This would have been the case, in his opinion, if the effect of the rule were to *prevent*

---

used by another trader, operated to the detriment of companies having their seats in other Member States thus suggesting some discriminatory effect.

[27] Case C-108/96 *D Mc Quen et al v Grandivision Belgium SA* [2001] ECR I-837, overruling Case C-61/89 *Bouchoucha* [1990] ECR I-3551.

[28] Case C-294/00 *Deutsche Paracelsus Schulen für Naturheilverfaharen GmbH v K Gräbner* [2002] I-6515; cf AG Micho's Opinion for a very critical assessment of the *Gebhard* approach.

[29] Case C-79/01 *Payroll Data Services (Italy) et al* [2002] ECR I-8923.

[30] There was no issue of mutual recognition since Italy had guaranteed that people qualified elsewhere would be able to register as labour consultants etc.

[31] It could be questioned whether the reasoning of the Court is correct: the Court based its findings on the non-necessity of the Italian legislation on the fact that a different regime applied to undertakings with more than 250 employees. However, it could be argued that a difference in regime was justified by the fact that big undertakings have in-house accountants and lawyers who are capable of ensuring that employment legislation is respected when calculating employees' salary and benefits.

[32] Case C-442/02 *Caixa-Bank* [2004] ECR I-8961.

subsidiaries of foreign institutions to *compete effectively*, a possibility which he did not exclude given the rigid structure of the banking market and the difficulties in raising capital for new market entrants which do not benefit from a large branch network. The Court followed a different path and found that the rules at issue fell within the scope of Article 43 EC, regardless of discrimination, since they constituted a 'serious obstacle' to the pursuit of foreign undertakings' activities through a subsidiary in France, affecting their access to the market. The rules, by restricting one of the most effective (in the Court's view) ways for foreign institutions to compete with domestic ones, made market access more difficult.[33]

It is clear that the broad approach to what is to be qualified as a restriction to the freedom of establishment has a deregulatory effect: thus, for instance, as a result of the ruling in *Caixa-Bank* the French rules were amended and banks are now allowed to compete in relation to remuneration for sight accounts. According to one's own understanding of what is the optimal level of market regulation, this might not be an altogether bad thing. However, it might be questioned whether such choice should be made by the Court rather than by the political institutions.

3. The Case Law on the Free Movement of Capital

This book is not concerned with the rules applying to the free movement of capital as such. However, it is worth mentioning some of the developments which have occurred in that field for two reasons: first of all, the free movement of capital is closely linked to the freedom of establishment since restrictions on, for instance, the possibility to acquire shares in a company constitute both a restriction to move capital, and a restriction on the possibility to buy a company. Secondly and more importantly, the Court in the free movement of capital cases has followed the same approach as that followed in freedom of establishment.[34] Thus, any rule which hinders or discourages movement is caught by Article 56 EC regardless of discrimination. From our perspective the most illustrative cases are those concerning 'golden shares', i.e. shares held by the Government which carry special powers (usually in privatized industries).[35] In particular, in the *BAA* case, the Court held that the limit on ownership (at 15 per cent) and the special rights attached to the United Kingdom golden share in BAA (the company that manages British

---

[33] For a critical assessment of the case, see E Spaventa 'Annotation on *Caixa-Bank*' (2005) 42 CMLRev 1151.

[34] Cf also Commission's Communication on certain aspects concerning intra-EU investments [1997] OJ C 220/15, esp. point 9.

[35] Case C-367/98 *Commission v Portugal* (Golden shares) [2002] ECR I-4732; Case C-483/99 *Commission v France* (Golden shares) [2002] ECR I-4781; Case C-503/99 *Commission v Belgium* (Golden shares) [2002] ECR I-4809; Case C-98/01 *Commission v UK* (BAA golden share) [2003] ECR I-4641. See also Cases C-282 and 283/04 *Commission v Netherlands* (Golden shares in the telecommunication sector) [2006] ECR I-9141; Case C-112/05 *Commission v Germany* (Volkswagen), case pending.

Airports) infringed Article 56 EC of the Treaty. In this case there was no issue of discrimination since the limits to ownership and voting rights applied to shareholders regardless of where they were incorporated. Nonetheless the Court found that since the rules affected the position of shareholders, they were 'liable to *deter* investors from other Member States from making such investments and, consequently, affect access to the market'.[36] Some of the rules struck down by the Court, such as the limit to ownership in the *BAA* case, did not have a *specific* effect on intra-Community movement of capital, and indeed the reasoning of the Court suggests that *mere existence* of special rules might discourage investors from investing in a company, and thus restrict market access. A similar broad approach can be seen in the case of *Burtscher*,[37] where the Court assessed the compatibility with Article 56 EC of non-discriminatory rules which provided that buyers of immovable property in Austria should make a declaration to the public authorities to notify the purchase within two years, lacking which the transaction would be declared retroactively invalid. The Court found the rules to be a restriction on the free movement of capital, and found that, at least in the case at issue, the penalty for non-compliance was disproportionate. In this case, yet again, the rules did not have a specific impact on cross-border transactions: rather, they imposed formal (non-discriminatory) requirements for the transaction to acquire full legal effects.

4. The *Gebhard* Test, Tax and Social Security Rules

As we have seen above, the *Gebhard* formulation is very broad,[38] encompassing any rule which is liable to hinder or even just discourage movement. This, of course, might give rise to problems since any rule is liable to fall within such a broad definition. In particular, it would be open to a claimant to argue that a high level of taxation or of social security contribution might discourage her/him to move to another Member State to take up an economic activity there. But if this were the case, fiscal regimes would be subject to a proportionality and necessity assessment hardly compatible with the refusal to remove the unanimity requirement (i.e. the power of veto) in relation to the exercise of Community competence in the field of direct taxation and welfare contribution.[39] In this field, more than in any other, the scrutiny of necessity and proportionality required by the free movement provisions would entail the substitution of policy choices made by national

---

[36] Case C-98/01 *Commission v UK* (BAA golden share) [2003] ECR I-4641, para 47 emphasis added. See also Case C-174/04 *Commission v Italy* (gas and electricity) [2005] ECR I-4933, where the Commission successfully challenged Italian rules which limited to 2 per cent the shares that could be held by public undertakings in the privatized Italian gas and electricity companies.
[37] Case C-213/04 *Burtscher* [2005] ECR I-10309.
[38] And yet not broad enough for some, e.g. E I Kaldellis 'Freedom of Establishment versus Freedom to Provide Services: An Evaluation of Case-Law Developments in the area of Indistinctly Applicable Rules' (2001) 28 LIEI 23.
[39] See Articles 95(2), 42 TEC, as well as Article 58(a) TEC.

legislatures with judicial assessment. It is not surprising then that, by and large, the Court has refused to extend the *Gebhard* formula to this area.

Thus, in most cases, tax and social security rules fall within the scope of the Treaty only if they directly or indirectly discriminate against foreigners, non-residents or migrants.[40] This is not to say that the Treaty provisions do not have a palpable effect on Member States' tax and social security rules, since those are likely to contain a territorial element, typically a distinction on grounds of residence, which brings the rules within the scope of the prohibition on indirect discrimination.[41] Whilst the Court has been willing to accept that, in some cases, such distinctions might be justified by an imperative requirement (e.g. the need to maintain the cohesion of the tax system), it has also made clear that such requirements must be truly necessary to achieve the proposed aim and it has been ready to scrutinize closely whether this is the case. As we shall see in Chapter 6, the introduction of Union citizenship has expanded the scope of the Treaty and, as a result, a residence requirement must always be justified regardless of whether a given social benefit falls within the scope of the Treaty,[42] or the claimant falls within the personal scope of the economic free movement provisions.[43]

Furthermore, in these cases, discrimination is widely construed, so as to include not only rules which directly or indirectly discriminate on grounds of nationality or residence, but also those rules which act to the detriment of movers. However, seldom does the Court have recourse to the wider 'discouragement' formula in relation to those rules,[44] and it has made clear that the 'Treaty offers no guarantee to a citizen of the Union that transferring his activities to a Member State other than that in which he previously resided will be neutral as regards taxation. Given the disparities in the tax legislation of the Member States, such a transfer might be to the citizen's advantage in terms of indirect taxation or not, according to the circumstances'.[45]

---

[40] The Court has indeed demonstrated its willingness to ensure – through a generous interpretation of the secondary legislation, or the free movement provisions as the case might be – that migrants would not be deprived of benefits because of the lack of co-ordination between social security rules. It is interesting to note that the Commission is somehow more cautious than the Court in cases relating to social security; e.g. Case C-124/99 *Borawitz* [2000] ECR I-7293; Case C-135/99 *Elsen* [2000] ECR I-10409; Case C-227/03 *A. J. van Pommeren-Bourgondiën* [2005] ECR I-6101.

[41] In the case of taxation, the assessment of the existence of discrimination must often be preceded by the assessment as to whether the resident and non-resident subject to tax are in comparable situations, see e.g. Case C-234/01 *Gerritse* [2003] ECR I-5933; cf also Article 58(1)(a) EC.

[42] Case C-192/05 *Tas-Hagen and Tas* [2006] ECR I-10451.

[43] E.g. Case C-403/03 *Schempp* [2005] ECR I-6421; Case C-224/02 *Pusa* [2004] ECR I-5763; Case C-406/04 *De Cuyper* [2006] ECR I-6947.

[44] Case C-165/91 *Van Munster* [1994] ECR I-4661; Case C-262/97 *Engelbrecht* [2000] ECR I-732; in Case C-18/95 *Terhoeve* [1999] ECR I-345 even though the Court referred to the discouragement formula, the rules were in fact discriminatory against movers.

[45] Case C-365/02 *Lindorfs* [2004] ECR I-7183, para 34 and see also Case C-403/03 *Schempp* [2005] ECR I-6421. Those cases were decided in relation to Article 18 EC (Union citizenship), but exactly the same approach has been adopted in relation to Article 39 EC in Case C-387/01 *Weigel* [2004] ECR I-9445, para 55.

This said, in relation to Article 49 EC, the Court maintains an ambiguous position which is slightly at odds with what was said above. For instance, in the *De Coster* case,[46] the Court qualified a heavy tax on TV satellite dishes as a non-discriminatory obstacle, thus suggesting that also tax rules might be caught by the Treaty regardless of discrimination. However, that case is not crystal clear since the Court did in any event assess the discriminatory effects of the tax in question by pointing out that the tax affected non-domestic broadcasters more than domestic ones, since the latter had unlimited access to the cable network, whilst the former necessarily had to rely on satellite transmission. In the later case of *Mobistar*, the Court reiterated, as a matter of principle, the fact that non-discriminatory rules (including tax rules) fall within the scope of the Treaty whilst at the same time excluding that a non-discriminatory tax on masts and pylon could fall within the scope of the Treaty free movement of services provisions if its only effect was to increase the cost of the service in question.[47] As we shall see in Chapter 7, there are two possible (and not mutually exclusive) explanations for this case law: first, that at least *de facto* if not *de jure* national tax rules are compatible with the Treaty unless they are discriminatory; second, as in the case of goods, the Court might want to leave the door open for the possibility to scrutinize tax rules should they be so high as to have the same effect as a prohibition on the relevant economic activity.

5. Conclusions

The past decade has been characterized by a constant expansion of the scope of the Treaty free movement of persons provisions, not only having regard to the fact that non-discriminatory barriers are now subject to judicial scrutiny in terms of proportionality and necessity, but also in that it is now considerably easier to bring oneself within the scope of the Treaty. The recent case law raises a number of important issues.

First, there appears to be no clear demarcation line as to which rules are capable of falling within the notion of 'barrier to movement'. As a result, we witness a variety of different approaches which very much depend on the rules under scrutiny. Tax and most social security rules are assessed having regard to a discriminatory test, and there seems to be very little scope in these cases for an assessment in terms of 'discouragement'; some rules, such as the ones in *Graf*, are assessed in relation to a market access test coupled with the doctrine of 'effect too uncertain and indirect'; other rules are excluded because they are considered

---

[46] Case C-17/00 *De Coster* [2001] ECR I-9445; and see also Case C-134/00 *Viacom Outdoor* Srl [2005] ECR I-1167, where a non-discriminatory tax on billboard advertising was excluded because its impact was too modest rather than because of the absence of any legal or factual discrimination.
[47] Joined Cases C-544 and C-545/03 *Mobistar* [2005] ECR I-7723, esp. para 31; J Meulman and H de Waele 'A Retreat from *Säger*? Servicing or Fine-Tuning the Application of Article 49 EC' (2006) 33 LIEI 207 argue that *Viacom* and *Mobistar* represent a fine-tuning of Article 49 EC (almost Keck-type).

inherent in the organization of the relevant activity. Finally, some rules are assessed having regard to the broad notion of discouragement, with little indication provided as to the rationale behind the Court's decision.

Secondly, the expansion of the free movement provisions comes at the expense of the Member States' regulatory powers, in that national regulatory choices are increasingly subject to a proportionality and necessity scrutiny. This raises two related issues. In the first place, a proportionality assessment of non-discriminatory rules implies a choice over conflicting values and interests which traditionally pertains to the legislature. In other words, as we shall see in detail in the next chapters, an increasing number of policy choices are now justiciable through the medium of Community law. This determines a partial loss of regulatory sovereignty by the Member States. In the second place, it is not self-evident that the Court's generous interpretation of the free movement provisions is supported by the Treaty which, as said before, does not give us any indication as to a preferred type of market economy. In other words, it could be argued that the effect of the Court's case law is to impose a diffuse scrutiny on the desirable *level* of market regulation, rather than just imposing a scrutiny on those rules which have a *specific* effect on intra-Community trade and movement. Those issues, of constitutional importance, will form a central part of our investigation in the rest of the book. We will first assess the explanations put forward by the scholarship, to then consider the case law on Union citizenship so as to offer a different perspective from which to consider the developments that have occurred in the last decade. Thus, it will be argued that the Court's case law can be justified if we redefine the rights granted by the Treaty and consider some of the developments under scrutiny as an effect of the introduction of Union citizenship.

Chapter 4

Providing a Framework to the Free Movement Provisions: The Narrow Approach

In the previous chapters we gave an overview of the current state of the law in the field of free movement; it is now time to turn our attention to the theoretical debate surrounding those provisions.

As said before, such debate is one of constitutional importance, since the broader the scope of the free movement provisions, the greater the impact on the Member States' regulatory discretion. The debate reflects two, not necessarily mutually exclusive, concerns. First, the need to provide a coherent framework capable of accommodating, if not all the nuances, at least the majority of the case law. Secondly, the need to provide a satisfactory normative justification for the proposed framework. As a result, the debate is as much focused on what *ought* to be, as it is on what actually *is*. Broadly speaking, there are two schools of thought.

One argues that the Treaty only justifies prohibitions on discriminatory/double burden measures, or, in a more elaborated version, that the Treaty imposes a principle of mutual recognition ('narrow approach').[1] The other argues that the Treaty should be interpreted as prohibiting also those measures which in one way or another affect market access ('broad approach').[2] Whilst the former advocates a

---

[1] E.g. N Bernard 'Discrimination and Free Movement in EC Law' (1996) 45 ICLQ 82; N Bernard 'La libre circulation des marchandises, des personnes et des services dans le Traité CE sous l'angle de la compétence' (1998) 33 CDE 11; N. Bernard *Multi Level Governance* (Kluwer Law International 2002); J Snell *Goods and Services in EC Law* (OUP Oxford 2002); G Davies *Nationality Discrimination in the European Internal Market* (Kluwer Law International, The Hague, 2003).

[2] E.g. AG Jacobs' Opinion Case C-412/93 *Société d'importation Éduard Leclerc-Siplec v TF1 Publicité SA* [1995] ECR I-179; S Weatherill 'After *Keck*: some thoughts on how to clarify the clarification' (1996) 33 CMLRev 885; C Barnard 'Fitting the remaining pieces into the goods and persons jigsaw? (2001) 26 ELRev 34. Of course, the scholarly debate is more nuanced than what suggested in the text; thus some authors argue for a different approach to goods and services on the

contraction of the scope of the free movement of persons' provisions, the latter advocates an expansion of the scope of Article 28 EC so as to have a uniform test for all four freedoms. Both views are problematic: the former because it does not reflect the state of the law; the latter because, whilst it offers a more coherent framework to explain the state of the law, it fails to provide a sufficient normative justification for such a broad interpretation of the Treaty free movement provisions. We are first going to analyze the narrow approach, to then turn to the broad view.

Those who support a discriminatory approach to the Treaty free movement provisions rely primarily on the fact that the Treaty does not make any choice as to a given model of market economy. Thus, the Treaty cannot be used to impose such choices on the Member States. Whilst both a literal and teleological interpretation support the elimination of all discrimination based on nationality (including indirect discrimination), there is no indication in the Treaty that other types of restriction come within its scope and should therefore be prohibited or even scrutinized according to the mandatory requirements doctrine. It should be remembered that the debate over the scope of the free movement provisions is not simply a debate on the outcome of the Court's case law, i.e. on whether the end result reached by the Court is acceptable. It is very much a debate over whether the Court can derive from the Treaty the very power of scrutiny over the proportionality of national rules which it arrogates to itself. Thus, what is important from a constitutional perspective is not whether the rules in, say, *Gebhard*, were justified or not; rather it is whether there is any basis in the Treaty to subject them to scrutiny under Community law, and thus interfere with the choices of national legislatures.

Those who support a narrow approach reject the idea that the Treaty can be construed as prohibiting anything more than frontier barriers and discriminatory measures. Frontier barriers are prohibited because the Treaty so indicates: thus the references to quantitative restrictions and free movement, together with the very idea of an internal market where there are no frontiers, point at the fact that total bans on imports, total bans on the provision of services, and restrictions on entrance should be scrutinized according to the Treaty derogations or the imperative requirements doctrine. Further, the letter and the aims of the Treaty also make clear that no discrimination should be permitted unless justified by one of the Treaty derogations, in the case of directly discriminatory rules; or an objective reason, in the case of indirectly discriminatory rules. As we shall see in more detail, those who support the discrimination theory consider rules which impose a double burden as being caught either because such rules are inherently discriminatory or because they are inimical to the very idea of an internal market.

---

one hand and establishment and workers on the other, e.g. L Daniele 'Non-discriminatory restrictions to the free movement of persons' (1997) 22 ELRev 191; some for a combined discrimination/market access test, e.g. J Meulman and H de Waele 'A Retreat from *Säger*? Servicing or Fine-Tuning the Application of Article 49 EC' (2006) 33 LIEI 207; and M Poiares Maduro has looked at the problem from the different perspective of correcting representative malfunctions, *We, the Court* (Hart Publishing Oxford 1998).

However, according to this view, there is no ground in the Treaty to justify interfering with the regulatory competence of the Member States when there is no issue of discrimination or double burden. Whilst the underlying policy and constitutional justifications for a narrow approach are similar, different conceptual frameworks have been suggested to support the narrow view. We are first going to consider the discrimination/double burden approach, to then turn to the mutual recognition approach suggested by Bernard.

1. Discrimination, Double Burden and Mutual Recognition

The debate about the appropriate scope of the Treaty, always a heated one, was reignited by the *Keck* ruling. Following the Court's decision to exclude as a matter of principle non-discriminatory selling arrangements from the scope of Article 28 EC, several authors argued that that Article now only prohibited discriminatory restrictions. The application of product requirements on imports always needs to be justified since those rules are inherently indirectly discriminatory. Once a product has been regulated in one of the Member States, it should not be subjected to further legislation unless the application of such legislation is required to protect a mandatory requirement of public interest. So if product requirements are inherently discriminatory, and selling arrangements, by explicit decision of the Court, are caught only if discriminatory, then, the argument goes, it is clear that Article 28 EC only covers quantitative restrictions (i.e. partial or total bans on imports) and discriminatory measures.[3] The Court should adopt a similar approach to persons as the one adopted in goods: thus, only frontier obstacles (entry restrictions and total bans on services); discriminatory rules (rules which discriminate against foreigners and migrants);[4] and rules which impose a double burden should be caught by the Treaty provisions. The latter are seen as inherently discriminatory since the migrant would be regulated twice whilst the domestic economic actor is regulated only once.

---

[3] It is a matter of discussion whether the scope of Article 28 EC can be accurately so described. There are a number of measures which are neither selling arrangements nor product requirements and that are caught regardless of discrimination, e.g. licence requirements in Case C-189/95 *H Franzén* [1997] ECR I-5909.

[4] And the very idea of how to define discrimination and how many types of discrimination might there be, is far from being uncontroversial; thus, certain authors identify a third type of discrimination, material discrimination, e.g. G Marenco 'Pour une interprétation traditionnelle de la notion de mesure d'effet équivalant à une restriction quantitative' (1984) 19 CDE 291 uses the notion of material discrimination (discrimination matérielle) then distinguishing between extrinsic and intrinsic discrimination. K Lenaerts 'L'égalité de traitement en droit communautaire' (1991) 26 CDE 3, uses the term 'discrimination matérielle' to indicate both different treatment of comparable situations and equal treatment of non-comparable situations. Most of the scholarship however does not recognize material discrimination as a separate category of discrimination, e.g. N Bernard 'Discrimination and Free Movement in EC Law' (1996) 45 ICLQ 82; C Hilson 'Discrimination in Community free movement law' (1999) 24 ELRev 445.

Double burden rules would be of special relevance in the case of Article 49 EC: since a service provider is regulated by its state of establishment, most rules imposed by the host State would have to undergo scrutiny under the imperative requirements doctrine. On the other hand, a double burden is unlikely to arise in the case of workers and establishment, since in those situations the person (or company) moves to the other Member State 'to participate, on a stable and continuous basis, in the economic life of a Member State other than his State of origin'.[5] The host State then becomes the main, if not only, regulator; and the risk of a double regulatory burden is much reduced. For this reason, in the case of workers and establishment, what is primarily relevant is discrimination on grounds of nationality and migration. Of course, the concept of indirect discrimination is given a broad interpretation: all rules which place the foreigner or migrant at a disadvantage because of their status, or which affect foreigners and migrants more than nationals/non-movers, are caught by Articles 39 and 43 EC and need to be objectively justified. Furthermore, in the case of Article 43 EC, rules which restrict the number of possible establishments, or dictate the form that such establishment should take (i.e. branch, agency etc), should be caught, regardless of discrimination, because they run against the very letter of the Treaty. As we said in Chapter 1, this was very much the framework followed by the Court until the early 1990s: a broad interpretation of indirect discrimination, double burden theory, letter of the Treaty. Thus, for instance, residence requirements, (domestic) qualification requirements, and language requirements were in principle caught by the Treaty provisions.

However, given the evolution of the case law in the last decade, it is now considerably more difficult to argue convincingly that the free movement of persons' provisions, as interpreted by the Court, encompass simply a prohibition on discriminatory restrictions, and indeed to do so risks rendering the concept of discrimination so broad as to become almost meaningless.[6] As said in the previous chapters, the rulings in *Gouda* and *Säger* signalled a clear departure from a discriminatory assessment of Article 49 EC. It has been suggested that those rulings are compatible with a double burden test. This might be true for *Säger*, where the service provider, a British company offering patent renewal services, had already been regulated in the UK and thus the imposition of further regulation by Germany, the Member State where the service was to be provided, resulted in a double regulatory burden.[7] However, it might be questionable whether a double burden or a discriminatory approach is of any help in the case of *Gouda*, where the Court accepted that a ban on Sunday advertising constituted a restriction on the freedom to provide advertising services.[8]

---

[5] Case C-55/94 *Gebhard v Consiglio dell'Ordine degli Avvocati e Procuratori di Milano* [1995] ECR I-4165, para 25.

[6] Cf for instance the interpretation given by J Snell *Goods and Services in EC Law* (OUP Oxford 2002).

[7] Case C-76/90 *M Säger v Dennemeyer & Co. Ltd* [1991] ECR I-4221.

[8] Case C-288/89 *Stichting Collectieve Antennevoorziening Gouda and Others v Comissariaat voor de Media* [1991] ECR I-4007.

Furthermore, the double burden approach is difficult to reconcile with the case law on restrictions imposed by the Member State of establishment. As said in Chapter 2, the Court in *Alpine* extended the scrutiny under Article 49 EC to a non-discriminatory restriction imposed by the provider's home state. Bernard (and later Snell) has argued that the ruling is consistent with the reallocation of regulatory competences endorsed by the double burden theory.[9] Thus, the rules in *Alpine* concerned the way the service was to be provided in another Member State and that is allegedly a matter for the recipient Member State. For this reason, the Netherlands, as the provider's state of establishment, had to justify its rules. Attractive as it is, this interpretation might not be consistent with the approach so far followed by the Court since, in the case of services, there seems to be an absolute presumption that the host-State is always required to justify the imposition of its own rules on a foreign service provider. However, if, as argued by Bernard, the guiding principle underlying *Alpine* is a reallocation of regulatory competences/double burden principle according to which the State of origin cannot impose rules concerning the *way* the service is to be provided in another Member State, then the State where the service is provided should be in no need to justify rules relating to the *way* the service is provided. This is clearly the approach followed in the post-*Keck* case law in the field of goods. The Member State of origin regulates the 'product' whilst the Member State of destination regulates the *way* the product is sold. For this reason the importing Member State is at liberty to apply its non-discriminatory selling arrangements to imported products. However, there is no evidence that such a framework is applied to the services provisions: thus, whilst it is true that in *Alpine* the Court required rules which determined the conditions on how a service was to be provided in another Member State to be justified, there is no evidence that, had such rules been imposed by the Member State of destination, they would have escaped judicial scrutiny. Indeed *Gouda*, where the Court found that a ban on Sunday advertising was caught by Article 49 EC, points to the opposite result: is not a Sunday ban on the provision of a service akin to a Sunday trading ban which, following *Keck*, is excluded from the scope of Article 28 EC?

Further, and as admitted by Snell,[10] more recent rulings demonstrate that the Court does not limit its assessment of the rules imposed by the Member State of establishment to those which discipline 'selling arrangements' in other Member States, or which are extra-territorial in nature. Thus, as pointed out before, the Court in *Gourmet* scrutinized a ban on advertisement imposed by the Member State of establishment. There was no double regulatory burden as Sweden, the

---

[9] N Bernard 'La libre circulation des marchandises, des personnes et des services dans le Traité CE sous l'angle de la compétence' (1998) 33 CDE 11, 34–35; as we shall see below, Bernard has elaborated upon his theory and has later espoused a mutual recognition approach; a very similar view to Bernard's 1998 approach has been rehearsed by J Snell *Goods and Services in EC Law* (OUP Oxford 2002) 93–94. See also G Davies *Nationality Discrimination in the European Internal Marker* (Kluwer Law International The Hague 2003).

[10] J Snell, *ibid*, 111 and ff.

state of establishment, was the only regulator; nor was there any other type of discrimination. The same can be said about the rulings in *Freskot* and *Carpenter*:[11] in neither case was there an issue of discrimination or double burden.

In relation to freedom of establishment, the *Gebhard* approach is also difficult to reconcile with a narrow reading of the free movement provisions.[12] The rule in *Gebhard*, a registration requirement for lawyers, did not impose a double regulatory burden as Mr Gebhard had his primary establishment in Italy, which therefore was the only regulator. Nor was the rule indirectly discriminatory, as it affected Italian lawyers just as severely as foreign lawyers and, as we shall see in more detail below, the rule did not have a *specific* effect on migrants.

As for workers, the rules at issue in *Bosman* did have a direct impact on free movement,[13] and for this reason might be considered as falling within Article 39 EC, even in its narrower reading proposed by those who support a discrimination approach. After all, if it had been a State which had required the payment of a fee in order to be able to take up employment in another Member State, the outcome of the case would have seemed less surprising. However, that was not the case in *Lethonen*, where a rule imposing deadlines for fielding players in a basketball championship was found to breach Article 39 EC.[14]

Thus, the merit of the discriminatory approach can only lie in a prescriptive rather than descriptive model. In other words, if the discriminatory/double burden approach is not capable of describing 'what the state of the law *is*', the approach might be valuable in indicating 'what it *ought* to be'.

2. The Mutual Recognition Approach

The other 'narrow' approach which deserves to be analyzed is that proposed by Bernard.[15] From a practical viewpoint, the mutual recognition approach is hardly different from a double burden approach, since of course ensuring mutual recognition means also ensuring that products and economic operators are not subject to a double regulatory burden. However, Bernard approaches the problem from a regulatory competence perspective.[16]

---

[11] Case C-355/00 *Freskot* [2003] ECR I-5263; Case C-60/00 *Carpenter v Secretary of State for the Home Department* [2002] ECR I-6279.

[12] Case C-55/94 *Gebhard v Consiglio dell'Ordine degli Avvocati e Procuratori di Milano* [1995] ECR I-4165. The *Gebhard* ruling will form part of detailed investigation in the next chapter.

[13] Case C-415/93 *Union Royal Belge des Sociétés de Football Association ASBL v Jean-Marc Bosman* [1995] ECR I-4921.

[14] Case C-176/96 *Jiry Lehtonen, Castors Canada Dry Namur-Braine ASBL v Fédération Royale Belge des Sociétés de Basket-ball ASBL* [2000] ECR I-2681.

[15] N Bernard *Multi Level Governance* (Kluwer Law International 2002), Ch. 2; see also N Bernard 'La libre circulation des marchandises, des personnes et des services dans le Traité CE sous l'angle de la compétence' (1998) 33 CDE 11.

[16] See also AG Mayras' opinion in Case 33/74 *J H Van Bisbergen Bestuur van der Berdifsvereniging voor de Metaalnijverheid* [1974] ECR 1299, at 1316.

Bernard identifies two main frameworks of analysis for the free movement provisions: the *Dassonville* approach,[17] and the *Cassis de Dijon* approach.[18] In the *Dassonville* approach, any rule is *prima facie* illegal under the Treaty and must be justified since any difference in the regulatory standards of the Member States is liable to impede intra-Community trade and movement. In Bernard's opinion, such an approach is centralizing, since it tends to encourage the substitution of national regulatory standards with a single Community standard.

On the other hand, the *Cassis de Dijon* is a mutual recognition approach, the one that Bernard advocates and suggests can be used as a conceptual framework to explain (almost all) the case law on free movement. The mutual recognition approach recognizes that Member States do in principle retain regulatory responsibility for the market place. However, in order to ensure free movement, Member States must recognize the regulatory choices made by other Member States and must therefore allow goods and services produced in another Member State to be marketed in their territory. Thus the Member State of destination cannot impose its own rules on imported products/services.[19] Bernard then explains how the mandatory/imperative requirements doctrine fits into the mutual recognition framework: mutual recognition and the ensuing competition between legal orders which derives from leaving the Member States' regulatory competence intact in relation to home produced goods/services, are only 'politically and socially acceptable when the divergences in regulatory policies between the Member States remain within reasonable limits'.[20] When 'divergences are so great as to frustrate significantly the autonomy of national regulators', Member States can impose their own standards by invoking the mandatory requirements doctrine.

There is no doubt that the mutual recognition principle is one of the conceptual frameworks underpinning the Court's case law: that much is clear from *Cassis* as well as from the case law on mutual recognition of qualifications. However, the real question, one that Bernard answers in the affirmative, is whether mutual recognition can provide a persuasive framework for *all* (or almost all) of the case law.

In relation to the free movement of goods, Bernard considers the *Keck* ruling[21] to be entirely consistent with a mutual recognition/repartition of regulatory competences approach. This said, conscious of the problems raised by the *Alpine* ruling[22] for this model, Bernard refines the repartition of regulatory competences model: thus, it is true that the Member State of origin is competent to regulate the production of the goods (product requirements), and that the Member State

---

[17] Case 8/74 *Procureur du Roi v Dassonville* [1974] ECR 837.

[18] Case 120/78 *Rewe-Zentrale AG v Bundesmonopolverwaltung für Branntwein* (Cassis de Dijon) [1979] ECR 649.

[19] In the context of Article 28 EC he Court has clarified that national law must contain a mutual recognition clause in order to be compatible with Community law, see Case C-184/96 *Commission v France* (Foiegras) [1998] ECR I-6197.

[20] N Bernard *Multi Level Governance* (Kluwer Law International 2002), 18.

[21] Case C-267/91 and C-268/91 *Keck and Mithouard* [1993] ECR I-6097.

[22] Case C-384/93 *Alpine Investments BV v Minister van Financiën* [1995] ECR I-1141.

where the product is sold is competent to regulate the modalities of sale (selling arrangements). However, in his analysis, Bernard shifts the focus from the home/host State dichotomy to the country of establishment. It is the latter that has regulatory competence over any aspect of the economic life of a person or a company established in its territory. In this regard, he considers the selling arrangements in *Keck* as part of country of establishment rules: the person regulated was the retailer attempting to resell the goods at a loss, who was established in France; the rules at issue did not seek to regulate a producer established in another Member State, who would be regulated by that Member State. In other words, to understand whether the rules fall within the scope of the Treaty we need to 'identify the country of establishment of the economic operator responsible for the marketing of the product'.[23] Thus, *Keck* and *Alpine* are consistent with each other: in *Keck* the products were marketed by a trader established in France, in *Alpine* the country of establishment was the Netherlands and therefore that country was the 'home-State' entrusted with the regulation of the company.

Leaving aside the fact that *Alpine*, as acknowledged by Bernard himself, was not decided along these lines, since the rules were indeed caught by Article 49 EC and had to be justified, this model is not entirely convincing. If the repartition of regulatory competences always resulted in home-State rules, even for selling arrangements, then a trader established in one Member State and selling directly the goods in another Member State would not have to comply with the latter's rules in relation to the way the product is sold. There is no indication in the case law that the Court has accepted such an approach and indeed there is case law to the contrary. Take for instance the recent case of *Schmidt*,[24] where the Court found that Austrian rules prohibiting door-to-door selling of jewellery were not caught by Article 28 EC, since they were non-discriminatory and could therefore be applied to a German importer/seller. In this respect, the traditional repartition of regulatory competence approach (home state regulates product requirements, host state regulates selling arrangements) is much more convincing. The objection that such framework does not allow for a competition between legal orders in relation to selling arrangements, or that it does not allow economic operators to devise a pan-European marketing strategy, is an objection to *Keck* itself, and the vision of

---

[23] N Bernard *Multi Level Governance* (Kluwer Law International 2002), at 25.

[24] Case C-441/04 *A-Punkt Schmuckhandel v Schmidt* [2006] ECR I-2043; see also Case C-20/03 *Burmanjer and others* [2005] ECR I-4133 and Case C-254/98 *TK-Heimdienst* [2000] ECR I-2487, where even though the situation which gave rise to the litigation was purely internal, the Court reasoned in 'abstract terms' as to whether the rules at issue would be discriminatory against providers *established* elsewhere. Most cases concerning selling arrangements do in fact relate to litigation between importers and their state of establishment, e.g. Case C-292/92 *Hünermund and others* [1993] ECT I-6787; Joined Cases C-401 and 402/92 *Tankstation't' Heukske and Boermans* [1994] ECR I-2199; Joined Cases C-418/93 et al. *Semeraro Casa Uno* [1996] ECR I-2975. However, even in those cases there is no indication that the ruling would be different had the trader been established in another Member State. It is another matter whether some of those rules could fall within the scope of Articles 43/49 EC even when excluded from the scope of Article 28 EC.

the internal market espoused in that ruling, rather than a new way to conceptualize the existing case law.

But even leaving aside nuances as to home-state principle and repartition of regulatory competences, the mutual recognition approach fails to explain the case law on the free movement of persons. Bernard himself acknowledges that the ruling in *Bosman*,[25] where the Court found the transfer fees to fall within the scope of Article 39 EC, cannot be reconciled with a mutual recognition approach; given that the rules were harmonized at European level by the Football Association, there could be no issue about mutual recognition. But apart from *Bosman* which, as said above, seems entirely consistent with a movement rationale, the rest of the case law on non-discriminatory restrictions sits at odds with a mutual recognition rationale. Take for instance those cases in which the Court allowed economic operators to challenge the rules of the Member State of establishment under either Article 49 EC on the grounds that they had clients abroad (*Sodemare*, *Gourmet* and *Carpenter*),[26] or under Article 43 EC on the grounds that they were foreigners (*Gebhard*, *Mc Quen*, *Payroll*[27] as well as probably the *BAA* case).[28]

In all those cases, the rules under attack were those imposed by the home-State and, in all those cases, there was no issue of mutual recognition. Having regarded, in particular, to the establishment cases, which seem to indicate a consistent pattern in the case law unlikely to be reversed, the deregulatory impact of the Court's approach is clear. Thus, take for instance the case of *Payroll* – there a company having its secondary establishment in Italy attacked Italian rules which reserved the exercise of an economic activity (the calculation of pay slips) to people possessing given qualifications.[29] The rules were under attack not because they failed to take into account qualifications obtained elsewhere in the Community, which would have clearly been a mutual recognition issue; rather, as in *Gebhard*, it was the very existence of the rules which was successfully attacked. The same can be said about the rules in *Caixa-Bank* which prohibited banks from remunerating sight accounts.[30] In those cases, once the Court finds a rule to be an unjustified barrier to intra-Community trade, the rule needs to be struck off the statute book tout court, since there is no realistic possibility that the rule could be applied selectively only to those who have not exercised their free movement right.

---

[25] Case C-415/93 *Union Royal Belge des Sociétés de Football Association ASBL v Jean-Marc Bosman* [1995] ECR I-4921.

[26] Case C-70/95 *Sodemare Sa and others v Regione Lombardia* [1997] ECR I-3395; Case C-405/98 *Konsumentombudsmannen (KO) v Gourmet International Products AB (GIP)* [2001] ECR I-1795; C-60/00 *Carpenter v Secretary of State for the Home Department* [2002] ECR I-6279; and see also Case C-355/00 *Freskot* [2003] ECR I-5263, where the existence of a purely potential out of state provider was enough to trigger the Treaty.

[27] Case C-55/94 *Gebhard v Consiglio dell'Ordine degli Avvocati e Procuratori di Milano* [1995] ECR I-4165; Case C-108/96 *D McQuen et al v Grandivision Belgium SA* [2001] ECR I-837; Case C-79/01 *Payroll Data Services (Italy) et al* [2002] ECR I-8923; and also Case C-442/02 *Caixa-Bank* [2004] ECR I-8961.

[28] Case C-98/01 *Commission v UK* (BAA golden share) [2003] ECR I-4641.

[29] Case C-79/01 *Payroll Data Services (Italy) et al* [2002] ECR I-8923.

[30] Case C-442/02 *Caixa-Bank* [2004] ECR I-8961.

It is difficult to argue that the mutual recognition model provides a satisfactory description of the state of the law. Whilst it is true that the non-discriminatory barriers cases are by far a minority, they are also by far too important a minority to be dismissed. This does not mean, however, that the narrower approach, whether the discrimination one or the mutual recognition one, is not conceptually useful: however its use lies more in its prescriptive arguments than in its descriptive analysis.

3. The Narrow Approach as a Prescriptive Model

The Court's broad interpretation of the free movement provisions can be criticized for several reasons.[31]

First of all, it needs hardly mentioning that a very extensive interpretation of the free movement provisions determines similar problems to those already experienced in the *Sunday Trading* saga. A proportionality assessment of rules which 'merely regulate the market' implies balancing market freedom against other competing values. Lacking a precise indication as to how those values have to be balanced, the end result might be rather subjective, depending on the 'eyes of the beholder'. Take *Gourmet*, where the Court's reasoning suggested that the total ban on alcohol advertisement could be proportionate, whilst the national court found the opposite.[32] A departure from a discriminatory assessment renders it extremely difficult to define the boundaries of the rights granted by the Treaty,[33] which in turn determines problems of legal certainty, both for the parties involved in the main proceedings and, more importantly, for the Member States. Further, the more imprecise the test, the more likely the possible discrepant application of Community law by national courts. A discrimination test would be, it is argued, a simpler, clearer and more consistent test which would solve those important practical problems.

Secondly, and more importantly, there is a legitimacy problem. It is argued that there is no basis in the Treaty to justify a broad and diffuse power of judicial scrutiny of national rules which do not have a specific impact on intra-Community trade or movement.[34] And only discriminatory rules, those which impose a double

---

[31] It has been suggested that the *Keck* approach should be extended also to the other freedoms, and particularly to services. However some authors consider that that is not necessary since they perceive that the free movement of services has been already somehow curtailed; W H Roth 'The European Court of Justice's Case Law on Freedom to Provide Services: Is *Keck* Relevant?'; and J L Hansen 'Full Circle: Is there a Difference between the Freedom of Establishment and the Freedom to Provide Services?' both in M Andenas and W H Roth (eds) *Services and Free Movement in EU Law* (OUP Oxford 2002) 1, 15; and 197, 203, respectively.

[32] Cf U Djuberg 'Historic decision lifts restrictions on commercial advertising in Sweden' (2003) 27 *European Lawyer* 13.

[33] This point will be fully addressed in Chapter 5 below.

[34] J Y Art 'Legislative Lacunae, the Court of Justice and Freedom to Provide Services' in D Curtin and D O'Keeffe (eds) *Constitutional Adjudication in European Community and National Law*

burden, and frontier measures, have a specific effect on intra-Community trade/movement. Once that specificity is lost, the Treaty is transformed into an economic constitution of liberal derivation, used to challenge the very level of regulation chosen by the Member State in the exercise of its regulatory competence. However, the Treaty does not endorse any *given* model of economic constitution in preference to any other. Surely it is a market economy model,[35] but there is nothing in the Treaty to give an indication as to a *desired* level of market regulation, and very little as to which values (if any) should take precedence over market/economic values.[36] The Court has recently clarified that non-economic fundamental rights might take precedence over the fundamental freedoms;[37] however, short of clashes between traditional constitutional rights, it is difficult to have any idea as to which values should be given preference. Take for instance the case of consumer protection, where the Court has been attacked for excessively lowering the standards by imposing its own view of the 'reasonably circumspect consumer', thus striking down legislation aimed at protecting more vulnerable consumers.[38] On the other hand, a discriminatory test would allow the Court a degree of 'agnosticism',[39] making sure that the judiciary is not called upon to make substantive, and subjective, decisions about the level of market regulation. Thus, the free movement provisions are only concerned with negative integration, not with positive choices as to the correct level of regulation. Those should be left to the national and Community legislatures.

Also, the scholarship arguing in favour of the discriminatory assessment highlights how the outcome of the cases would seldom be different. In relation to non-discriminatory barriers, the Court's assessment of the proportionality of the rules at issue tends to be not very intrusive – thus most of the rules that were brought within the scope of the Treaty were in any case found to be justified

---

(Butterworths Dublin 1992) 121, agues on the contrary that the Court should intervene in the case of legislative paralysis. Thus, its pro-active approach is justified by the Treaty aims. Others have argued that the Court should also correct representative malfunctions, i.e. the fact that rules which might affect foreigners are chosen by a legislature which does not represent them, M Poiares Maduro *We, the Court* (Hart publishing Oxford 1998) esp. Ch 5; see also S Weatherill 'Pre-emption, Harmonisation and the Distribution of Competence to Regulate the Market' in C Barnard and J Scott (eds) *The Law of the Single European Market. Unpacking the premises.* (Hart Oxford 2002), 41. Contrast W H Roth 'The European Court of Justice's Case Law on Freedom to Provide Services: Is *Keck* Relevant?' in M Andenas and W H Roth (eds) *Services and Free Movement in EU Law* (OUP Oxford 2002), 1, 9.

[35] Article I–3(3) CT which lists as one of the Union's objectives the achievement of a 'social market economy'.

[36] We are referring only to pre-harmonization market regulation since when harmonizing the Treaty imposes some constraints on the institutions such as – for instance – a high level of health, consumer and environmental protection; Cf Art. 95 TEC.

[37] Case C-112/00 *Schmidberger* [2003] ECR I-5659.

[38] See e.g. Case C-470/93 *Mars* [1995] ECR I-1923 and S. Weatherill 'Recent caselaw concerning the free movement of goods: mapping the frontiers of market deregulation' (1999) 36 CMLRev 51; the Court seems to have partially retracted from its rigid view of who is the consumer to be protected in Case C-220/98 *Estée Lauder v Lancaster* [2000] ECR I-117.

[39] N Bernard 'Discrimination and Free Movement in EC Law' (1996) 45 ICLQ 83, 105.

because the Court, mindful of the difficulties of assessing such regulatory choices, adopted a very loose proportionality test. Therefore, the theory goes, if one looks at the end result in the majority of cases, the rules which were found to conflict with the Treaty free movement provisions were in any case indirectly discriminatory, and the small minority of cases where that was not true were wrongly decided.[40]

Lastly, it is argued, if the internal market is concerned with the efficient allocation of resources, a mutual recognition approach is the best way to ensure such an efficient allocation without imposing upon domestic values. Thus, a narrow approach allows not only for regulatory pluralism, but also for the economic operator's choice as to where to locate itself. This determines a healthy competition between legal orders: if a company or a person is not satisfied with the rules of the Member State of establishment, it can relocate itself in another Member State, with the certainty of not being excluded, for this only reason, from the market of its original state.[41] This in turn could trigger a competition between the States to provide the most attractive regulatory environment and eventually this could lead to States ending up converging towards the most efficient regulatory model. The competition between legal orders would also allow greater choice: citizens would then be able to express their preferences both through their vote and through their choices as economic actors. On the other hand, a broader approach which goes beyond double regulatory burden/discrimination would lead to deregulation rather than competition between legal orders. If Mr Gebhard can in any case challenge the rules of his Member State of establishment, then he would have no incentive to relocate in another Member State which provides a friendlier regulatory environment. Rather, the host State would have no choice but to amend its rules – there being little chance of a different regime for foreign people who establish themselves in the territory, and domestic providers.

Whilst it could be seriously doubted that non-corporate actors would really vote with their feet, in that in the case of individuals emotional (and economically irrational) factors might well be more important than the desire to be more or less regulated, most of those objections have compelling force. Furthermore, it should be noted how the expansion of the scope of the free movement provisions might create further constitutional problems in relation to the possible concurrent expansion of Community harmonizing competence.[42] The Court has clarified that the

---

[40] Truly non-discriminatory rules were found unjustified restrictions to the free movement provisions in Case C-79/01 *Payroll Data Services (Italy) et al* [2002] ECR I-8923; Case C-60/00 *Carpenter* [2002] ECR I-6279; Case C-442/02 *Caixa-Bank* [2004] ECR I-8961.

[41] See generally D Esty and D Geradin (eds), *Regulatory Competition and Economic Integration: Comparative Perspectives* (Oxford, OUP, 2001).

[42] Articles 44 and 95 EC. The opposite problem might arise in relation to the *Keck* exclusion of certain rules from the scope of Article 28 EC; but see G. Davies 'Can selling arrangements be harmonised' (2005) ELRev 370 who argues that the *Keck* ruling does not affect the Community's harmonizing competence. Of the opposite advice, K Mortelmans 'The Relationship between the Treaty Rules and Community Measures for the Establishment and Functioning of the Internal Market – Towards a Concordance Rule' (2002) 39 CMLRev 1303; J Snell 'Who's Got the Power: Free Movement and Allocation of Competences in EC Law' (2003) YEL 323.

Community can exercise internal market harmonizing competence only to the extent to which harmonization is necessary to remove obstacles to free movement or/and an appreciable distortion of competition.[43] A broad reading of what constitutes an obstacle in relation to the Treaty provisions might either expand Community competence; or create a dichotomy between the notion of obstacle for negative and positive integration purposes respectively. Both outcomes are constitutionally problematic. In relation to the first problem, take as an extreme example the *Carpenter* case, which related to UK immigration rules as applied to own citizens. The UK has negotiated an opt out from Title IV of the EC Treaty, and is thus bound by legislation adopted in relation to third country nationals only to the extent to which it decides to opt in.[44] But if we were to take the Court's ruling literally, a rule harmonizing the status of own nationals' third country spouses might fall within the competence of the Community to eradicate obstacles to the free movement of services. This would be politically impossible, and legally questionable. However, if that is not the case, if the ruling in *Carpenter* cannot be used as authority to extend Community competence, then it is arguable that one of the results of such case law is to create a difference in the definition of obstacle for the purposes of establishing incompatibility with one of the free movement provisions, on the one hand, and the Community harmonizing competence, on the other. As a matter of theory, this could lead to a judicially created gap in regulatory competences: if the rule needs to be disposed of in the national context and cannot be replaced by a harmonized rule for lack of Community competence, then there would be no authority capable of regulating in that field. As a matter of practice though, and as we shall see in more detail in Chapter 6, in those extreme cases such as *Carpenter* the Court declares the incompatibility with the Treaty, not of the national legislation as a whole, but of the way such legislation is applied to *that particular person*, in *that particular circumstance*.

This said, the acceptance of a certain degree of dissonance between the notion of obstacle in relation to negative and positive integration might still produce constitutionally questionable results. Take for instance the case of the proportionality assessment performed by the Court. The intensity of review of proportionality in relation to Community rules tends to be much lighter than that of national rules creating obstacles to intra-Community trade.[45] This is natural having regard to the fact that, in the case of harmonizing rules, the Court is balancing market freedom with other public interests, whilst in the case of national rules the Court is balancing the Treaty free movement rights vis-à-vis national interest. However, once we step out of a discrimination rationale, the balancing exercise becomes one of economic freedom vis-à-vis competing interests, and a different interpretation of the proportionality of the rules at issue is more difficult to justify. Take the case of *Caixa-Bank*: there France prohibited the remuneration of sight accounts. The

---

[43] Case C-376/98 *Germany v Parliament and Council* (Tobacco Advertising) [2000] ECR I-8419.

[44] See Protocol 4 to the TEU on the position of the United Kingdom and Ireland.

[45] See generally G De Búrca 'The Principle of Proportionality and its Application in EC Law' (1993) YEL 105.

Court found that such a prohibition was an unjustified barrier to the freedom of establishment. The rule clearly reflected a policy choice. It is very unlikely, though, that the same policy choice would be deemed non-proportionate if it were made by the Community legislature.[46] In that case the Court would be hesitant in substituting its own assessment for that of the legislature. This produces a fracture in the system which is difficult to explain.

4. Conclusions

Those who support a narrow approach to the free movement provisions argue that, following *Keck*, the Court has espoused a discriminatory reading of the scope of Article 28 EC. Thus, in their opinion, a similar approach should drive the interpretation of the free movement of persons' provisions. Since it is accepted that some of the case law in this field cannot be reconciled with a discriminatory approach, those who argue in favour of a narrow approach rely primarily on legitimacy and policy considerations. Thus, their view is, at least in the case of Articles 39, 43 and 49 EC, prescriptive rather than descriptive. The free movement provisions do not justify interference with the Member States' regulatory competence (beyond the elimination of discriminatory rules). In the absence of Community harmonizing legislation, it is for national legislatures to decide as to the appropriate level of regulation and the social or cultural values which should take precedence over market values. Whilst some of the policy arguments put forward by such scholarship have compelling force, the narrow approach does nothing to provide us with a normative framework capable of accommodating the developments in the case law. As it has been noted at the beginning of this chapter, there is no indication that the Court is going to overrule its *Gebhard* approach. A prescriptive approach is therefore of limited use. We now turn our attention to the market access test, examining first whether it reflects the case law, and then its normative justification. As it will be shown, the market access approach is capable of offering an explanation for much, if not all, the case law. However, the main problem with that model is that it does not offer a normative justification for the Court's interpretation: thus, whilst it might describe the rationale behind the case law, it fails to offer a persuasive explanation as to why the Treaty should be interpreted in such a broad fashion. It therefore fails to overcome the objections raised by that part of the scholarship which supports a narrower interpretation of the Treaty.

---

[46] See also M Dougan 'The Constitutional Dimension to the case law on Union citizenship' (2006) 31 ELRev 613.

Chapter 5

Market Access: A Concept in Search of a Definition[1]

There is no pleasing European lawyers. Thus, if those who support a narrow approach to the Treaty free movement provisions are displeased about the developments which have occurred in the field of free movement of persons, those who support a wider approach are critical about the *Keck* a priori exclusion of some rules from the reach of Article 28 EC.

The case in favour of rethinking the *Keck* approach was forcefully made by Advocate General Jacobs in *Leclerc-Siplec.*[2] In his opinion, whilst the *Keck* presumptions (product requirements affect intra-Community trade, non-discriminatory selling arrangements do not) might be useful guidelines, the automatic exclusion of some rules from the scope of the free movement of goods provisions carries the risk of leaving too much outside. Some selling arrangements, he argued, might have an effect on intra-Community trade even when non-discriminatory. For instance, restrictive rules on where a product can be sold might affect intra-Community trade by depriving traders in other Member States of outlets for their products. In his view, the fact that a similar restriction affects in the same way domestic producers is immaterial. This type of rule might well have an effect on intra-Community trade, and therefore there should be no absolute presumption that, lacking a discriminatory effect, they fall outside the scope of the Treaty. Advocate General Jacobs' objections were taken on board by the scholarship and several authors have since argued in favour of a 'market access' test.

From a conceptual viewpoint, those who argue in favour of a market access test rely on several considerations. First of all, the right to access another state's

---

[1] This Chapter draws from E Spaventa 'From *Gebhard* to *Carpenter*: towards a (non-)Economic European Constitution' (2004) 41 CMLRev 743.

[2] Case C-412/93 *Société d'importation Éduard Leclerc-Siplec v TF1 Publicité SA* [1995] ECR I-179.

market must be a necessary and natural consequence of the rights to move granted by the Treaty. Indeed the latter would be worthless if Member States were to be able to erect barriers to market access. The very reason why a trader, a worker, or a self-employed person moves is in order to access a new market. Secondly, it is clear that, in the case of the free movement of persons' provisions, market access is relevant in assessing a possible breach of the Treaty. Since the free movement provisions all share the same underlying rationale (a free market economy?), the Court should adopt a 'global approach' in interpreting them.[3] Thirdly, it would make the case law more consistent. At present, advertising restrictions fall in principle outside the scope of application of Article 28 EC, only to be subject to full scrutiny under Article 49 EC. A market access approach would not only remedy this oddity, but would also allow a more careful policing of those rules which might have a disproportionate effect on traders' ability to penetrate a foreign market.

The market access test, attractive as it is, does not come without its own problems: indeed, it risks falling hostage to the same definitional failure which created the *Sunday Trading* monster. The ransom to be paid to ensure unfettered access to the market might then well be too high: it is difficult to define the boundaries of the Treaty freedoms. Further, it is a matter of debate as to whether the Treaty provides sufficient basis for such a broad interpretation of the free movement rules. We shall now look at how the market access test relates to the case law,[4] to then turn our attention to whether the market access test is justified by the Treaty.

1. Market Access as (Almost) a Descriptive Model: The Case Law on Persons

There are various different versions of the market access test, and we will analyze them in detail in the next sections. In this section, we will just look at how the market access test relates to the case law. For this purpose, it is unnecessary to look at the nuances of the various tests, since those are primarily intended to make sure that some rules are excluded from the scope of application of the Treaty.

Those who support the market access test propose that rules which hinder access to a (foreign) market should be caught by the Treaty, together of course with directly discriminatory restrictions. Thus, indirectly discriminatory rules, such

[3] The term 'global approach' is borrowed by L Daniele 'Non-discriminatory restrictions to the free movement of persons' (1997) 22 ELRev 191, who used it in arguing against it.

[4] It is beyond the scope of this book to analyze whether the market access model correctly describes the scope of Article 28 EC. It seems however that the Court still relies on a comparative/discrimination approach in relation to selling arrangements, and that, at least in those cases in which market access is not totally precluded, such rules are caught only to the extent to which they make access to the market of imported products more difficult than access to the market of domestic products; e.g. Case C-322/01 *Deutscher Apothekerverband eV v 0800 DocMorris NV* [2003] ECR I-14887; Case C-20/03 *Burmanjer and others* [2005] ECR I-4133.

as residence and qualification requirements, hinder market access since they make it more difficult for the migrant to access a foreign market. Non-discriminatory measures also are caught but only insofar as they affect (directly/substantially/formally, depending on the test) access to the market. Thus, the market access test is capable of explaining the application of the free movement provisions beyond discrimination; and in many ways, it provides us with a coherent framework to explain most of the developments in the field of the free movement of persons. It also provides us with a simpler framework than even the discrimination approach since in order to accommodate what is primarily a non-discriminatory assessment in a discriminatory framework, some difficult intellectual gymnastics are occasionally required.[5] Those who support the market access approach have then a reasonable claim that it reflects the state of the law better than the discrimination approach, not least since the case law on persons is rich in references to market access.

Thus, in *Alpine*, the Court held that the rules under scrutiny could not be excluded from the reach of Article 49 EC because they 'directly affected access to the market in services in the other Member State'.[6] And indeed *Alpine* might be convincingly explained having regard to the market access test: by imposing restrictions on the way providers could advertise their financial services in other Member States, the Dutch rules clearly affected the provider's ability to contact clients in other Member States, and consequently its ability to gain access to foreign markets. In this respect, the fact that the restriction applied also to the advertising of its services to domestic clients was immaterial.

In *Bosman*, the Court referred to the fact that the transfer fee for footballers directly affected 'players' access to the employment market in other Member States'.[7] And again, the market access approach might well provide a better explanation for the ruling in *Bosman*: a rule which requires a prospective employer to pay a fee in order to employ a worker clearly discourages the employer from hiring that person, and consequently reduces the worker's possibility to access that market (whether in that State or in another country). Again, it is irrelevant whether the restriction applies internally as severely as it applies externally. Furthermore, market access also explains the exclusion of the applicability of the free

---

[5] E.g. Snell, *Goods and Services in EC Law* (OUP Oxford 2002) p. 96 and ff. Considerable difficulties arise also in holding that the scope of Article 28 EC post-*Keck* is limited to a prohibition on discriminatory obstacles, not the least because in absence of domestic production of a product in competition with an imported product there cannot be any discrimination (see Case C-47/88 *Commission v Denmark* [1990] ECR I-4509; and also Case C-391/92 *Commission v Greece* (processed milk for infants) [1995] ECR I-1621). However, product requirements are always caught, regardless of whether there is domestic production. Cf also M Poiares Maduro 'The Saga of Article 30 of the Treaty: To Be Continued' (1998) 5 MJ 298, 310, who considers that cases in which there is no national production should be looked at with suspicion not because of risk of discrimination, which cannot be there, but because of a 'risk of under-representation [in the national political process] of the interests represented by the imported products'; cf also M Poiares Maduro *We, the Court* (Hart Publishing Oxford 1998).

[6] Case C-384/93 *Alpine Investments BV v Minister van Financiën* [1995] ECR I-1141, para 38.

[7] Case C-415/93 *Union Royal Belge des Sociétés de Football Association ASBL v Jean-Marc Bosman* [1995] ECR I-4921, para 103.

movement provisions in *Graf*. In that case, the Court itself made clear that for non-discriminatory rules to be considered as obstacles to movement, they must 'affect access of workers to the labour market'.[8] And a rule which provides for compensation for dismissal does not affect in any way the worker's right to access the market. It might, at worst and in a very loose sense, discourage her/him moving just as many other factors might discourage a person from doing so (cost of living, salary, employment benefits, social security rules, house prices etc).

Furthermore, the case law on total bans on the provision of a service (or the exercise of an activity) can also be explained with reference to a market access approach. The rules in *Schindler*, by outlawing large-scale lotteries, prevented access to part of the Community market.[9] And so did the advertisement rules in *De Agostini*, which by outlawing advertisement aimed at children prevented service providers established in other Member States from offering advertisement in Sweden.[10]

The *Gebhard* case law on requirements necessary to exercise a profession might also fit well into this framework, even though the Court fails to mention market access in those cases.[11] To impose a requirement that lawyers be enrolled at the bar before being allowed to use the title *avvocato*, or to restrict eye examinations to qualified ophthalmologists,[12] regulates, and therefore restricts, access to the market. The same can be said for the rules prohibiting remuneration of sight accounts in *Caixa-Bank* which did not allow the Spanish bank to use a marketing technique which would have made it easier for it to compete and gain market share from banks already established in France.[13]

However, even in relation to persons, there are cases which are difficult to reconcile with a market access test. Take, for instance, the services section of the ruling in *Gourmet*.[14] It should be recalled that, in that case, Swedish rules forbade, almost completely, alcohol advertising. GIP, a Swedish company, successfully argued that the rules restricted its possibility to offer advertising spaces to *potential* clients established abroad, and therefore restricted its freedom to offer intra-Community services contrary to Article 49 EC.[15] *Gourmet* cannot properly be reconciled with a market access approach since in that case the rules forbidding the advertising of alcoholic beverages did not have an impact on access to a foreign market; rather they *excluded* the existence of a domestic market altogether. If the

---

[8] Case C-190/98 *V Graf v Filzmoser Maschinenbau GmbH* [2000] ECR I-437, para 23.

[9] Case C-275/92 *HM Customs Excise v Schindler* [1994] ECR I-1039.

[10] Case C-34 to 36/95 *Konsumentombudsmannen (KO) v De Agostini (Svenska) Förlag AB and TV Shop I Sverige AB* [1997] ECR I-3843.

[11] Case C-55/94 *Gebhard v Consiglio dell'Ordine degli Avvocati e Procuratori di Milano*[1995] ECR I-4165.

[12] Case C-108/96 *D McQuen et al v Grandivision Belgium SA* [2001] ECR I-837.

[13] Case C-442/02 *Caixa-Bank* [2004] ECR I-8961.

[14] Case C-405/98 *Konsumentombudsmannen (KO) v Gourmet International Products AB (GIP)* [2001] ECR I-1795.

[15] The Court then left it to the national court to determine whether the restriction on the free movement of services (and on the free movement of goods) was proportionate. The national court found that such was not the case, see U Djuberg 'Historic decision lifts restrictions on commercial advertising in Sweden' (2003) 27 *European Lawyer* 13.

rules had been challenged by a provider established in another Member State, then they would have been caught by Article 49 EC; however, the rules were challenged by a provider established in Sweden. From that perspective, since advertisement was forbidden, there simply was no domestic market in advertisement, access to which was being hindered. The same goes for the ruling in the *BAA* case:[16] it is difficult to maintain that market access would be affected by the existence of a share carrying special powers; or for the ruling in *Burtscher*,[17] where the rules at issue simply imposed formalities for the lawful acquisition of immovable property. In *Freskot*,[18] where the State had devised a system of compulsory insurance for farmers, the rules might have had some effect on market access for insurance companies established in another Member State: however, such effect should have been negligible since it concerned insurance for a given risk which affected a limited number of people and, of course, the ruling in *Carpenter*, where the rules at issue provided for the deportation of those who had overstayed their leave to enter into the UK, cannot be reconciled even with the broadest notion of market access.[19]

In any case, market access cannot be seen as the only concept underlying the case law, and there can be hardly any doubt that discrimination on grounds of nationality and movement is still relevant. Thus for instance, the scrutiny of social security rules cannot be properly explained in relation to a market access rationale since the worker in those cases has already successfully accessed the labour market. Rather, what is relevant is whether the application of the rules at issue is likely to put the migrant at a disadvantage in comparison with the non-migrant. Market access can then explain a good part of the case law, but not all of it. It has in any case to be sided by the notion of 'discouragement' to moving, and discrimination against migrants.[20] This said, we should now attempt a more precise definition of market access.

2. Market Access: A Concept in Search of a Definition?

In economics there are, broadly speaking, two views of what constitutes a barrier to market access.

At one extreme, a barrier to market access is understood as being a barrier to entry, whether created by circumstances or by legislation.[21] Barriers to entry are 'barriers that make it more costly for new firms to enter an industry'.[22] In economic

[16] Case C-98/01 *Commission v UK* (BAA golden share) [2003] ECR I-4641.
[17] Case C-213/04 *Burtscher* [2005] ECR I-10309.
[18] Case C-355/00 *Freskot* [2003] ECR I-5263.
[19] Case C-60/00 *Carpenter v Secretary of State for the Home Department* [2002] ECR I-6279.
[20] See also AG Tizzano's Opinion in Case C-442/02 *Caixa-Bank* [2004] ECR I-8961.
[21] Of course we are concerned only with obstacles to access raised by regulations, or individual behaviour, not with 'natural' obstacles (such as geographic conditions).
[22] F E Foldovary *Dictionary of free market economics*, (Edward Elgar Publishing Inc, Northampton Massachusetts USA 1998), 48. See also J Black *Oxford Dictionary of Economics* (OUP Oxford 2nd

terms, therefore, a barrier to market access is defined through a comparative assessment.[23] Market access is thus construed as the ability for an economic actor to gain access to a market on an *equal footing* with other economic operators. This definition seems entirely consistent with the Court's view in the *Keck* ruling,[24] but for the fact that the Court makes it clear that a rule preventing market access (i.e. a total barrier) falls within the definition, regardless of discrimination.[25]

At the other extreme, *any* regulation can be seen as a potential barrier to access, since *any* regulation imposes and implies compliance costs. In order to discern acceptable and non-acceptable barriers to market access, regard is paid to whether the measure is arbitrary or not, rather than on its disparate effect. So for instance, a ban on Sunday trading might not be considered arbitrary, since aimed at protecting workers or/and cultural and social traditions. On the other hand, a rule which restricted the sale of newspapers to two hours a day could be seen as an arbitrary restriction to market access. This approach is more similar to that followed by the Court in the free movement of persons cases, and indeed the imperative requirements doctrine can be seen as a refined version of the 'arbitrariness' test. The rule is not arbitrary *only* if it pursues an interest consistent with Community law, and if the restriction it imposes is necessary and proportionate.

The tension between these two meanings which can be given to the concept of market access is reflected both in the case law of the Court (*Keck* vis-à-vis the case law on persons), and in the scholarly debates. Those who support the market access test place themselves in between the two extremes: whilst they reject a purely discriminatory approach, there is nevertheless a clear effort aimed at delimiting the breadth of the formula so as to exclude some rules from the reach of the Treaty. Thus they seem to adopt an *intuitive* approach to market access. We will first consider the tests proposed by Advocate General Jacobs and Weatherill.[26] Neither of them specifically considered the application of the market access test to justify the scrutiny of the *Gebhard* type rule.[27] For this reason, after having

ed 2002) entry 'market access' which defines market access as the 'freedom to sell in a market', and identifies as institutional obstacles restrictions on entry, tariffs and quotas.

23 A ban on advertisement is then considered a barrier to entry if, for instance, the product aims at competing with national established products since it would make it more difficult for the imported product to penetrate the new market. On similar lines see the Court's reasoning in Case C-405/98 *Konsumentombudsmannen (KO) v Gourmet International Products (GIP)* [2001] ECR I-1795.

24 Case C-267/91 and C-268/91 *Keck and Mithouard* [1993] ECR I-6097; the Court stated that non-discriminatory selling arrangements fall outside the scope of Article 28 EC since 'the application of such rules to the sale of products from another Member State meeting the requirements laid down by that State is not by nature such as to prevent their access to the market or to impede access any more than it impedes the access of domestic products' (para 17).

25 Cf Case 34/79 *Henn and Darby* [1979] ECR 3795. From an economic viewpoint, it is a matter of discussion whether a non-discriminatory barrier which prevents market access is to be considered a barrier to entry.

26 AG Jacobs' Opinion Case C-412/93 *Société d'importation Éduard Leclerc-Siplec v TF1 Publicité SA* [1995] ECR I-179; S Weatherill 'After *Keck*: some thoughts on how to clarify the clarification' (1996) 33 CMLRev 885.

27 It should be noted that AG Jacobs' Opinion predates the ruling in *Gebhard*.

considered their tests, we will turn to a more detailed analysis of the case law on establishment. We will then consider the test proposed by Advocate General Fennelly, since he took into consideration the problems arising from the case law on Article 43 EC.

3. Substantial Hindrances to Market Access: An Intuitive View?

In *Leclerc-Siplec*,[28] Advocate General Jacobs proposed an alternative to the *Keck* test. He argued that the ruling in *Keck* produced two main shortcomings. First of all, it was not appropriate to introduce a rigid distinction between different categories of rules and to impose different tests for each type of rule. In his opinion, the difference in the effect that selling arrangements might have on intra-Community trade is one of degree, not one of quality. Thus, if some selling arrangements might well have little impact (such as the prohibition on advertising outside pharmacies in *Hünermund*), other rules (such as rules severely limiting the outlets in which a product can be sold) might have a very restrictive impact on intra-Community trade. Secondly, it is inappropriate to introduce a discriminatory test, since an obstacle to intra-Community trade does not cease to exist merely because the rules affect domestic producers to the same extent. A discriminatory test would lead to fragmentation of the single market across national borders, since traders would have to adapt their arrangements to meet the demands of different Member States. Restrictions to trade should not be tested against local conditions, but against the aim 'of access to the entire Community market'.[29] In his opinion, the guiding principle which provides the appropriate test for the scope of Article 28 EC is that 'all undertakings which engage in a legitimate economic activity in a Member State should have *unfettered access to the whole of the Community market*, unless there is a valid reason for denying them full access to a part of that market'.[30] In order to limit the breadth of this principle, he then suggested the introduction of a form of *de minimis* test. Thus, in Advocate General Jacobs' opinion, only rules which impose a *substantial* restriction on access should be scrutinized in relation to the mandatory requirements doctrine. Of course, the *de minimis* test would not apply to directly discriminatory rules, since in that case the Treaty provides for an outright prohibition. Similarly, product requirements always have a substantial effect on intra-Community trade and thus would always be scrutinized.

The test proposed by Advocate General Jacobs raises several problems, in that it does little to explain why the effect of the Treaty should be to endorse a sort of positive harmonization through negative integration. Take his example of a rule which severely limits outlets for the sale of a given product. It is quite clear that

---

[28] Case C-412/93 *Société d'importation Éduard Leclerc-Siplec v TF1 Publicité SA* [1995] ECR I-179.
[29] *Ibid*, para 40 of the Opinion.
[30] *Ibid*, para 41 of the Opinion, emphasis added.

such a rule would impose a substantial hindrance to market access. The rule would then have to be justified, and the assessment would depend very much on the values which are given precedence. If the local hostility towards that product is considered an acceptable competing value, the rules will be upheld (and if such a degree of leeway is to be given to local preferences, there seems little point in imposing any scrutiny in the first place). However, if market freedom is to take precedence, and the rules are considered not justified, the State will have little choice but to amend its legislation – since it is unthinkable that it would allow only imported products to be more widely sold. As Joliet has noted, in the case of at least some selling arrangements, the scrutiny of non-discriminatory rules affects the State's ability to choose the level of regulation even for its own traders.[31] Whilst, in the case of product requirements, it is possible to insert a mutual recognition clause which, whilst forfeiting regulatory competence on imported products, allows retention of that competence in relation to domestic products, this is not always possible in the case of marketing rules. Consequently the step beyond discrimination in this case necessarily affects the Member State's competence to regulate the market and strike its preferred balance between market and competing values. This objection can be made in relation to any of the market access tests and indeed in relation to the Court's approach to the free movement of workers and freedom of establishment.

Further, and as noted by the scholarship, a *de minimis* approach might be difficult to apply. The *de minimis* approach is derived from competition law and in that context it relates to an objective factor, i.e. the company's turnover. But it is less viable in the case of a free movement-related barrier to intra-Community trade, where the Court has consistently excluded the relevance of quantitative assessments, partially because of their complexity, but also because the effect of the rules might well be to act as a barrier to the development of new markets.[32] Furthermore, it should be queried whether a *de minimis* approach is different from an *ex ante* proportionality assessment. In other words, to say that a rule does not substantially affect market access might well mean that the effect of the rule is not disproportionate, i.e. it does not affect the traders' ability to access the market in a disproportionate way. Thus, the Sunday trading rules might be excluded because the restriction they impose is deemed proportionate; a total ban on advertisement imposes what seems to be a non-proportionate restriction and thus needs to be scrutinized as to its aims and the way it pursues those aims.

Given the problems to which a *de minimis* assessment gives rise, other authors have attempted to encapsulate the market access test in qualitative rather than

---

[31] R Joliet 'The Free Circulation of Goods: the *Keck and Mithouard* decision and the new directions in the case law' (1995) 1 Columbia J Eur L 436.

[32] AG Tesauro in his Opinion in Case C-292/92 *Hünermund and Others v Landesapothekerkammer Baden-Württemberg* [1993] ECR I-6787, delivered before AG Jacobs' Opinion in *Leclerc Siplec* stated that, given the fact that Article 28 EC applies also to rules which have only a potential effect on trade, a *de minimis* test would introduce a 'probatio diabolica' (para 21).

quantitative criteria. Weatherill, also criticizing the *Keck* distinction based on the type rather than on the effect of the rules, suggested that non-discriminatory measures should escape scrutiny if they impose 'no direct or substantial hindrance to the access of imported goods or services'.[33] Admitting that it is problematic to define what is a direct and substantial hinderance to market access, the author referred to existing case law to illustrate the application of the principle. Thus, for instance, the total ban on lotteries in *Schindler* created a direct and substantial hindrance to market access; whilst the rules in *Peralta*, which merely increased transportation costs by prohibiting discharge of toxic substances into the sea, failed to meet the direct and substantial hinderance threshold. The rules in *Bosman* would be an example of a direct hindrance to market access; however, rules which merely regulated the *exercise* of an occupational activity would not constitute a hindrance to access, and thus would fall out of the reach of the Treaty.[34] Further, Weatherill suggested that this test could be applied also to exports, thus partially addressing the issue of reverse discrimination. Relying on the ruling in *Alpine*, and seeking consistency between the approach adopted in the case of 'export' of services and the approach adopted in relation to export of goods,[35] he proposed that the home State should be able to apply its rules provided they are non-discriminatory *and* they do not impose 'a direct and substantial hindrance' to access to the markets of other Member States.

The tests proposed by Advocate General Jacobs and Weatherill might well seem attractive because they are in some ways easier to apply than a very broad discriminatory test. Indeed, cases like *Alpine* and *Bosman* might be more easily explained having regard to substantial hindrances to market access than with reference to a broad discriminatory/double burden test (even though they could be as easily explained having regard to the equally simple notion of barriers to movement). Both tests might also provide a more convincing solution to the long-running problem of advertisement and long distance selling techniques such as internet and television sales. Given the crucial role of advertisement in market penetration, and the possibilities which new technologies afford to marketing, this might be more sensible.

---

[33] S Weatherill 'After *Keck*: some thoughts on how to clarify the clarification' (1996) 33 CMLRev 885, 897. On almost the same lines C Barnard 'Fitting the remaining pieces into the goods and persons jigsaw?' (2001) 26 ELRev 34, with the only difference that the test would apply also to discriminatory rules since those always either prevent or substantially impede market access.

[34] The distinction between rules which regulate *access* to an occupational activity, and rules which regulate the exercise of that activity had been made by AG Lenz in Case C-415/93 *Union Royal Belge des Sociétés de Football Association ASBL v Jean-Marc Bosman* [1995] ECR I-4921, para 205.

[35] Currently, Article 29 EC prohibits only directly discriminatory rules, see e.g. Case 237/82 *J Kaas BV et al. v Dutch Government Central Organ Zuivelkontrole* [1984] ECR 483, para 22; and more recently Case C-388/95 *Belgium v Spain* (Rioja) [2000] ECR I-3123; to restrict the scope of Article 29 EC in this way might be problematic in relation to internet sales, where a prohibition on sales imposed by the State of production might clearly have a substantial effect on intra-Community trade even when it is not discriminatory. Weatherill's proposal would address this problem.

If, however, this *intuitive* approach might be useful in the case of services and goods,[36] where the division of regulatory competences is clearer and it is easier to assess the specificity of the intra-Community situation, it does little to provide a clear indication of what would fall outside of the scope of the provisions relating to free movement of workers and freedom of establishment.[37] Thus, it shows its definitional deficiency when used in the context of non-discriminatory barriers to establishment and workers, where there might be no *specificity* of the intra-Community situation to help us discern rules which should be scrutinized from rules which should fall outside the scope of the Court's analysis. Whilst in the case of services and goods a barrier to market access might also be a barrier to movement which *specifically* affects cross-border trade in goods or services, it is less obvious that that is the case in relation to workers and establishment. The inclusion within the scope of Article 43 EC of formalities required in order to exercise a profession, even when there is no issue of double burden or discrimination, is problematic because, whereas those rules might well affect access to the market, they do not *specifically* affect access to the market of someone who is taking advantage of her/his Community rights.

In other words, these tests lack clarity in that they fail to identify *why* given rules do not affect market access whilst others do.[38] Thus if 'in *Keck* and *Leclerc-Siplec* (...) the limit of commercial freedom could not be directly connected to any cross-border aspect of the activity',[39] and thus the rules at issue did not directly or substantially hinder market access, why was that not also the case in *Gebhard*? After all, the registration requirement was in no way connected to 'any cross-border aspect of the activity'. It was a formality required to use the title *avvocato* and if the market access test also catches rules which do not have any cross-border specificity, is it really justified by a neutral reading of the Treaty, or is it not rather endorsing a given (liberal?) type of economic constitution? And if that is so, is there any indication in the Treaty that this might be what the free movement provisions demand?

---

[36] L Daniele 'Non-discriminatory restrictions to the free movement of persons' (1997) 22 ELRev 191, advocates a different approach for goods and services on one hand and workers and establishment on the other. However, his approach is a double burden approach all across.

[37] It is interesting to note that the two examples given by Jacobs (ban on advertising and television sales) would not necessarily fall outside the scope of Article 28 EC even after *Keck*. As said above it is accepted that a ban on advertising might very well have a discriminatory impact because, as the Court held in *Gourmet*, it might act to the detriment of imports, and AG Jacobs himself concedes that this would be a likely result even in the post-*Keck* era. On the other hand the ban on television sales might be seen as a rule imposing a double burden, in that to impose the rule of country of destination in such case would mean that the person would have to comply with two set of rules in relation to the same event.

[38] On the lack of a precise definition of the notion of market access see also P Craig and G De Burca *EU Law* (OUP Oxford 3rd ed 2002), 656. They suggest market access to be a means to an end, the end being 'to maximize sales/profits for the individual producer, and to enhance optimal allocation of resources for the Community as a whole'.

[39] S Weatherill 'After *Keck*: some thoughts on how to clarify the clarification' (1996) 33 CMLRev 885, 905.

We are first going to consider the *Gebhard* case law in detail, then assess it against the various market access tests, to see whether it is possible to provide a coherent market access test capable of delimiting the scope of the workers and establishment provisions.

4. The *Gebhard* (R)evolution

As said many times, in *Gebhard*, the Court expanded the scope of the free movement provisions so as to encompass any:

> rule liable to hinder or make less attractive the exercise of fundamental freedoms guaranteed by the Treaty.[40]

It is true that the Court accepts that *in principle* non-discriminatory rules regulating an economic activity can be imposed on persons established within the territory and that, in any event and for this reason, those rules are generally found to be justified, being subject to a 'lighter' proportionality assessment. However, this does not make the *Gebhard* step less significant. What is crucial from a constitutional perspective is that the Court brings these rules within the ambit of application of the Treaty, thus accepting to scrutinize their aim and proportionality.

In *Gebhard* the rules at issue required lawyers to register at the local bar in order to provide their services using the title *avvocato*. This requirement had to be satisfied by any established lawyer and did not impose any specific burden on foreigners willing to exercise their profession solely in the host State (Italy). For sure, had such rules been imposed on a service provider they would have been a (justified) barrier to movement falling within the scope of Article 49 EC.[41] However, the case at issue related to Article 43 EC. In relation to this provision, Mr Gebhard's situation was by no means different from that of any other lawyer in Italy; and, arguably, there was nothing in the rule which was capable of affecting *specifically* migrants. Despite the use of a similar formulation in *Kraus*,[42] the difference between the two cases is clear: in *Kraus* the rules were not movement-neutral; those who went abroad for a course of study would suffer a disadvantage once they came back in the home-State for the sole reason of having moved. In *Gebhard* the rules were movement-neutral: they were not able to impose a barrier to movement any more than a high level of taxation or social contribution would have created such a barrier.

---

[40] Case C-55/94 *Gebhard v Consiglio dell'Ordine degli Avvocati e Procuratori di Milano* [1995] ECR I-4165, para 37 and operative part of the ruling.

[41] Directive 77/249 to facilitate the effective exercise by lawyers of freedom to provide services [1977] OJ L 78/17, provides that lawyers offering services in another Member State shall do so using the title used in the Member State from where they come; Mr Gebhard could have indeed offered his services using the title *Rechtsanwalt*, but could not offer them using the title *avvocato* before registering with the local bar which would be responsible to ensure that he possessed the relevant qualification.

[42] Case C-19/92 *Dieter Kraus v Land Baden-Württemberg* [1993] ECR I-1663.

By allowing Mr Gebhard to question those rules, thereby imposing that a necessity and proportionality assessment be carried out, the Court severs the link between a *specific* effect on free *movement* and the rules at issue. It is this very lack of *specificity* of the intra-Community situation, specificity which is there when there is a double burden or a cross-border issue, which brings about a qualitative change. If, before the developments under examination, the internal market[43] could be defined as a market without 'frontiers' in which persons could move freely, and could not be penalized for so doing, now the internal market becomes rather different, requiring something which goes beyond negative integration, if by that we mean the acceptance by the Member States of each other's regulatory standards in the absence of Community harmonizing legislation.

The move towards a non-discriminatory assessment of the workers and establishment provisions is therefore problematic; in these cases the person or the company establishes her/itself in the host country. By so doing the person ceases, for most purposes, to be regulated by her country of origin. Thus, there is usually no issue of a double regulatory burden. When people establishing themselves in another country could question only discriminatory and indirectly discriminatory rules, the double burden theory, with its stress on the inherent division of regulatory competences, provided an accurate explanation of the rationale behind the Court's interpretation. Thus, the internal market required that Member States were prohibited from applying discriminatory rules (both on grounds of nationality and on grounds of movement). Further, it required that only one set of regulations applied for any given activity, since otherwise the person exercising her right would be penalized for so doing.[44] However, the double burden theory ceases to be a viable explanation when the Court allows persons established in the host Member State to attack rules which are neither directly nor indirectly discriminatory, and which do not impose a double regulatory burden or a direct cross-border hindrance. The same is true when the Court started allowing service providers to attack rules imposed by the Member State of establishment even when there is no issue of a double regulatory burden or of a direct barrier to the cross-border provision of services.[45] Take *Gourmet*. In this case a prohibition on advertising imposed by the Member State of establishment was scrutinized on the sole grounds that it prevented domestic service providers to offer advertising space in their

---

[43] The very definition of the internal market is contested. Thus for instance AG Mischo in his Opinion in Case C-79/01 *Payroll Data Services (Italy) et al* [2002] ECR I-8923, criticizes the *Gebhard* case law arguing that the 'big internal market' might be achieved only through harmonization and not through an extensive interpretation of the establishment provisions (paras 28 and ff). See also his Opinions in Case C-108/96 *D McQuen et al v Grandivision Belgium SA* [2001] ECR I-837 and in Case C-294/00 *Deutsche Paracelsus Schulen für Naturheilverfaharen GmbH v K Gräbner* [2002] I-6515.

[44] This for the persons' provisions. Of course the expansion of the scope of Article 28 EC in the eighties could not be so justified. See the discussion on the *Sunday Trading Cases* in chapter 2 above.

[45] In Case C-224/97 *E Ciola v Land Voralberg* [1999] ECR-I2517, the Court also accepted to scrutinize a rule which applied to an established service provider on the grounds that it was providing a service to foreigners. However, that case is different because the rule was a directly discriminatory rule which directly affected (if not even prevented) the service provider to offer its services to foreigners. No wonder then that the rule fell within the scope of application of the Treaty.

publications (to be sold and distributed in the home state) to potential clients abroad.[46] Thus, in principle, the fact that a service is provided for foreign recipients is enough to be able to question regulations imposed by the home country. *Gourmet* was allowed to challenge rules which did not have a *specific* cross border effect: those rules did not prevent *access* to a foreign market, rather they prevented the very *existence* of a domestic market. Similarly, in *Freskot* the Court allowed the claimant to challenge a system of compulsory insurance for natural risks imposed by its Member State of establishment on the grounds that (*potential*) foreign service providers *might* be restricted in their freedom to offer insurance for that risk in that Member State.[47] Taken at face value the *Gourmet/Freskot* approach would, for instance, allow someone to challenge the unlawfulness of prostitution services on the grounds that some of his/her clients might be foreign, or that some foreign prostitutes might want to offer those services in that state.

For these reasons, the developments in *Gebhard*,[48] as confirmed in *Gourmet*, represent not only a step towards a considerable expansion of the scope of the free movement provisions, but also a *qualitative* leap in the content of the free movement rights. Thus, if previously the Court's interpretation of the persons' provisions was instrumental – or could be so explained and justified – to the achievement of the internal market, the move towards a non-discriminatory assessment adds a new dimension to the rights conferred upon individuals by the Community. After the developments in *Gebhard* (and *Gourmet*), it is possible to attack rules – at least to a certain extent – which merely regulate an economic activity even though there is *no double burden*, or *any intra-Community specificity*.[49] As a result Member States' competence to regulate the exercise of an economic activity for those established within their territory is affected, in that such rules have now to undergo the proportionality assessment. Furthermore, the very prohibition of an economic activity might also have to be justified under Article 43 EC.[50] But also, as a result of the *Gebhard* approach, the freedom of establishment and the freedom to provide services seem to fade into one another

---

[46] Case C-405/98 *Konsumentombudsmannen (KO) v Gourmet International Products (GIP)* [2001] ECR I-1795, esp. para 38.

[47] Case C-355/00 *Freskot* [2003] ECR I-5263.

[48] Case C-55/94 *Gebhard* [1995] ECR I-4165. A registration requirement was found to infringe Articles 12, 43 and 49 EC in Case C-264/99 *Commission v Italy* (Haulage) [2000] ECR I-4417; however lack of reasoning together with the reference to three different Treaty articles does not make the ruling good material for analysis.

[49] As we have seen in Chapter 3, the *Gebhard* approach is now established case law, e.g. Case C-108/96 *D M Quen et al v Grandivision Belgium SA* [2001] ECR I-837; Case C-294/00 *Deutsche Paracelsus Schulen für Naturheilverfaharen GmbH v K Gräbner* [2002] I-6515; Case C-79/01 *Payroll Data Services (Italy) et al* [2002] ECR I-8923; Case C-442/02 *Caixa-Bank* [2004] ECR I-8961, and it applies also to the free movement of capital, e.g. Case C-367/98 *Commission v Portugal* (Golden shares) [2002] ECR I-4732; Case C-483/99 *Commission v France* (Golden shares) [2002] ECR I-4781; Case C-503/99 *Commission v Belgium* (Golden shares) [2002] ECR I-4809; Case C-98/01 *Commission v UK* (BAA golden share) [2003] ECR I-4641; Case C-213/04 *Burtscher* [2005] ECR I-10309.

[50] Case C-294/00 *Deutsche Paracelsus Schulen für Naturheilverfaharen GmbH v K Gräbner* [2002] I-6515, para 40.

since the same rules (of the host State) can be equally attacked by an established person and a temporary service provider.[51] This is true even though the service provider is regulated elsewhere, whilst the established provider might well be regulated only by the State of establishment.

If the *Gebhard* approach is problematic because of its lack of intra-Community specificity, it also has some practical consequences. Admittedly, at least in *Gebhard*, the alleged obstacle to movement arose, to put it in Advocate General Tesauro's words,[52] not out of differences between national regulatory standards, but because of the very *existence* of such rules in the host State. It was immaterial to Mr Gebhard's freedom of establishment, and it surely did not form part of the Court's considerations, whether Germany (the State of origin) had the same rules as Italy. It was the very existence of the registration requirement which, in the Court's opinion, created a barrier to the freedom of establishment. But if the specificity of the intra-Community situation is lacking, how is it possible to provide a test capable of curtailing its application, and to give some indication as to which rules should be scrutinized and which should be considered as not affecting intra-Community movement and thus be reserved to the socio-cultural preferences of the Member States? It is clear that neither a discriminatory nor a double burden test is of any help in these cases. The question is then whether a market access test can justify the *Gebhard* ruling, whilst also providing valuable discerning tools as to the scope of the Treaty freedoms. This is the issue which some authors,[53] and Advocate General Fennelly in particular, have attempted to solve.

5. Formal Restrictions to Market Access: Not All that Glitters is Gold

In his opinion in *Graf*,[54] Advocate General Fennelly provided a detailed analysis of the case law, at the same time attempting to qualify the extent to which non-discriminatory restrictions fall within the scope of Articles 39 and 43 EC.

It might be recalled that in *Graf*, the plaintiff challenged national rules which provided for compensation only upon dismissal and not upon voluntary

[51] In Case C-58/98 *J Corsten* [2000] ECR I-7919, para 44, the Court hinted at the fact that the necessity and proportionality assessment might differ according to whether the provider is established or not. However this does not change the fact that this case law, by subjecting the rules of the State of establishment to scrutiny, constitutes a considerable expansion of Article 43 EC.

[52] Cf AG Tesauro's Opinion in Case C-292/92 *Hünermund and Others v Landesapothekerkammer Baden-Württemberg* [1993] ECR I-6787.

[53] E.g. C Barnard and S Deakin 'Market Access and Regulatory Competition' in C Barnard and J Scott (eds) *The Law of the Single European Market. Unpacking the premises.* (Hart Oxford 2002), 197, who draw extensively on AG Fennelly's test.

[54] Case C-190/98 V *Graf v Filzmoser Maschinenbau GmbH* [2000] ECR I-437; a comparable test has been put forward by Advocate General Tizzano in Case C-442/02 *Caixa-Bank* [2004] ECR I-8961; he suggested that only discriminatory rules and rules which directly affect access to the market by directly impeding the taking up of an economic activity should be caught by Article 43 EC.

resignation. Mr Graf argued that the prospect of losing such compensation discouraged him from taking up employment in another Member State, and fell thus within the scope of the *Bosman* ruling. Whilst Mr Graf's contention might seem rather preposterous, the problem it raised was of no minor importance. The breadth of the *Bosman* formula needed to be curtailed so as to provide guidance as to which rules fell in principle within the free movement provisions and which rules were not as such capable of affecting the freedoms granted by the Treaty. In order to provide some guidance as to the scope of application of the Treaty, Advocate General Fennelly analyzed the cases in which the Court scrutinized non-discriminatory restrictions and divided them into three categories.

The first category is that in which rules imposing a limitation on the number of establishments (and one could add on the type of establishment)[55] were found to conflict with the Treaty. In those cases, it is the letter of Article 43 EC itself that suggests that such rules require judicial scrutiny. The rights under Article 43 EC encompass a right to create secondary establishments (branches agencies etc) in a Member State other than that of primary establishment. It is not surprising, then, that discrimination should not be relevant in those cases, and indeed *Klopp*, the case in which the Court first established this principle by holding that the prohibition for lawyers to have more than one establishment was caught by the Treaty, was decided well before the expansion of Article 43 EC to encompass non-discriminatory barriers.[56]

The second category is that of rules concerning qualifications for posts or professional activities. Those cases can be conceptualized both as discriminatory against migrants, and as imposing a double burden on migrants who have already gained their qualification in another Member State.[57]

The third category is that of the *Bosman*-type of restrictions. In Advocate General Fenelly's opinion, judicial scrutiny of this type of rules is justified since they directly affect a 'step in the exercise of free movement, that is, the chance of taking up of employment'.[58]

Advocate General Fennelly then argued that these three types of rules all share the same attribute, that of being '*formal* restrictions on access to economic activity in a Member State. Conditions are prescribed by law or regulation non-compliance with which constitutes an absolute bar to taking up the activity in question'.[59] In Advocate General Fennelly's opinion, when an alleged obstacle does not arise from

---

[55] Case C-101/94 *Commission v Italy* (Dealing in transferable securities) [1996] ECR I-2691.

[56] Case 107/83 *Ordre des Avocats au Barreau de Paris v O Klopp* [1984] ECR 2971, and indeed when the scope of Article 43 EC might have been even narrower. More recently see Case C-104/03 *Commission v Greece* (opticians) [2005] ECR I-3177.

[57] Cf Case C-340/89 *Vlassopoulou* [1991] ECR I-2357.

[58] Case C-190/81 *V Graf v Filzmoser Maschinenbau GmbH* [2000] ECR I-437, Opinion para 27.

[59] *Ibid*, para 28, emphasis in the original. AG Fennelly considers that only the rulings in Case C-19/92 *Kraus v Land Baden-Wü rttemberg* [1993] ECR I-1663, and in Case 16/78 *Criminal proceedings against M Choquet* [1978] ECR 2293 are inconsistent with this model. However, it should be noted that the conditions for recognition and use of foreign titles in *Kraus* were arguably indirectly discriminatory against migrants (who are more likely to possess a foreign academic title); and in

a *formal* restriction to market access, but rather 'from some neutral material barrier or disincentive deriving from national regulations, the prejudice to the exercise of Community law rights must be established',[60] i.e. some sort of disadvantage arising from the fact that a free movement right has been exercised. Thus, neutral rules can be considered as '*material* barriers to market access, if it were established that they had actual effects on market actors akin to exclusion from the market'.[61] This test has the merit of attempting to reconcile the nuances of the case law with the market access approach, and indeed it might well explain the *Gebhard* case law since, undeniably, rules which impose mandatory registration (or a qualification requirement) in order to be able to exercise a profession impose a formal restriction on market access. However, there are two main problems with this approach.

First, it does not explain all the case law. For instance, why were the rules on fielding players in *Lethonen* a formal barrier to market access, whilst the selection rules in *Deliège* were not treated as such?[62] After all, both set of rules related to requirements which, if not met, would prevent the exercise of the activity. Mr Lehtonen could not play in the basketball championship because his club had not fielded him on time; Ms Deliège could not take part in the international judo competitions because she had not been selected by the relevant sporting association. Even should we take a pragmatic approach to those two cases, (the rules in *Lethonen* were caught because they favoured non-EU nationals over EU nationals), subsequent case law does not fit comfortably in this categorization. After all, the prohibition on remunerated bank accounts in *Caixa-Bank* did not constitute a precondition to take up an economic activity.

Secondly, the Advocate General argued that the *Bosman*-type rules affect the chance of taking up employment and therefore affect the right to free movement. That might have been the case in *Bosman*, in which the barrier created by the transfer fee directly affected Mr Bosman's chances of taking up employment in another Member State. However, Advocate General Fennelly argued in favour of an *absolute* presumption that *formal* barriers to market access always affect the right to free movement, without explaining why that is. He also failed to clarify why *only* in the case of *material* barriers such prejudice to the right granted by the Treaty needs to be demonstrated.

To see it from a different perspective, what is the basis to include *formal* barriers to market access within the scope of the Treaty provisions on workers and establishment? Only if there is a *specific effect* (a prejudice to free movement?) of those barriers on intra-Community movement, it is possible to

---

Choquet, where the obligation to convert a driving licence was at stake, the Court expressly refers to the principle of non-duplication of requirements.

[60] Case C-190/81 *V Graf v Filzmoser Maschinenbau GmbH* [2000] ECR I-437, Opinion para 31.

[61] *Ibid*, para 33.

[62] Case C-176/96 *Jiry Lehtonen, Castors Canada Dry Namur-Braine ASBL v Fédération Royale Belge des Sociétés de Basket-ball ASBL* [2000] ECR I-2681; Joined Cases C-51/96 and C-191/97 *C Deliège v Ligue Francophone de Judo et Disciplines Associées ASBL et al* [2000] ECR I-2549.

draw a demarcation line to the scope of the free movement provisions. But if this specificity is lacking, it might be difficult to conceptualize these developments so as to exclude the fact that the Treaty might have become of more general application, maybe granting a right to exercise economic activities, albeit in other Member States, rather than just a right to move. Those aspects will be now subject of our investigation.

6. Market Access and the Internal Market

Advocate General Fennelly's suggestion is that rules non-compliance with which bar a person from exercising an activity are caught by Articles 43 and 39 EC. But why would that be? The wording of the Treaty does not seem to support this claim: Article 43 EC provides that freedom of establishment shall be exercised under the conditions laid down in the host state, and Article 39 EC provides for the abolition of any discrimination based on nationality. Whilst the wording of both articles suggests that the right to equal treatment is not the only right that employed and self-employed persons derive from the Treaty,[63] it does suggest that, once in the territory of the host State, individuals should abide by the (non-discriminatory) laws of that State.

If a literal interpretation does not provide any justification for the Court's approach, it is necessary to assess whether a teleological interpretation of the Treaty, i.e. the internal market rationale, might support such claim; and if so, whether the notion of formal barriers to market access might be a useful tool in delimiting the effect of the free movement provisions upon the regulatory competences of the Member States. There are three main arguments which can be used to support the idea that formal barriers to market access should in principle be scrutinized.

6.1. Formal Barriers and Absolute Bans

First, the formal barrier test is reminiscent of the case law on goods and services concerning absolute bans on imports and the provision of services respectively. Thus, one could argue that since absolute barriers to the import of goods and absolute bans on the provision of services are caught by the Treaty even when non-discriminatory, that should be the case also for the other free movement provisions. Analogical reasoning would then lead us to request Member States to justify rules such as those identified by Advocate General Fennelly, since they also, when not satisfied, 'bar' the exercise of an economic activity. However, the analogy would be misplaced. There are in fact two ways, by no means mutually exclusive, to explain the case law on goods and services.

A total barrier to imports runs against the prohibition on quantitative restrictions contained in the Treaty. This was the argument used by the Court in *Henn and Darby*,

---

[63] Thus those articles state that the freedoms shall *include* (or *entail*) the right to equal treatment.

where the Court held that a prohibition on the import of pornographic material constituted a zero quota and was therefore a quantitative restriction which needed to be justified on one of the grounds contained in Article 30 EC.[64] Similarly, the prohibition on the provision of a given service might be seen as an absolute restriction which, according to the wording of the Treaty, would have to be justified.[65] But more importantly, both a ban on imports and a ban on the provision of services run against the mutual recognition principle.[66] Once a product/service has been lawfully produced, i.e. has been *regulated somewhere* in the Community, it should be able to move freely unless there is a good reason to stop it.[67] However, if the product (or service) has not been lawfully produced then there should be no issue of free movement.[68]

This reasoning cannot be automatically transposed to persons established in another Member State, since there the migrant might have not been subject to any regulation, and as soon as she moves her residence she would not, for most purposes, come under the regulatory jurisdiction of the Member State of origin. A lawyer established in Italy is wholly regulated by Italian legislation and professional rules.

Similarly, in cases where a service provider can rely on Article 49 EC against its Member State of establishment merely on the grounds that it provides a service for recipients established abroad, even though there is no barrier to cross-border activities, the economic actor is allowed to question its main (and maybe only) regulator.[69] The idea that a formal bar to activities of established persons should be subject to judicial scrutiny is, in this case again, not justified by a regulatory repartition/mutual recognition approach.

6.2. Formal Barriers and Internal Market

Secondly, it might be that the relevant factor which brought about the Court's scrutiny in the cases on establishment examined above is the underpinning internal market assumption that, once a person is exercising a profession somewhere in the

---

[64] Case 34/79 *R v Henn and Darby* [1979] ECR 3795.

[65] Article 49 EC prohibits the 'restrictions on freedom to provide services within the Community'. The Court does not consider the prohibition to provide a service as an absolute barrier, since it allows the Member States to rely on the mandatory requirements, Case C-275/92 *HM Customs & Excise v Schindler* [1994] ECR I-1039.

[66] On mutual recognition see K Armstrong 'Mutual Recognition' in C Barnard and J Scott (eds) *The Law of the Single European Market. Unpacking the premises* (Hart Oxford 2002), 225–267.

[67] This case law is entirely consistent with the internal market and the attempt to eradicate any protectionist measure. Pretend Member State A produces only beer, and prohibits both production and import of wine. It is obvious that judicial scrutiny of such a measure would be entirely consistent and necessary for the establishment of a true internal market.

[68] A different and more complicated issue relates to whether the Member State of destination would be entitled to check compliance with the rules of the Member State of origin, or whether the Member State of origin is the only State entitled to perform checks.

[69] See the discussion on *Sodemare*, *Gourmet* and *Freskot* above and in Chapter 2.

Community, she should be allowed to exercise that profession in other Member States unless there is a good reason to prevent her.[70] This could be the rationale behind *McQuen* and *Payroll* (and maybe *Caixa-Bank*):[71] in those cases the parent companies were lawfully providing the service in their State of primary establishment, and wanted to extend their market to other Member States. One could argue that the fact that they were doing so through the establishment of subsidiaries should not affect their freedom to elaborate a pan-European strategy and gain access to other markets.[72] In other words, it could be argued that in those cases a disparity in national rules would in itself be an obstacle, since it would require those who wanted to extend their market beyond the confines of one Member State to adapt to different rules in different Member States. In this respect, to construe Article 43 EC as encompassing only discriminatory restrictions would allow for the fragmentation of the Community market in 27 different markets to be maintained. Thus, in those cases there might have been an intra-Community specificity which justified the Court's scrutiny.

However, this was not the case in *Gebhard* and *Gräbner*.[73] In those cases, there was no attempt to elaborate a pan-European strategy; and indeed those cases – surely the latter, probably the former – related to primary, rather than secondary, establishment. Furthermore, in all those cases, the Court's reasoning does not suggest that there is any assessment of a specific barrier to intra-Community movement. As in the case of goods in the 1980s,[74] if there is a two-limb test – to fall within the scope of the Treaty prohibition the rule needs a) to *hinder* or *discourage* movement, and b) to be not justified – the Court is focusing primarily on the second part of the test, i.e. on an assessment of the proportionality of the measures at stake. It is only in a few cases (those in which the alleged limitation imposed has very little connection to the exercise of the economic activity such as *Graf*, or is inherent in the very existence of the economic activity such as *Deliège*), that the first limb of the test is deemed not to have been satisfied and thus there is no need to address the proportionality of the measures at stake. But by doing so, by focusing on the second limb of the test, by focusing directly on the proportionality of the measure rather than on whether there is a barrier to intra-Community movement, the Court is construing potentially *any rule* as an obstacle in need of justification. The focus on the proportionality assessment, rather than on the existence of a barrier to intra-Community movement, makes it more difficult to find

---

[70] I am particularly grateful to Michael Dougan for raising this objection.
[71] Case C-108/96 *D McQuen et al v Grandivision Belgium SA* [2001] ECR I-837; Case C-79/01 *Payroll Data Services (Italy) et al* [2002] ECR I-8923.
[72] This reasoning is similar to that adopted in Case 382/87 *Buet* [1989] ECR 1235, esp. para 7. Following the ruling in *Keck* however the existence of disparities in rules concerning advertising is not per se enough to constitute an obstacle to trade within the meaning of Article 28 EC.
[73] Case C-294/00 *Deutsche Paracelsus Schulen für Naturheilverfaharen GmbH v K Gräbner* [2002] I-6515 and also Case C-98/01 *Commission v UK* (BAA golden share) [2003] ECR I-4641; and Case C-213/04 *Burtscher* [2005] ECR I-10309, see Chapter 3 above.
[74] See Chapter 2.

an intra-Community specificity to the rules under scrutiny so as to provide some guidance as to the rationale behind their inclusion within the scope of Article 43 EC.

6.3. Formal Barriers and Movement

Thirdly, it could be argued that the formal barrier to market access test is justified by a 'movement rationale'. The Treaty grants a right to move to exercise an economic activity. If the Member States impose conditions on the exercise of economic activities, they are indirectly imposing a restriction on the individual's right to move, in that, given the hindrance to the exercise of the economic activity (the very reason why the migrant would migrate), the individual might be discouraged from moving and thus discouraged from exercising her right. This approach reflects very much the reasoning of the Court in *Bosman* and *Gebhard*, and thus might provide a more accurate representation of the current situation. However, the case law of the Court does not seem to support a distinction between formal and material barriers to market access. Whilst it is undeniably true that the rules in *Gebhard* (registration for lawyers), *McQuen* (ophthalmologists) and *Gräbner* (naturo-therapists) represented *conditio sine qua non* for exercising an economic activity, this is not true for the rules in *Caixa-Bank* (restriction on sight accounts), in *BAA* (restrictions on shareholders' rights), in *Burtscher* (penalty for failure to register the acquisition of immovable property). Even leaving aside the ruling in *Carpenter*, which might be seen as a (full Court) oddity, the scope of the free movement provisions seems not to be restricted to *formal barriers*. Rather, there is increasing evidence that any rule regulating the exercise of an economic activity might be construed as a direct or indirect hindrance to movement that needs justifying.

If that is so, however, the market access test loses any ability to distinguish between rules which should be scrutinized and rules which should not. It would be just as well to say that, as construed by the Court, the free movement of persons' provisions are capable of encompassing virtually any rule. To interpret such regulations as a barrier (formal or substantive) to market access means that we are embracing a broad notion of market access whereby potentially any rule relating to the exercise of an economic activity can be construed as a barrier to market access. This is not to say, however, that *all* rules will be so construed. In its erratic way of proceeding, the Court does adopt different tests in relation to different rules, not least for social security and tax rules which, as said in Chapter 3, are usually subject to a discriminatory rather than hindrance/discouragement assessment,[75] and might well exclude some rules (such as the selection rules in *Deliège*) because of an a priori assessment of their legitimacy.

---

[75] See Chapter 3; Cf also Case C-451/99 *Cura Anlagen GmbH* [2002] ECR I-3193, the Court found that an indirect tax on vehicles was in breach of Article 49 EC because it was not proportionate since it

For these reasons, it seems that the formal market access test does not help much in providing a coherent conceptual framework capable of delimiting the scope of the free movement provisions. If, on the one hand, it has the merit of providing a good descriptive model, in that it accommodates most of the case law (but not the oddity *Lehtonen/Deliège*, nor the *Gourmet/Carpenter* approach), on the other hand, it does not convincingly explain the rationale underlying the case law. Similarly, the substantial/direct hindrance to market access approach might provide a good *intuitive* model, but it fails to clearly define the boundaries of the free movement provisions. If the answer is not to be found in the existence of intra-Community specificity, i.e. in a *specific* impact of the rule on the cross-border situation (there was none in *Gebhard*, in *Lehtonen*, in *Gourmet*, in *Carpenter*, in *Brutscher*, in *Caixa-Bank*, and in *Freskot*), then again it seems that the real issue is whether there is a (substantial?) hindrance to the exercise of an economic activity. In other words, if the specificity of the intra-Community situation is lost, and a challenge is allowed to those rules which do not have a specific impact on those who move, when the obstacle arises not from the difference of regulatory standards in the Community, nor from the lack of mutual recognition, then it seems that the barrier arises from the *very existence* of national rules. If this is true, then there is a shift in focus when assessing the existence of a barrier.

The underlying rationale seems that of guaranteeing that those who have exercised their right to move are not subject to unnecessary regulation, to a disproportionate interference with their right to pursue an economic activity. If we define this as a right to market access, then we are giving such a broad meaning to this concept (resembling the broad view where any rule might be construed as a barrier and is acceptable only insofar as it is not arbitrary) that it becomes synonymous to the right, known in national constitutional traditions, to pursue an economic activity without being unduly restricted by regulation. The *Gebhard* approach might well be seen in this light, and so can *Gourmet*. The rules in *Gebhard*, *Mc Quen*, *Payroll* and *Caixa-Bank* all restricted the exercise of an economic activity, the rules in *Gräbner* and *Gourmet* prohibited an economic activity. It is for this reason that they were scrutinized. Furthermore, it should be noted that the fact that in most cases the rules have been found to be justified does not affect the significance of this shift in focus:[76] what is relevant in assessing the limits to the Member States' regulatory powers as imposed by the Treaty free movement provisions, is to what extent national rules are subject to judicial scrutiny in terms of proportionality. In other words, the (Economic) Constitution arises from the *very existence* of a power of scrutiny. The extent to which national

---

could have been imposed in a way which would not discriminate against leasers established in another Member State.

[76] Cf N Bernard *Multilevel Governance in the European Union* (Kluwer Law International The Hague 2002), 30 et *ff*, who considers *Gebhard* an ambiguous ruling because the rules at issue were justified, and finds in *Bosman* a case endorsing the idea of a European Economic Constitution. Others consider *Gebhard* as concerning indirectly discriminatory rules; e.g. J L Hansen 'Full Circle: Is there a Difference between the Freedom of Establishment and the Freedom to Provide Services?' in M Andenas and W H Roth *Services and Free Movement in EU Law* (OUP Oxford 2002), 197.

(and Community) rules are justified, on the other hand, relates to the 'substantive content' which is given to that Constitution, i.e. to the way in which different values (economic, social, integrationist) are balanced.

Thus, there has been yet another development in the internal market, which has never been a static concept,[77] whereby the free movement provisions can be used as a weapon to challenge the regulatory behaviour of the Member States. Further, it is not only protection from unnecessary market regulation that the Court is affording to European citizens. There are some indications that the Court might well be willing to step beyond the idea of *market* citizens to protect citizens simply as *citizens*. *Carpenter* is the best example of this trend, but the health cases could also be seen in that light.[78]

7. Conclusions

The ambiguity surrounding the market access test does little to help the quest for clarity which characterizes the debate over the scope of the free movement provisions. The problem is that either a discriminatory approach is accepted, similar to the Court's approach in *Keck*, or potentially almost any regulation might be seen as a restriction to market access. If the latter view is accepted, the test loses any meaningful ability to distinguish between rules which are subject to a proportionality assessment and rules which do not need to be so assessed. We should therefore query whether the notion of market access is the test which is best apt to unveil the consequences of the Court's interpretation, or rather whether it is an 'internal market blanket' covering a state of affairs which some might perceive as rather uncomfortable. The market access test might indeed attempt to conceal the fact that the Court's interpretation of the free movement provisions no longer finds in the internal market rationale its sole inspiration.

The ruling in *Gebhard* signals the emergence of a new constitutional dimension, which is departing from the internal market rationale, if we mean by this concept that which relates to the establishment of free movement from a negative integration viewpoint. In other words, the internal market rationale in its traditional meaning provides no justification by itself for allowing a challenge to rules which bear no relation to the individual's ability to move around the

---

[77] P Craig 'The Evolution of the Single Market' in C Barnard and J Scott (eds) *The Law of the Single European Market. Unpacking the premises.* (Hart Oxford 2002), 1.

[78] See Chapter 2 above. Another interesting question relates to the impact of the expansion of the scope of the free movement provisions on the Community's internal market competence under Article 95 EC. See Case C-376/98 *Germany v Parliament and Council* (Tobacco advertising) [2000] ECR I-8419; D Wyatt 'Constitutional Significance of the Tobacco Advertising Judgment of the European Court of Justice' in *The ECJ's Tobacco Advertising Judgment* (CELS Occasional Paper No. 5 Cambridge 2001); and 'Community Competence to Regulate Medical Services' in M Dougan and E Spaventa *Social Welfare and EU Law* (Hart Publishing 2005), 131; G Davies 'Can Selling Arrangements be Harmonised?' (2005) 30 ELRev 371.

Community. The 'free movement' right is no longer construed as a mere right to move, but rather as a right to pursue an economic activity in another country. The Community right then becomes akin to the claim that citizens have against their own state, in national contemporary liberal democracies, not to be *unjustly* limited in their freedom – be this freedom economic or of another kind. A new layer of protection to personal freedom is added: the very claim which traditionally pertains to the realm of national constitutional law, the right not to be restrained without there being a good reason, becomes a Community right, albeit restricted mainly to the economic dimension – but also, as we shall see in the next chapter, going beyond that dimension.

In *Gebhard*, the Court leaves behind 'economic agnosticism' to espouse instead a notion of liberal market economy.[79] However, this does not mean that the Court is embracing a *neo-liberal* approach, i.e. *hostile* to regulation, believing that it is for the market to regulate itself. Rather, it is embracing a *liberal* approach, in the sense of protecting the individual from *unnecessary* regulation. It is exactly this preference towards the 'individual' rather than just towards the 'market' that explains the case law where there is no issue of barrier to movement (*Gebhard*, *Gourmet*, *Freskot*), or where the economic-right dimension is minimal if not altogether inexistent (*Carpenter*). The fact that the Court is not endorsing a neo-liberal approach is demonstrated not only by its case law on the compatibility of harmonizing rules with the free movement provisions (where it clearly leaves a wide margin of discretion to the Community legislature as to the necessary level of regulation),[80] but also by the fact that the Court uses a 'light touch' on proportionality when dealing with this type of restrictions (thus ensuring that the Member States retain the power to balance different values in deciding the regulatory threshold).[81]

This said, to conceptualize the scope of the free movement of persons provisions as encompassing a right to exercise an economic activity in another Member State rather than a broad right to market access tells us nothing about a possible normative justification for such a step. Such normative justification is, in the writer's opinion, to be found in the introduction of Union citizenship. Thus, not

[79] I borrowed this expression from N Bernard 'Discrimination and Free Movement in EC Law' (1996) 45 ICLQ 82, 105.

[80] See N Bernard *Multilevel Governance in the European Union* (Kluwer Law International, The Hague, 2002) and his point that were the Court to have embraced a neo-liberal view of the Economic Constitution, it would have to be much more heavy handed in its review of Community legislation.

[81] In all cases but *Payroll* and *Caixa-Bank* the Court found the measures to be justified. On the different intensity of proportionality review in Community law *cp* De Búrca 'The Principle of Proportionality and its Application in EC Law' (1993) 13 YEL 105; the different standard of review for harmonized rules has led K Mortelmans 'The Relationship between the Treaty Rules and the Community Measures for the Establishment and Functioning of the Internal Market – Towards a Concordance Rule' (2002) 39 CMLRev 1303, to argue in favour of introducing an explicit provision in the Treaty explicitly subjecting the Community legislature to the free movement provisions.

only in the Court's case law is there visible a certain element of concern for the protection of the individual which is entirely consistent with citizenship discourse, but also the hermeneutic technique adopted in relation to Articles 17 and 18 EC sheds some light on the (earlier) developments in the case law on economic migration.

We shall now turn to the case law on Union citizenship, to then suggest an alternative explanation for the ruling in *Carpenter*. In the last chapter we will then try to offer a different perspective from which to appreciate the developments which have been the main focus of this book.

Chapter 6

Union Citizenship

Any account of the law on the free movement of persons would be incomplete without at least a summary discussion of Union citizenship; however, and as said in the previous chapter, it is not only for the sake of completeness that we are going to analyze this topic. Rather, and as it will be seen in the next chapter, the case law on citizenship serves as a basis to provide normative legitimacy for the case law on economic migrants.

We have seen in the previous chapters that economically active citizens derive extensive rights from the Treaty. We have focused primarily on State regulations that migrants are able to challenge under Community law by claiming that such rules constitute barriers to their right to move and exercise an economic activity in another Member State; but, as we have seen in the first chapter, economically active migrants also enjoy a general right of residence and, when resident, rights of equal treatment in relation to contributory and non-contributory benefits.[1] Being active participants in the host State's society, economically active migrants also have a right to become active claimants and, as we have seen, the Court has, unsurprisingly, construed the notion of economically active migrants generously.

Further, some rights accrue also to those who are passively economically active, i.e. those who travel to another Member State not to exercise an economic activity but to receive a service provided for remuneration. Even though the right to equal treatment in this case does not extend to benefits which can be defined as an expression of social solidarity (such as health care, unemployment benefits etc.), since those are not provided for remuneration, tourists might still participate

[1] In the case of a worker (or someone falling within the Treaty economic free movement provisions), Article 12 EC might be of use for those benefits which do not fall either within Article 39 EC, since they do not relate to conditions of employment, nor within Regulation 1612/68, since they cannot be qualified as social advantages; e.g. Case C-411/98 *A Ferlini v Centre Hospitalier de Luxembourg* [2000] ECR I-8081.

in some of the social advantages financed by the public purse. We have seen that service recipients have a right to equal treatment in relation to anything directly or indirectly connected to the service they receive, such as preferential museum tariffs.[2] Tourists also enjoy a right to be protected from crime on the same grounds as residents, and thus may claim compensation for crime on the same grounds as nationals;[3] and have a right to stand trial in another language if that right is available to residents.[4]

This said, before the introduction of Union citizenship, economically inactive citizens had limited rights under Community law. They did not fall within the Treaty free movement provisions, but were covered by the three Residence Directives adopted in the early 1990s.[5] Those Directives provided that, in order to gain a right of residence, the economically inactive needed to have sufficient resources and comprehensive health insurance. Those conditions were imposed in order to ensure that economically inactive migrants would not become a burden on the welfare resources of the host state.[6]

This framework was criticized because of the link between activity/resources and rights under Community law. The Community project, it was said, directly benefited only the 'strongest' members of society – those who could exercise an economic activity or who had their own resources – to the exclusion of the weakest members of society, the poor, those who are unable to work etc. The effect of the Treaty was then (and to a certain extent still is) to create a subclass of citizens who were unable to enjoy rights under Community law and who might, in their own Member States, enjoy less rights than their more entrepreneurial migrant peers.

This basic framework is still in place; however, there is no doubt that it has been conceptually and, to a lesser extent, practically affected by the introduction of Union citizenship. This was inevitable since there is a clear and in many ways natural tension between the notion of supra-national citizenship and welfare states which are primarily divided across national borders. Thus, the problem lies not in recognizing a right to move or even to reside to other Union nationals. It lies with the extent to which other Union nationals might become active claimants of social welfare provision without having established a link of belonging, traditionally

---

[2] Case C-45/93 *Commission v Spain* (Museum admission) [1994] ECR I-911; and Case C-388/01 *Commission v Italy* (Italian museums) [2003] ECR I-721. Directive 2004/38 has codified and extended the right to equal treatment to all citizens. Thus, migration is enough to trigger the right to equal treatment and it is no longer necessary to establish a connection with Article 49 EC (but see below on the limits of equal treatment). For a more detailed analysis of Union citizens' rights and of Directive 2004/38 see A Arnull, A Dashwood, M Dougan, M Ross, E Spaventa and D Wyatt *Wyatt and Dashwood's EU Law* (5th ed., Sweet and Maxwell 2006), Chapter 17.

[3] Case 186/87 *Cowan v le Trésor Public* [1989] ECR 195.

[4] Case C-274/96 *H O Bickel and V Franz* [1998] ECR I-1121, examined in detail in the next section.

[5] Directive 90/364 on the right of residence [1990] OJ L180/26; Directive 90/365 on the right of residence for employees and self-employed persons who have ceased their occupational activity [1990] OJ L180/28; Directive 93/96 on the right of residence for students [1993] OJ L317/59; the three residence directives have now been repealed by, and subsumed in, Directive 2004/38.

[6] Students need only to assure the authorities that they have sufficient resources, Article 1 Directive 93/96, and now Article 7(c) Directive 2004/38.

created either through birth or through active economic contribution.[7] If, on the one hand, the Member State has a legitimate interest in protecting its limited welfare resources from undeserving claims, on the other hand, Union citizens might well have a reasonable expectation to enjoy some benefits in the host welfare society even when they have not, or are not, exercising an economic activity.

It is therefore not surprising that the case law on citizenship reflects this tension between the need to shelter the national welfare systems from a general equal treatment obligation, and the recognition of a broader notion of solidarity which goes beyond the territorial confines of the single Member State. Indeed, the Court has proceeded with caution in giving effect to the rights enshrined in Article 18 EC, trying to balance the full effectiveness of a Treaty fundamental provision with the budgetary constraints to which welfare systems are subject.

In this chapter we are going first to outline the case law on citizenship, to then offer an alternative reading of the *Carpenter* case and argue in favour of the elimination of reverse discrimination through the medium of Community law. In the next chapter we will then try and offer a unitary vision of the developments which have occurred in the field of the free movement of persons.

1. From *Sala* to *Baumbast*: The Tortuous Path Towards Union Citizenship

Article 17 EC of the Treaty establishes Union citizenship, and Article 18 EC provides that every citizen of the Union has a right to 'move and reside freely within the territory of the Member States, subject to the limitations and conditions laid down in the Treaty and by the measures adopted to give it effect'. Whilst some authors argued from the very beginning that the citizenship provisions were capable of granting enforceable rights to individuals,[8] the Court moved only slowly towards the recognition of the direct effect of Article 18 EC.

---

[7] See generally M Dougan and E Spaventa (eds) *Social Welfare and EU Law* (Hart Publishing Oxford 2005) and G de Búrca (ed) *EU Law and the Welfare State. In Search of Solidarity* (OUP Oxford 2005).

[8] E.g. S O'Leary *The Evolving Concept of Community Citizenship* (Kluwer The Hague 1996) and contrast with B Wilkinson 'Towards European Citizenship? Nationality, Discrimination and Free Movement of Workers in the European Union' (1995) 1 EPL 417. The view that Article 18 EC should have direct effect was endorsed by all the Advocates General who examined the issue; see e.g. AG La Pergola's Opinion in C-85/96 *M M Martínez Sala v Freistaat Bayern* [1998] ECR I-2691; AG Cosmas' Opinion in Case C-378/97 *F A Wijsenbeek* [1999] ECR I-6207, esp. para 84 and ff; AG Alber's Opinion in Case C-184/99 *R Grzelczyk v Centre public d'aide social d'Ottignies-Louvain-la-Neuve* [2001] ECR I-6193. The literature on citizenship is extensive; e.g. E. Meehan *Citizenship and the European Community* (Sage Publications, 1993); D O'Keeffe 'Union Citizenship' in D O'Keeffe and PM Twomey (eds) *Legal Issues of the Maastricht Treaty* (Chancery Law London 1994), Ch 6; A Rosas and E Antola (eds) *A Citizens' Europe: in search of a new order* (Sage Publications London 1995); UK Preuβ 'Problems of a Concept of European Citizenship' (1995) 1 ELJ 267; M Everson 'The Legacy of the Market Citizen' in J Shaw and G More (ed) *New Legal Dynamics of the European Union* (Clarendon Press Oxford 1995), 73; S O'Leary 'The Relationship between Community

In *Sala*,[9] a Spanish citizen living in Germany was denied a child raising allowance on the grounds that, even though she was lawfully resident in Germany by virtue of a bilateral Treaty with Spain, she did not have, nor could obtain, a residence permit. German nationals did not need such a permit to be eligible for the allowance. It was not entirely clear whether Mrs Sala, who had been previously employed, could be considered as a worker and thus be entitled to equal treatment in respect of social advantages pursuant to Regulation 1612/68, and family benefits pursuant to Regulation 1408/71. Leaving it to the national court to determine whether Mrs Sala was a 'worker' for the purposes of Community law, the Court clarified that in any event Mrs Sala fell within the scope of the Treaty by virtue of being a Union citizen lawfully resident in another Member State, and for this reason she was entitled to equal treatment pursuant to Article 12 EC in relation to all matters falling within the scope *rationae materiae* of the Treaty. Since the benefit in question fell within the scope of the Treaty, Mrs Sala was protected by the principle of non-discrimination in respect of the allowance, even were she not to be considered a worker. Whilst the Court relied on Article 18 EC to broaden the scope of the Treaty, it did not address the issue as to whether Article 18 EC was capable of conferring a directly effective right to movement and residence.

In *Bickel and Franz*,[10] as we have seen in Chapter 2, the Court was similarly elusive as to the effect of Article 18 EC. It should be recalled that, in this case, an Austrian and a German national undergoing trial in the bilingual South Tyrol region in Italy claimed a right to have the proceedings conducted in German. Residents in the province had such a right, but non-residents had to face trial in Italian. Given that a residence requirement always amounts to indirect discrimination, the issue for the Court was whether the situation fell within the scope of application of the Treaty so that the principle of non-discrimination would apply. In deciding that it did, the Court preferred to find in Article 49 EC the trigger for Article 12 EC, rather than to rely directly on the citizenship provisions,

---

Citizenship and the Protection of Fundamental Rights in Community Law' (1995) 32 CMLRev 519; D O'Keeffe and M Horspool 'European Citizenship and the Free Movement of Persons' (1996) 31 The Irish Jurist 145; J Shaw 'The Many Past and Futures of Citizenship in the European Union' (1997) 22 ELRev 554; S Douglas Scott 'In Search of Union Citizenship' (1998) 18 YEL 29; R W Davis 'Citizenship of the Union ... Rights for All' (2002) 27 ELRev 121; C Jacqueson 'Union citizenship and the Court of Justice: something new under the sun? Towards social citizenship' (2002) 27 ELRev 260; M Dougan and E Spaventa 'Educating Rudy and the (non-)English Patient: A Double Bill on Residency Rights under Article 18 EC' (2003) 28 ELRev 699; E Guild *The Legal Elements of EU Identity: EU Citizenship and Migration Law* (Kluwer Law International 2004); R C A White 'Free Movement, Equal Treatment and Citizenship of the Union' (2005) 54 ICLQ 885; C Barnard 'EU Citizenship and the Principle of Solidarity' in M Dougan and E Spaventa *Social Welfare and EU Law* (Hart Publishing Oxford 2005), Ch. 8; K Hailbronner 'Union citizenship and access to social benefits' (2005) 42 CMLRev 1245; M Dougan 'The constitutional dimension to the case law on Union Citizenship' (2006) 31 ELRev 613.

[9] Case C-85/96 *M M Martínez Sala v Freistaat Bayern* [1998] ECR I-2691; S O'Leary 'Putting flesh on the bones of European Union citizenship' (1999) 24 ELRev 68.

[10] Case C-274/96 *Bickel and Franz* [1998] ECR I-7637.

which however it mentioned in order to strengthen its reasoning.[11] Thus, the Court found that Article 49 EC applied to those Union citizens who visit another Member State and receive or intend to receive services in that State; and, the Court added, the freedom of movement enshrined in Article 18 EC would be enhanced if citizens were to be able to use their own language on the same basis as German speaking residents of the region in communicating with the host-State's authorities.

In *Wijsenbeek*,[12] the Court once again refrained from clarifying whether Article 18 EC was capable of having direct effect. In this case, the Court found that the right to move contained in Article 18 EC did not pre-empt the Member States' power to carry out frontier controls. Thus, the effect of Article 18 EC was limited to imposing an obligation that the sanction for failure to show an identity document at the border be proportionate.[13]

Progressively, however, the Court relied more and more on Union citizenship. In *Elsen*,[14] a German national working in Germany transferred her residence to France and acquired the status of frontier worker. Her son was born when she was residing in France, and after having been on maternity leave she did not resume her occupational activity. She subsequently asked the German authorities to take into account her child-rearing period for the purposes of calculating old age pension. That claim was denied on the grounds that the child rearing had taken place abroad. The Court found that Mrs Elsen's child-rearing period had to be taken into account by the competent institution. In reaching this finding, the Court referred to Article 18 EC in a way which seemed to imply that, indeed, such provision alone was capable of having direct effect. The case is particularly significant since arguably the Court could have reached the same conclusion by simply relying on Article 39 EC and Regulation 1408/71.[15] This said, however, it is not until the triptych *Grzelczyk*, *D'Hoop* and *Baumbast* that the Court gave a clear indication of the effect of Union citizenship.

In *Grzelczyk*,[16] a French citizen who was studying in Belgium applied, during the last year of his studies, for the *minimex*, a non-contributory benefit reserved to own nationals and those Union citizens covered by Regulation 1612/68 (i.e. workers and workers' family members).[17] The benefit was denied on the ground

---

[11] *Ibid,* para 15.
[12] Case C-378/97 *F A Wijsenbeek* [1999] ECR I-6207.
[13] This was an obligation which would have arguably arisen anyway since according to consistent case law Member States cannot impose disproportionate sanctions for breaches of rules in any way connected with the exercise of a Community right; Case 118/75 *L Watson and A Belmann* [1976] ECR 1185; Case 157/79 *Pieck* [1980] ECR 2171; Case 8/77 *C Sagulo, G Brenca et A Bakhouche* [1977] ECR 1495; Case C-265/88 *L Messner* [1989] ECR 4209; Case C-193/94 *Skanavi* [1996] ECR I-929.
[14] Case C-135/99 *U Elsen v Bundesversicherungsanstalt für Angestellte* [2000] ECR I-10409.
[15] Cf AG Saggio's Opinion who does not even mention citizenship. The rules at issue in the case worked to the disadvantage of migrant workers.
[16] Case C-184/99 *R Grzelczyk v Centre public d'aide social d'Ottignies-Louvain-la-Neuve* [2001] ECR I-6193.
[17] This was consistent with a previous ruling of the Court, Case 197/86 *S M Brown v Secretary of State for Scotland* [1988] ECR 3205.

that Mr Grzelczyk was neither a Belgian national nor did he fall within the scope of Regulation 1612/68. The case revolved around whether such discrimination fell within the scope of the Treaty. In particular, could Mr Grzelczyk, a student whose right of residence derived from Directive 93/96, rely on Article 18 EC and on the *Sala* ruling to establish his entitlement to a social advantage? Not surprisingly, the Belgian Government (supported by other Member States), argued that Article 18 EC was not constitutive of new rights and could not be interpreted as granting rights beyond those conferred in the three Residence Directives which, by making residence conditional upon resources, clearly excluded non-economically active from welfare benefits. The Court found that:

> Union citizenship is destined to be the *fundamental status* of nationals of the Member States, enabling those who find themselves in the same situation to enjoy the same treatment in law irrespective of their nationality, subject to such exceptions as are expressly provided for.[18]

Mr Grzelczyk was lawfully resident in Belgium and therefore, consistently with the *Sala* ruling, he fell within the personal scope of the Treaty. Since the *minimex* fell within the material scope of the Treaty, Article 12 EC applied and any discrimination on grounds of nationality was prohibited.

The Court next turned to the relationship between Article 18 EC and Directive 93/96, which expressly excluded any right to equal treatment in relation to maintenance grants for students. The Court acknowledged that Article 18 EC refers to 'limitations and conditions' contained in other parts of the Treaty and in secondary legislation adopted to give it effect, and it found that the requirements provided for in Directive 93/96 (sufficient resources and health insurance) constituted such 'limitations and conditions'. Thus, it is open for a Member State to terminate the right of residence of a Union citizen when, and if, the citizen does not meet any longer the requirements provided in Directive 93/96 (or in one of the other Residence Directives),[19] and becomes an unreasonable burden on the welfare system of the host State. However, termination of residence cannot be an automatic consequence of the student's reliance on welfare provision in the host-Member State since, in the Court's view, in adopting the three Residence Directives the Member States accepted a limited degree of financial solidarity. As a result, entitlement to the *minimex* could not be made conditional upon nationality. Thus, *Grzelczyk*, consistently with the *Sala* ruling, confirmed that Union citizens who have moved to another country fall within the scope *rationae personae* of the Treaty, and thus, provided the situation falls within the scope *rationae materiae* of the Treaty, they can rely on Article 12 EC to claim equal treatment also in relation to benefits. However, the case also indicated that the right to equal treatment might be limited by the Member States: should the Union citizen rely excessively on the host-State's welfare provision, then her/his residence

[18] Case C-184/99 *Grzelczyk* [2001] ECR I-6193, para 31, emphasis added.
[19] Cf Case C-456/02 *Trojani* [2004] ECR I-7573.

right might be terminated and with it the right to equal treatment would go as well.

This reasoning is further elaborated upon in *D'Hoop*.[20] Belgian law provided for a tide-over allowance for young people seeking their first employment. One of the conditions to be satisfied in order to be eligible for the benefit was to have received secondary education in Belgium.[21] Ms D'Hoop was a Belgian national who, having received her secondary education in France, failed to fulfil that condition. Thus even though she had received her university education in Belgium, she was not eligible for the tide-over allowance. The Court, consistently with *Grzelczyk*, found that movement together with Union citizenship is enough to bring oneself within the scope *rationae materiae* and *personae* of the Treaty. This is true even when the citizen is economically inactive. Using familiar reasoning,[22] the Court held that a Member State could not treat less favourably its own citizen who had taken advantage of her right to move, than it would have done if she had not exercised her Treaty freedom. To penalize Ms D'Hoop for having taken advantage of her free movement rights granted by Article 18 EC would be inconsistent with that freedom.[23] Thus, a difference in treatment between those who have exercised their free movement rights and those who have not can be accepted only insofar as it is based on objective reasons and it is proportionate to the legitimate aim pursued by the national rules.

In the case at issue, the legitimate purpose of the restriction was to ensure that there was a real link between the applicant and the geographic employment market concerned. However, in the Court's view, the rules at issue went beyond what was necessary to ensure that link, since the fact that a person completed her secondary education abroad is not in itself representative of the connection between applicant and geographical labour market. In *Bidar*,[24] which we shall examine in more detail in the next chapter, the Court confirmed that a person lawfully resident in a Member State other than that of her/his origin is entitled to equal treatment in respect of welfare benefits, including maintenance grants and loans for attending university. Mr Bidar was a French citizen residing with his grandmother in the UK; he had been in the UK for four years during which time he attended secondary education. Mr Bidar then enrolled at university and applied for a maintenance loan,

---

[20] Case C-224/98 *M N D'Hoop v Office national d'emploi* [2002] ECR I-6191, noted A Illiopoulou and H Toner 'A new approach to discrimination against free movers? *D'Hoop v Office National de l'Emploi*' (2003) 28 ELRev 389.

[21] Exception given for children of migrant workers.

[22] See e.g. in the context of workers, Case C-370/90 *Singh* [1992] ECR I-4265.

[23] In this respect, see also Case C-224/02 *Pusa* [2004] ECR I-5763; Case C-406/04 *De Cuyper* [2006] ECR I-6947; Case C-192/05 *Tas-Hagen and Tas* [2006] ECR I-10451.

[24] Case C-209/03 *Bidar* [2005] ECR I-2119; noted C Barnard (2005) 42 CMLRev 1465; O Golynker 'Student Loans: the European concept of social justice according to *Bidar*' (2006) 31 ELRev 390; M Dougan 'Fees, grants, loans and dole cheques: who covers the the costs of migrant education within the EU?' (2005) 42 CMLRev 943; A P van der Mei 'EU Law and Education: Promotion of Student Mobility versus Protection of Education Systems' in M Dougan and E Spaventa (eds) *Social Welfare and EU Law* (Hart Publishing Oxford 2005), Ch. 10.

which was refused on the grounds that he was not 'ordinarily resident' in the United Kingdom for the purposes of English law. It should be recalled that students relying on the students' directive (now on Article 7 (c) Directive 2004/38) are excluded from the right to equal treatment in relation to maintenance grants and loans.[25] The Court, however, found that Mr Bidar was lawfully resident in the UK by virtue of the general Residence Directive[26] and not of the students' directive. For this reason, and subject to objective justifications, he was entitled to equal treatment in respect of all benefits, including maintenance loans.

In the cases examined above, the Court linked Union citizenship/equal treatment rights to lawful residency. In *Baumbast*, it was finally made clear that Article 18 EC granted a directly effective right of residence.[27] Here, a German national living in the UK was denied renewal of his residence permit on the grounds that he did not fulfil the conditions set out in Directive 90/364, which, like Directive 2004/38 now, made the right to reside in another Member State conditional upon having sufficient resources and comprehensive health insurance. Although Mr Baumbast had sufficient resources and health insurance in Germany, where he and his family would go to receive health treatment, he did not have insurance for emergency treatment in the UK and thus was not insured for *all* health risks as required by Directive 90/364. The issue was then whether Article 18 EC grants a free standing right to residence even when the situation does not fall within the scope of one of the three Residency Directives (and now of Directive 2004/38).[28] Further, the Court had to consider what weight should be given to the specification contained in Article 18 EC that the right to move and reside is subject to the limitations and conditions laid down in the Treaty and by the measures adopted to give it effect.

The Court stated that Article 18 EC conferred 'on every citizen the right to move and reside freely within the territory of the Member States'.[29] Consistently with its reasoning in *Grzelczyk*, the Court held that that right to residence is subject to the limitations contained in secondary legislation, i.e. sufficient resources and comprehensive health insurance so as not to become a burden on the host welfare system. However, since these 'limitations and conditions' limit a right conferred directly by the Treaty, they must be applied consistently with the general principles of Community law and, in particular, with the principle of proportionality. Not to allow Mr Baumbast to reside in the UK only because he was not covered by emergency treatment insurance would be a disproportionate interference with the substance of the right of residence which he derived directly from the Treaty. Thus,

---

[25] See Article 3 Directive 93/96 and now Article 24(3) Directive 2004/38. The latter provides that prior to the acquisition of permanent residence (which occurs after five years of continuous lawful residence) economically inactive Union citizens (who are not family members of economically active Union citizens) do not have a right to maintenance aid for studies.

[26] Directive 90/364, now subsumed in Directive 2004/38.

[27] Case C-413/99 *Baumbast and R v Secretary of State for the Home Department* [2002] ECR I-7091.

[28] Directive 90/364; Directive 90/365; Directive 93/96.

[29] Case C-413/99 *Baumbast and R v Secretary of State for the Home Department* [2002] ECR I-7091, para 81.

Mr Baumbast was allowed to stay despite not meeting *all* the requirements of Directive 90/364. This said, in *Trojani*,[30] the Court clarified that Union citizens have to satisfy at least to a certain extent the conditions in the Residence Directives (and now in Directive 2004/38) and that Article 18 EC does not confer a right to reside upon those who do not have sufficient resources within the meaning of Directive 90/364. However, if the Union citizen is lawfully resident, the *Grzelcyk* ruling applies and the citizen will be entitled to equal treatment in respect of all benefits, even though recourse to welfare provision might justify termination of residence (though never automatically).

Following these recent developments, the situation for economically inactive people seems to be as follows.[31]

First of all, Union citizens who lawfully reside in another Member State are entitled to equal treatment in respect of all benefits falling within the scope of Community law. Since Article 39 EC and Regulations 1612/68 and 1408/71 cover most welfare benefits, with the exclusion only of those which are conferred upon the economically active by virtue of the special relationship of nationality, such as benefits linked to participation in military conflicts,[32] then most welfare benefits are in principle available also to non-economically active Union citizens lawfully residing in the host-State. However, excessive reliance on this right might be ground for the host-State to terminate the right to residence itself, subject to the general principles of Community law, and in particular to the principle of proportionality. For this reason, reliance on the right to equal treatment cannot automatically justify termination of residence (*Grzelcyck*)[33] and the personal circumstances of the claimant must be taken into consideration (*Baumbast*).

Secondly, Member States are not prevented from introducing criteria which, whilst distinguishing between Union citizens, are objectively justified and proportionate to the legitimate aim pursued by the rules. Thus, the ruling in *D'Hoop* suggests that the Member States might be entitled to make some benefits conditional upon a link between the claimant and the territory. This has been confirmed by the ruling in *Collins* where,[34] as we have seen in the first chapter, the Court held that Member States can make a work-seekers' allowance conditional upon the claimant having established a genuine link with the domestic employment market.

Thirdly, Union citizens now derive their right to residence (and movement) directly from Article 18 EC, having before derived it from secondary legislation.

---

[30] Case C-456/02 *Trojani* [2004] ECR I-7573.

[31] These issues have been thoroughly examined in M Dougan and E Spaventa 'Educating Rudy and the (non-)English patient: A double-bill on residency rights under Article18 EC' (2003) 28 ELRev 699, and the conclusions in the text draw from that analysis.

[32] See recently e.g. Case C-386/02 *Baldinger* [2004] ECR I-8411. Even though such benefits do not fall within the scope *rationae materiae* of the Treaty, Member States cannot refuse to grant such benefits on the sole ground that the beneficiary (own national) is resident in another Member State, Case C-192/05 *Tas-Hagen and Tas* [2006] ECR I-10451.

[33] Now codified in Article 14(3) Directive 2004/38.

[34] Case C-138/02 *Collins* [2004] ECR I-2703; O Golynker 'Jobseekers' rights in the European Union: challenges of changing the paradigm of social solidarity' (2005) 30 ELRev 111.

That right to residence might be subject to conditions as contained in secondary legislation, and especially the sufficient resources and comprehensive health insurance requirements. Thus, in principle, Union citizenship does not entitle the individual to become an 'unreasonable' burden on the welfare system of the host-State.[35] However, what is to be considered 'unreasonable' very much depends on the case at issue, and in any event the Member States have to comply with the principle of proportionality and with fundamental rights as general principles of Community law. Particularly relevant in this respect is the right to family life.[36]

As a result, the effect of Article 18 EC is to sever only partially and to a very limited extent the right to reside from 'economic' elements. In this respect, the cases of *Baumbast* and *Trojani*[37] can be usefully juxtaposed: Mr Baumbast was an economically active wealthy citizen, who was unlikely to rely heavily (if at all) on the UK health system; the extent to which his permanence in the United Kingdom demanded some solidarity from British citizens was therefore very limited. On the other hand, Mr Trojani, a French citizen who, whilst taking part in a socio-reintegration programme in Belgium, claimed the *minimex* and clearly needed the support of his fellow Union citizens to a greater extent than Mr Baumbast, was in principle excluded from the benefits of the Treaty since he did not have sufficient resources.[38]

The case of *Trojani* might also be usefully juxtaposed to the ruling in *Collins*.[39] There, the Court decided that it had to reinterpret Article 39 EC in the light of Union citizenship. As a result, the right to equal treatment provided for in Article 39(2) EC was extended to cover work-seekers, for whom such right was previously limited to the right to access employment. On the other hand, in *Trojani* the Court refused to 'update' its interpretation of what constitutes a 'real and effective' economic activity to include work which aims (also) at the reintegration of less fortunate members of society. Activities which, even if remunerated, do not form part of the 'normal labour market' fall outside the scope of the Treaty. Thus, the fact that Mr Trojani worked for the Salvation Army for about 30 hours a week, and that he received remuneration for that work, was deemed not to be relevant because such an activity was part of a socio-occupational reintegration scheme. It is clear then that Article 18 EC is of very limited impact in addressing the problems of exclusion created by the EC Treaty. This, however, does not subtract from its conceptual and constitutional relevance. In particular, the effect of Article 18 EC is to reshape, at least partially, the relationship between Union citizens, in terms of relaxing the link of belonging necessary to be able to claim solidarity from the host-community.

---

[35] Cf Article 14(c) Directive 2004/38.

[36] E.g. Case C-413/99 *Baumbast and R v Secretary of State for the Home Department* [2002] ECR I-7091; Case C-200/02 *Chen* [2004] ECR I-9925.

[37] Case C-456/02 *Trojani* [2004] ECR I-7573.

[38] In practice however he was allowed to rely on the Treaty since he was lawfully resident in Belgium: thus in order to exclude him from the right to welfare assistance, the Belgian authorities would have to terminate his right to reside.

[39] Case C-138/02 *Collins* [2004] ECR I-2703.

Fourthly, Article 18 EC can be of use also to establish the right of residence in one of the Member States of a non-Union national family member. In *Baumbast and R*, the Court made clear that once the children of a worker have exercised their right to reside and enter into education in the host-State, their primary carer (both in the case of the parents' divorce and in the case in which the worker has ceased her/his occupational activity),[40] derives a right of residence from the children's right to reside in the host-State. Otherwise, the Court reasoned, the children's right to stay in the host-country and pursue their education there would be rendered meaningless.

The same reasoning applies in cases where the child/minor derives her/his right of residence directly from Article 18 EC rather than deriving it indirectly from her/his parents' exercise of one of the economic free movement provisions. This is so even when Article 18 EC is used instrumentally to elude immigration rules. Thus in *Chen*,[41] Mrs Chen, a Chinese national, gave birth in Belfast to a baby girl, Catherine. The only reason why Catherine's parents had chosen Belfast was because of the Irish nationality rules which, as they stood at the time, provided that anyone born in the island of Ireland (i.e. including anyone born in Northern Ireland) would be eligible for Irish nationality. Having acquired Irish nationality without having ever set foot in the Republic of Ireland, Catherine and her mother sought to establish themselves in Wales by relying on Article 18 EC. They argued that, as an Irish national, Catherine had a right conferred directly by the Treaty to establish herself in any of the Member States and that her mother, as her primary carer, needed to be able to establish herself with her, or else Catherine's right would be deprived of all substance. The Court accepted both propositions: the reasons why a Union citizen wishes to rely on her rights are immaterial; and it was clear that Catherine's right to reside in the UK would have been rendered meaningless if Mrs Chen had not been given the right to stay in Wales with her daughter.

2. The Right to Challenge National Rules Falling Within the Scope of the Treaty, and Beyond

Article 18 EC can also be invoked to obtain an increased level of protection, in the form of judicial review, of national rules which affect in any way the exercise of the free movement rights and, in this sense, the right to equal treatment might well be relevant beyond the confines of purely economic interests. We have seen above that, in *Bickel and Franz*, Article 18 EC was mentioned by the Court in relation to rules concerning the language of proceedings in a bi-lingual region of Italy. However, in that case the Court relied primarily on Article 49 EC to impose the equal treatment obligation. More representative of the potential of Articles 17 and 18 EC in fostering

[40] This has now been codified in Directive 2004/38, see Articles 12 (3) and 13 (2)(b).
[41] Case C-200/02 *Chen* [2004] ECR I-9925.

Union citizens' rights is the case of *Garcia Avello*.[42] Here, Article 17 EC was successfully invoked to challenge the application of Belgian rules on the determination of surnames. Mr Garcia Avello was a Spanish citizen married to a Belgian national and residing in Belgium. The couple wished their children's surname to be determined following the Spanish custom of having the father's last name followed by the mother's last name and, accordingly, they registered their children in the Spanish embassy with the double surname. However, the Belgian authorities refused to register the children with the double surname and instead imposed the use of the father's surname. The first question for consideration was whether there was any connection with Community law. Belgium argued that the situation was purely internal since the children had never resided in Spain. The Court relied on the children's Spanish nationality to find the cross-border element capable of triggering the Treaty. After all, the children were Spanish citizens residing in Belgium, and the fact that they were also Belgian citizens was immaterial. Since the situation fell within the scope of the Treaty, Article 12 EC applied. The prohibition of discrimination contained in that article requires not only that comparable situations be treated equally but also that non-comparable situations be treated in a different way. The Belgian practice failed to respect the principle of equality in the latter sense: it treated non-comparable situations in the same way, by treating dual nationals like those who held only Belgian nationality. Belgian-only nationals were, in the Court's opinion, in a different situation from nationals bearing dual nationality because the latter might wish in the future to move to the Member State of their other nationality. In this case it would be inconvenient for the children to have all the documents relating to their life in Belgium (such as diplomas etc) in a name different from that that they were going to use in the other Member State (Spain). The Garcia Avello children were therefore in a different situation from that of children bearing only Belgian nationality and, accordingly, they should be treated in a different way.

It should be noted that one of the effects of the ruling in *Garcia Avello* is that Union citizens who are nationals of more than one Member State are, for that sole reason, protected by the Treaty with no need to establish any other 'movement' credential. More importantly, from our perspective, is the fact that the Court's reasoning is not entirely convincing. On the one hand, the Court clearly stated that the citizenship provisions cannot be used to broaden the scope of the Treaty; on the other hand, the reference to a purely hypothetical future desire of the children to go and live in Spain in order to establish the discriminatory effects of the rules at issue seems rather farfetched and, it should be noted, the Court refers to Article 17 EC, which simply establishes Union citizenship, rather than to Article 18 EC which

---

[42] Case C-148/02 *Garcia Avello* [2003] ECR I-11613; see also Case C-168/91 *Konstantinidis* [1993] ECR I-1191, where the Court relied on an economic link to protect a Greek citizen from the mis-transliteration of his name.

guarantees the right to free movement.[43] Whilst it could be said that there was an intra-Community dimension to the case since had Mr Garcia Avello not taken advantage of his movement rights, the situation would have not arisen, the case is a useful indication of the far reaching effects of the Treaty citizenship provisions.

If in *Garcia Avello*, dual nationality alone was enough to trigger the Treaty, in *Schempp* movement was enough to trigger Articles 18 EC and 12 EC in relation to German tax legislation.[44] Even though the challenge in itself was unsuccessful, the case is interesting because the Court accepted that the situation fell within the scope of the Treaty. Here, Mr Schempp divorced from his wife, who then went to live in Austria. Following the transfer of his ex-wife's residence, Mr Schempp found that he could not deduct the alimony he was paying her from his taxable income. German rules provided that, if the money was paid to a person resident outside Germany, it could be deducted only if it was taxed in the place of residence of the ex-spouse. According to Austrian tax rules, however, the alimony was tax-free and, as a result, Mr Schempp could not deduct the amount he paid to his ex-wife. This was the case even though his ex-wife was not paying taxes when she was residing in Germany because her income was below the minimum taxable income. The Court found that Article 18 EC had been triggered by Mr Schempp's former wife, since she had taken advantage of her free movement rights in transferring her residence from Germany to Austria. For this reason, the situation was not purely internal and Article 12 EC applied. The ruling is not entirely convincing, since it suggests that the situation would have been different had Mr Schempp's ex wife not been a Union citizen, whilst arguably the detriment to Mr Schempp arising from a distinction based on residence should have been sufficient to bring the situation within the scope of Community law. But in any event, it confirms that movement alone is, as a result of Article 18 EC, enough to trigger the Treaty, with all the advantages deriving not only from the applicability of Article 12 EC, but also more broadly from the possibility of invoking judicial review of national legislation in terms of its proportionality and fundamental rights compliance. Furthermore, the Court has clarified in *Tas-Hagen and Tas* that this reasoning applies even in those cases in which the object of the claim falls altogether outside the scope of the Treaty.[45] In that case, it found that a Member State could not refuse the payment of a pension for civilian war victims, a matter excluded from the scope *rationae materiae* of the Treaty, to a legitimate beneficiary on the sole ground that

---

[43] In a similar case brought following the ruling in *Garcia Avello*, the Court refused jurisdiction on the grounds that the body which referred the question was not a 'court or tribunal' for the purposes of Article 234 EC, Case C-96/04 *Standesamt Stadt Niebüll* [2006] ECR I-3561. AG Jacobs found that even though there was no discrimination in the case at issue, the rules were an unjustified obstacle to movement falling within the scope of Articles 17 and 18 EC.

[44] Case C-403/03 *Schempp* [2005] ECR I-6421. See also Case C-224/02 *Pusa* [2004] ECR I-5763; Case C-406/04 *De Cuyper* [2006] ECR I-6947; and Case C-318/05 *Commission v Germany* (taxation of school fees), Opinion delivered 21 September 2006, case still pending at the time of writing, paras 90 and 91.

[45] Case C-192/05 *Tas-Hagen and Tas* [2006] ECR I-10451; see also Case C-520/04 *Turpeinen* [2006] ECR I-10685.

she/he had gone to live in another Member State. As a result, it seems clear that, lacking an objective justification, Member States are not allowed to distinguish on grounds of residence in relation to benefits, tax advantages etc.

3. Mr Carpenter as a Citizen

In the cases mentioned above, the Court finally gave effect to the Union citizenship provisions, making it clear that, far from being a piece of rhetoric, such provisions are of constitutional significance in that they are redefining the relationship between individual and Member States. As we shall see in the next chapter, the introduction of Union citizenship has had an impact also on the case law on economic migrants, and can serve to provide a more coherent constitutional framework for such case law. Before turning to that case law, however, it is necessary to analyze the *Carpenter* case since, in the writer's opinion, that is one of the cases that most highlights the Court's concern for the protection of the individual as a citizen rather than as a market actor. Whilst the case was decided on the grounds of Article 49 EC, the reasoning adopted is unconvincing and *result-oriented*. In this respect, a more convincing normative basis for the ruling in *Carpenter* can be found in the combined reading of Articles 17 and 12 EC. Those provisons offer the tools to eliminate reverse discrimination, so as to truly fulfill the demands of equality which are inherent in any concept of citizenship, be it domestic or supra-national.

As seen in Chapter 2, the *Carpenter* case arose in relation to UK immigration rules.[46] It might be recalled that Mrs Carpenter was a Philippines national who, having overstayed her entry permit to the UK, married a British national. She then sought leave to remain in the UK, which was denied and a deportation order was made. Even though her marriage was genuine, according to British immigration rules she was to leave the UK and then seek, from abroad, leave to enter as the spouse of a UK citizen. Mr Carpenter, her husband, had a business in advertising and a 'significant proportion' of his trade was with operators established elsewhere in the Community. He thus travelled to other Member States in order to pursue his business.[47] Mrs Carpenter claimed that her deportation would have affected Mr Carpenter's right to carry on his activity, since he would have had either to go and live with her in the Philippines, or be separated from his family. The Court found that Mr Carpenter was a service provider within the meaning of Community law, since he provided services for recipients in other Member States. It then found that his separation from his wife would be 'detrimental to their family life and, therefore, to the conditions under which Mr Carpenter exercise[d] a fundamental

[46] Case C-60/00 *M Carpenter v Secretary of State for the Home department* [2002] ECR I-6279; noted A Acierno 'The *Carpenter* judgement: fundamental rights and the limits of the Community legal order' (2003) 28 ELRev 398.

[47] It is interesting that the order for reference does not mention how often he had to go away, nor was the issue discussed at the hearing.

freedom. That freedom could not be fully effective if Mr Carpenter were to be *deterred* from exercising it by obstacles raised in his country of origin to the entry and residence of his spouse'.[48]

The ruling is difficult to explain in relation to the free movement provisions. Both statements, i.e. that Mr Carpenter was a service provider, and that deportation of one's spouse is a disruption to family life, are indeed true. However, it is the link between the two which is missing. In other words, whilst it is obvious that emotional distress affects one's working abilities, it is not clear how such distress might be construed as a barrier to one's ability to provide services across the Community. The rest of the ruling demonstrates that the Court's worries lay not with Mr Carpenter's ability to provide services, but rather with the fact that the deportation order affected his right to family life as guaranteed by Article 8 of the European Convention of Human Rights. The fact that the Treaty was triggered allowed the Court to assess the compatibility of the UK rules with the Convention.[49] The Court, by severing the link between service provision and obstacle, guaranteed that the individual's rights in the case at issue would be upheld. However, these rights had nothing to do with a right to free movement. Rather, the case underlines the Court's self-perception as a guarantor of rights, a court which ensures that the individual is protected from executive/legislative misbehaviour. If, despite the Court's attempt to anchor the situation in Article 49 EC, the *Carpenter* ruling cannot be properly understood in the context of the freedom to provide services, it might be normatively justified having regard to Union citizenship. In particular, it could be argued that Article 17 EC read together with Article 12 EC can provide a more convincing framework to explain *Carpenter*, as well as eliminate the injustices created by the 'purely internal situation' rule in those cases where the rules at stake do not affect the exercise of an economic activity.

3.1. The Purely Internal Situation

According to orthodox thinking and case law, the Treaty free *movement* provisions do not apply in purely internal situations, i.e. when there is no cross-border element to have triggered the Treaty. This fact has led to the possibility of so called 'reverse discrimination', according to which nationals of a Member State who have not

---

[48] Case C-60/00 *M Carpenter v Secretary of State for the Home department* [2002] ECR I-6279, para 39 emphasis added.

[49] It is difficult to assess whether this ruling overrules, *de facto* if not *de iure*, Case C-168/91 *Konstantinidis v Stadt Altensteig, Standesamt und Landratsamt Calw, Ordnungsamt* [1993] ECR I-1191 (not even mentioned in the Court's ruling), where the Court rejected AG Jacobs' suggestion that whenever one falls within the scope of Community law one should be protected by fundamental rights as general principles of Community law (but only in another Member State), even if the breach of fundamental rights complained of has nothing to do with the free movement right. In that case the Court rejected this submission and ruled that fundamental rights as general principles of Community law would apply only in so far as instrumental to the Treaty freedoms.

exercised their right to free movement might be at a disadvantage when compared with Community nationals who have exercised their right to move.[50] The problem of reverse discrimination appears evident in those cases in which the claimant is seeking to establish intra-Community credentials in order to benefit from the Community regime in relation to the immigration rights of his/her family members. Given that Union migrants have a right to invoke the protection of Community law (also in relation to the status of their family members) when returning to their Member State of origin, the problem of 'reverse discrimination' arises mainly, if not only, in relation to static Community citizens. In this respect, consider the facts of *Carpenter* and compare them with the facts of *Akrich*. In both cases, Article 10 of Regulation 1612/68 was not relevant and, for this reason, the only applicable rules were the British immigration rules which clearly affected those in a purely internal situation and those in a cross-border situation not regulated by secondary Community law (i.e. British citizens who had married illegal migrants) in the same way. However, in *Akrich*,[51] fundamental rights scrutiny was ensured by the fact that the couple, well advised on the niceties of Community law, had moved to Ireland and then back to the United Kingdom. Thus, the Treaty had been effectively triggered. In *Carpenter*,[52] that was not the case. Whilst it is true that the Carpenters got their fundamental rights recognized even more effectively that the Akrichs, this was done only by a rather imaginative use of the concept of barrier. Had the Court been true to its case law, the situation should have been defined as wholly internal and it would have fallen outside the scope of Community law.

Since only movement triggers the free movement provisions, and since most EU citizens are static, the phenomenon of reverse discrimination is, as a matter of Community law, problematic. It is true that in many Member States this problem is tamed by national law, and especially by the constitutional guarantees of equality according to which own citizens cannot be treated in a less favourable way than foreigners.[53] However, this is not true, for instance, for the United Kingdom which has no such provision. Furthermore, and more importantly, it might be questioned whether such 'built-in' inequality is consistent with the demands of Union citizenship.

3.2. Giving Effect to Article 17 EC

As indicated above, when compared with the (later) case of *Akrich*, it is clear that Mr Carpenter was being discriminated against on the sole grounds that he had not

[50] As we have seen in the previous chapters, the scope of the 'purely internal' rule is greatly reduced in those cases in which the rules affect the right to pursue an economic activity, since in those cases the establishment of a connection with a purely potential client/provider abroad is sufficient to establish a connection with Community law. See also the discussion in the next chapter.

[51] Case C-109/01 *Akrich* [2003] ECR I-9607.

[52] Case C-60/00 *Carpenter* [2002] ECR I-6279.

[53] This is the case e.g. in Italy, France, Austria. See references to this effect in Joined Cases C-321 to 324/94 *Pistre and others* [1997] ECR I-2343; and Case C-254/98 *TK-Heimdiest Sass GmbH* [2000] ECR I-2487. In relation to Italy see e.g. judgment of the Italian Constitutional Court 30 December 1997, n. 443.

exercised his right to move. In order to solve this problem, the Court held that Mr Carpenter's right to provide services in other Member States was affected by the British immigration rules. However, it is possible that a more coherent conceptual explanation might be provided by relying on the combined effect of Articles 17 and 12 EC.

Article 17 EC establishes Union citizenship. The subsequent articles detail some of the rights that citizens derive from such provisions, such as the right to move and reside in any of the Member States, the right to vote in local and European elections, the right to consular protection and so on. Article 12 EC, on the other hand, provides that, within the scope of the Treaty, any discrimination on grounds of nationality is prohibited. In *D'Hoop*,[54] the Court clarified that the prohibition of discrimination also encompasses a prohibition on discrimination on grounds of movement; therefore own citizens are entitled to Treaty protection upon returning in their Member State after having moved. The question therefore is whether a citizen who has not exercised her free movement rights can fall within the scope of application of the Treaty and benefit of the non-discrimination right in relation to matters falling within the material scope of the Treaty.[55] In other words, is it normatively possible to argue that a Union citizen, regardless of movement, has the same rights as migrants unless the situation of the migrant and of the static citizen is non-comparable?

The argument in favour of such an interpretation is not very complex: Article 17(2) EC provides that 'Union citizens shall enjoy the rights conferred by this Treaty and shall be subject to the duties imposed thereby'. Now, there can be hardly any doubt that the right not to be discriminated against on grounds of nationality is a right conferred by the Treaty (Article 12 EC). Why then should such right be limited to those who have moved when there is no explicit indication of such a limitation in the text of the Treaty? After all, if Union citizenship is destined to be the fundamental status of all Union's nationals, it would be hermeneutically inconsistent to depart from established interpretation whereby fundamental Community rights are given a broad interpretation and any limitation to those rights is construed in a narrow way. This said, there are several objections which could be raised against such interpretation.

First of all, it could be argued that Article 17 EC was not intended to create such effects and that a right to equal treatment for *static* Union citizens has not been expressly provided for. However, it can be easily rebutted that the intention of the

---

[54] Case C-224/98 *M N D'Hoop* [2002] ECR I-6191, paras 30 and ss.

[55] The elimination of reverse discrimination has been advocated by many authors, see e.g. E. Johnson and D O'Keeffe 'From discrimination to obstacles to free movement: Recent developments concerning the free movement of workers 1989-1994' (1994) 31 CMLRev 1313; N Shuibhne 'Free movement of persons and the wholly internal rule: time to move on?' (2002) 39 CMLRev 731. However, other authors are against the expansion of the Treaty free movement provisions to embrace wholly internal situations; e.g. P Oliver and W H Roth 'The internal market and the four freedoms' (2004) 41 CMLRev 407, at 429 and ff.

Treaty drafters is not decisive;[56] that it is unlikely that the drafters intended Article 18 EC to be directly effective; and that there is no reason why the list of citizens' rights in the Treaty should be deemed exhaustive. To a certain extent the Court has already allowed Union citizens to rely on Article 17 EC, thus indicating that that provision produces at least some legal effects. For instance, in the *Gaumain-Cerri and Barth* case, which will be examined in more detail in the next chapter,[57] the Court relied on Articles 17 and 12 EC in order to ensure that the benefits at stake would be available to the claimants regardless of their place of residence. The Court held 'The status of Union citizenship enables nationals of the Member States who find themselves in the same situation to enjoy within the scope of the Treaty the same treatment in law, subject to such exceptions as are expressly provided for'.[58] Thus, at least in this case, the Court did not link equal treatment to migration. Similarly, in *Garcia Avello* the trigger for the Treaty was found in Article 17 EC, not in Article 18 EC.[59] Whilst it is true that *Gaumain-Cerri and Barth* concerned a cross-border situation, and *Garcia Avello* related to a dual-nationality case which might therefore be seen as inherently involving a cross-border element, the cases are a powerful indication of the fact that Article 17 EC might be of some legal relevance.

Secondly, it could be argued that the scope of the Treaty free movement of persons' provisions is inherently limited to migrants. However, whilst this might have been true for economic migrants, since Articles 39, 43 and 49 EC indicate that they are concerned with those who have moved,[60] and whilst this might be true on similar grounds for Article 18 EC, the wording of Article 17 EC does not mention movement nor are all the rights conferred on Union citizens linked to movement. Thus, for instance, the rights to good administration (ombudsman, access to documents) and voting rights are, quite naturally, not restricted to migrants. In relation to voting rights for the European Parliament, for instance, the Court has clarified that the principle of non-discrimination, as a general principle of Community law, applies to the situation of a Dutch citizen who is deprived of the voting rights for the European Parliament when residing in a Dutch overseas country or territory. Thus, since Dutch law recognized the right to vote to the European Parliament for Dutch nationals residing in a non-Member State, it could not deprive its nationals residing in one of its territories of such a right.[61] And, it should be recalled, movement is not always a pre-requisite for the exercise of Treaty rights.[62]

---

[56] With the notable exception of the conditions for standing for non-privileged applicants contained in Article 230 EC, e.g. Case C-50/00 *Unión de Pequecños Agricultores v Counci* [2002] ECR I-6677.
[57] Joined Cases C-502/01 and C-31/02 *Gaumain Cerri and Barth* [2004] ECR I-6483.
[58] Joined Cases C-502/01 and C-31/02 *Gaumain Cerri and Barth* [2004] ECR I-6483, para 34.
[59] Case C-148/02 *Garcia Avello* [2003] ECR I-11613.
[60] Although part of the scholarship has long argued that that is not necessarily true, especially in relation to Article 39 EC; e.g. H U J D'Oliveira 'The Community Case - Is Reverse Discrimination Still Permissible Under the Single European Act?' in T M de Boer (ed) *Forty years on: the Evolution of Postwar Private International Law in Europe*, Kluwer Law International, Amsterdam, 1990, 71.
[61] Case C-300/04 *Eman and Sevinger* [2006] ECR I-8055.
[62] E.g. Article 141 EC applies regardless of migration.

Thirdly, it could be argued that, to interpret Article 17 EC as producing some legal effects, even if only when read in conjunction with other provisions of Community law, would unduly expand the scope of application of the Treaty. After all, the European Court of Justice has held that 'Citizenship of the Union, established by Article 17 EC, is not, (. . .), intended to extend the scope *ratione materiae* of the Treaty also to internal situations which have no link with Community law'.[63] It could be argued then that to allow a citizen to trigger the Treaty without having actively exercised any of her Treaty rights, and in particular the right to movement, would be inconsistent with the Court's own understanding of the effect of Union citizenship. However, it should be noted that to give such an effect to Article 17 EC would expand the scope *rationae personae* of the Treaty, not its material scope. In any event, the Court's statement that the scope of application of the Treaty has not been expanded by the introduction of Union citizenship should be tested against the Court's own case law.

Thus, in *D'Hoop,* the Court stated that movement in *itself* is enough to bring oneself within the *personal* and *material* scope of the Treaty. In other words, once a Union citizen has exercised her right to move, there is no need to prove that the subject matter falls within the material scope of the Treaty in order for it to be brought within the scope of Article 12 EC and for the non-discrimination obligation to apply.[64] And the ruling in *Garcia Avello* demonstrates that the principle of non-discrimination applies beyond the material scope of the Treaty.[65] In that case, the Court applied the principle of non-discrimination in relation to national rules determining individuals' last names, a field which falls within the exclusive competence of the Member States. Whilst it is true that the Court refers to a possible and future barrier to movement that the application of such rules might create, it is clear that such alleged barrier, according to the Court's own case law, should have been deemed too remote and indirect to bring the matter within the material scope of the Treaty.[66]

Even regardless of these considerations, the material scope of the Treaty is construed in very broad terms. Thus, any matter upon which the Community has legislated, or which is referred to in the Treaty, is deemed to be within the material scope of Community law for the purposes of the application of the principle of equality in relation to Union citizens. This is the case even in instances where the exercise of Community competence was directed also at *excluding* the very existence of the right at issue. Take by way of example the *minimex* in *Grzelczyk*,[67] or the student loan in *Bidar*.[68] The requirement of sufficient resources and comprehensive health insurance in the three Residence Directives had been provided

---

[63] Case C-148/02 *Garcia Avello* [2003] ECR I-11613, para 26.

[64] See also Case C-192/05 *Tas-Hagen and Tas* [2006] ECR I-10451.

[65] And arguably in Case C-274/96 *H O Bickel and V Franz* [1998] ECR I-1121, since the judicial proceedings were in no way connected with the exercise of the Treaty free movement provisions.

[66] Case C-190/98 *V Graf v Filzmoser Maschinenbau GmbH* [2000] ECR I-437.

[67] Case C-184/99 *Grzelczyk* [2001] ECR I-6193.

[68] Case C-209/03 *Bidar* [2005] ECR I-2119.

for in order to *exclude* non-economically active individuals from being able to rely on the host-State's welfare assistance. As for maintenance loans, foreign students' entitlement to maintenance grants was explicitly excluded by the students' directive, and now by Directive 2004/38.[69] As a result of the broad understanding of the material scope of the Treaty for citizenship purposes, the exercise of any competence, even merely complementary, affects the material scope of the Treaty; and, the exercise of competence in relation to other areas, such as (for instance) in relation to economic migrants, has the effect of imposing a general equal treatment obligation in relation to all migrant Union citizens. The Court's statement that the scope of the Treaty has not been affected by Union citizenship seems not to be entirely accurate and, whilst it could be argued that the citizenship provisions should not affect the material scope of the Treaty, it is difficult to maintain that the personal scope of the Treaty has not been affected by the introduction of Union citizenship, since it is that provision which has brought non-economically active people within the scope of the Treaty.

3.3. The Elimination of Reverse Discrimination – Articles 17 and 12 EC

If there is no hermeneutic reason to prevent construing Article 17 EC so as to bring any Union citizen within the personal scope of the Treaty. However, this does not mean that the scope of the Treaty would be unduly expanded since, in order to rely successfully on Article 12 EC, the citizen would have to prove that she/he is discriminated against only because she/he has not exercised her right to move; and also that she is in a comparable situation to those who actively claim rights in Community law. Thus, for instance, following the clarification in *Akrich*,[70] migration rights conferred upon family members by Directive 2004/38 would be available only to those family members who are lawfully present in the territory before relying on Community law rights. In this case, it is unlikely that the static Union citizen would have to rely on Article 17 and 12 EC in order to gain residence rights for her family, since it is likely that migration rights would follow in any event from national migration law.[71] Nor would this interpretation help those in a same-sex partnership in countries which do not recognize such partnerships since Directive 2004/38 makes the rights of registered partners conditional upon the country of destination recognizing such relationships.

In relation to the *Carpenter* situation, i.e. to those cases in which the partner/spouse is not lawfully present in the territory of a Member State when claiming

[69] Directive 2004/38 provides for the full right of equal treatment (i.e. also as regards maintenance grants) for Union citizens who have gained the permanent right of residence, which matures after five years of continuous lawful residence in the host State.

[70] Case C-109/01 *Akrich* [2003] ECR I-9607.

[71] Albeit the Community interpretation might be more favourable to the migrants than the domestic interpretation of migration rules thanks to the applicability of the principle of proportionality, see e.g. Case C-1/05 *Yunying Jia v Migrationsverket*, judgment of 9 January 2007, nyr.

immigration rights, the Court has clarified in *Akrich* that the only obligation flowing from Community law for the national court is that of taking into due account the claimants' fundamental rights, an obligation which in any case follows from international Treaties and in particular from the European Convention on Human Rights. To recognize that Articles 17 and 12 EC confer a right on own nationals to be treated on an equal footing with Union migrants would thus not unduly expand the scope of Community law.

The abolition of reverse discrimination by means of Articles 17 and 12 EC would have also positive effects beyond that of ensuring that equality is truly a general principle of Community law. Thus, it would eliminate the need for certain intellectual gymnastics which do very little for the coherence of the legal system. In this way, the ruling in *Carpenter* can be accommodated in a more coherent framework and the random outcomes to which Community law might give rise would be disposed of. Furthermore, the abolition of reverse discrimination would come through the medium of Community rather than national law therefore ensuring real equality between citizens. Finally, if we were to understand *Carpenter* as a citizenship case, we would also eliminate the problems arising from the possible definition of migration rules for spouses of own static citizens as a barrier to movement. In this respect, consider that such a definition could lead to the conclusion that the Community has internal market competence to eliminate such barriers, something which would be inconsistent with the special regime provided for in Title IV EC.[72]

A last clarification is necessary: the abolition of reverse discrimination would not transform Article 17 EC in a free standing position; it would only serve the purpose of triggering Article 12 EC. In other words, Article 17 EC would not be used to establish a free standing right of review in terms of fundamental rights and proportionality. Rather, the right of the Union citizen would be limited to a true right not to be discriminated against on grounds of nationality or movement.

4. Conclusions

In this chapter we have analyzed the case law on Union citizenship as a result of which Union citizens derive wide ranging rights from Community law. Thus, as a result of such case law, Union citizens derive a right to be treated proportionately in relation to all matters which might affect their right to move and reside in another Member State; they derive a right not to be discriminated against on grounds of nationality or residence, and such right is broadly interpreted. Overall, Union citizens derive an enhanced right of judicial review of legislation, including a right to review of how such legislation is applied and of the effects it might have on their personal circumstances. Lastly, it has been argued that Union citizenship should also be understood as requiring the elimination of reverse discrimination so that

---

[72] See Chapter 4 above.

citizens who find themselves in comparable circumstances should be treated equally regardless of whether they have moved or not. This would allow for Union citizenship to acquire a more convincing constitutional status by removing unjustifiable inequalities, without unduly expand the scope of the Treaty. It would also allow for a more persuasive explanation for the ruling in *Carpenter*.

This said, it should be remembered that Union citizenship has also had an impact on the other free movement provisions. This spill-over effect is sometimes clear, such as when the Court refers explicitly to Union citizenship whilst analyzing cases falling within one of the other free movement rights, and sometimes less evident. In particular, the case law on Union citizenship might help in providing a more satisfactory theoretical framework to explain the developments which have occurred in the past 15 years in the field of the economic free movement rights. It is now time then to look at the more general impact that Union citizenship has had on the free movement provisions.

Chapter 7

Mr Gebhard Meets Mr Baumbast: Towards a More Coherent Theory of Free Movement

It has been highlighted above how the expansion of the scope of Articles 39 and 43 EC to encompass non-discriminatory barriers lacks a coherent conceptual framework. Whilst the market access test might provide a useful descriptive model, it does not provide a normative justification for the Court's case law. In particular, it has been argued that, as the case law stands at present, the right conferred by the Treaty encompasses also a right not to be unduly restricted in the exercise of an economic activity in the territory of (another) Member State. The effect of Articles 39 and 43 EC is to allow economic migrants to demand the scrutiny of (almost) any market regulation in terms of proportionality and necessity. This is the case even when the rule does not have a specific effect on movement or a cross-border specificity. Thus, from a constitutional perspective, the effect of the Court's case law is to introduce a diffuse judicial scrutiny of rules disciplining an economic activity.

Furthermore, the free movement provisions also constrain Member States in the *way* they adopt regulations. In particular, even when a rule is in principle justified, the principle of proportionality might require the national court to assess whether the application of the rule to *that* particular case is justified;[1] and it might require Member States to leave economic operators a sufficient time to adapt to regulatory changes.[2] The result of the Treaty free movement provisions is therefore to empower the individual, as an economic migrant, allowing her/him to demand

---

[1] E.g. Case C-60/00 *Carpenter* [2002] ECR I-6279.

[2] Case C-463/01 *Commission v Germany* (reusable packaging) [2004] ECR I-11705; Case C-320/03 *Commission v Austria* (ban on heavy lorries) [2005] ECR I-9871. Those rulings were delivered in the context of the free movement of goods, but there is no reason why the same approach should not apply to the other free movement provisions.

that Member States refrain from imposing unnecessary regulation, and that Member States take into account the effect of regulation on personal circumstances and vested economic interests. In this way, the Court's interpretation creates a result reminiscent of traditional constitutional rights, where there are inherent limits imposed on the regulatory discretion of the legislature, especially in terms of proportionality and fundamental rights. Such inherent limits, however, are traditionally cognisable only by specialized or superior courts. Through the case law of the Court, such rights to review become communitarized and, in being so, afford more effective protection to citizens through the principle of direct effect and supremacy, allowing any court to review national (economic) legislation.

The problem is whether such pervasive effects in domestic constitutional systems can be justified having regard to the Treaty. Here, traditional free movement orthodoxy is of little help in providing a normative justification for such constitutional developments. However, citizenship discourse might help in two ways. First of all, it is clear that the right not to be constrained in one's activity without there being a good reason can be seen as an aspect of a more fundamental citizenship right, if citizenship is also to be understood as an empowering status which transforms the relationship between government and governed, and inherently limits the power of the former over the latter. In this respect the enhanced right to judicial review, to a further scrutiny over the actions of executive and legislative authorities which is afforded by Community law through the case law of the Court, can be seen as an aspect of enhanced (Union) citizenship rights. Secondly and, for our purposes, more importantly, the reasoning adopted by the Court in relation to Union citizenship might usefully be transposed to justify the expansion of the Treaty economic free movement of persons' provisions.

In order to show how the citizenship and the persons provisions are (naturally) inter-related we will start by recalling those cases in which the citizenship provisions have had a direct impact on the economic migration provisions, to then draw attention to the similarities in the hermeneutic techniques adopted by the Court in the health and citizenship cases. We will then turn to analyze the *Gebhard* line of case law, arguing that it can be better explained and normatively justified having regard to the stance later taken by the Court in *Baumbast.* In that case, the Court held that any limitation or condition to the rights granted by Article 18 EC must pursue a legitimate public interest, as well as being compatible with the general principles of Community law and in particular with the principle of proportionality. Once we redefine the right granted by the economic free movement provisions as a right to pursue an economic activity in another Member State, then we can apply the *Baumbast* reasoning to hold that any limitation or condition imposed by a Member State to that right must pursue a legitimate interest and must comply with the general principles of Community law including proportionality and fundamental rights. Seen in this way, the developments which have occurred in the past decade can be considered consistent with the overall European constitutional framework developed by the Court.

1. Union Citizenship and the Other Free Movement of Persons' Provisions: Creating the 'Fundamental Status' of Union Citizens

As said above, the Court has declared Union citizenship to be the fundamental status of Union citizens.[3] Such fundamental status is relevant not only in establishing rights of residence and equal treatment for those citizens that are not otherwise protected by the Treaty, but is also informing the Court's interpretation of the other free movement provisions.[4] Thus, for instance, and as already mentioned in Chapter 1, in *Collins* the Court revisited its own interpretation of the scope of Article 39 EC in the light of the introduction of Union citizenship.[5] In particular, the Court had previously limited the rights that work-seekers derive from that article to a right to enter and stay in any of the Member States for a reasonable time; and to a right to equal access in relation to employment.[6] However, access to welfare benefits was excluded. Following the ruling in *Collins*, this is no longer the case. Thus, the Court held: '[i]n view of the establishment of *citizenship* of the Union and the interpretation in the case law of the right to equal treatment enjoyed by citizens of the Union, it is no longer possible to exclude from the scope of Article 48(2) [now 39(2)] of the Treaty – which expresses the fundamental principle of equal treatment, guaranteed by Article 6 [now 12] of the Treaty – a benefit of a financial nature intended to facilitate access to employment in the labour market of a Member State'.[7]

A similar link between the economic free movement provisions and Union citizenship was also made in relation to the interpretation of the public policy derogation contained in Article 39(3) EC. Thus, in *Orfanopoulos*, the Court held that a 'particularly restrictive' interpretation of the derogations from the free movement of workers (thus even stricter than that already given before) is 'required by

---

[3] E.g. Case C-184/99 *Grzelczyk* [2001] ECR I-6193, para 31.

[4] On the relationship between the broad interpretation of the Treaty free movement provisions and citizenship (the latter as consistent development of the former), also AG La Pergola's Opinion in Case C-85/96 *M M Martínez Sala v Freistaat Bayern* [1998] ECR I-2691, esp. para 23. And M Poiares Maduro 'Striking the Elusive Balance Between Economic Freedom and Fundamental Rights' in P Alston (ed) *The EU and Human Rights* (OUP Oxford 1999).

[5] Case C-138/02 *Collins* [2004] ECR I-2703.

[6] Case C-292/89 ex parte *Antonissen* [1991] ECR I-745; Case C-278/94 *Commission v Belgium* [1996] ECR I-4307, and above Chapter 1.

[7] Case C-138/02 *Collins* [2004] ECR I-2703, para 63, emphasis added; noted by H Oosterom-Staples (2005) 42 CMLRev 205, who argues that the Court should distinguish more clearly between the scope of application of Article 18 EC and the scope of application of the economic free movement provisions. However, in this writer's opinion there is no normative or rational justification for adopting such a rigid compartmentalization. An economic migrant is also a citizen. Thus she benefits of the more generous regime accorded to economic migrants by virtue of the general principle that *lex specialis derogat generalis*; and also benefits from all of the rights that pertain to Union citizens when those are not already provided for by the economic provisions. The ruling in *Collins* has been confirmed in Case C-258/04 *Ioannidis* [2005] ECR I-8275.

virtue of a person's status as a citizen of the Union'.[8] In *Gaumain-Cerri and Barth*,[9] the Court relied on Article 17 EC in relation to benefits falling within the scope of Regulation 1408/71 on the co-ordination of social security schemes. Here, litigation ensued from the German's authorities' refusal to pay old age pension contributions for non-professional carers of patients insured in Germany, on the sole ground that the carers were established outside Germany. The benefits fell within the scope of Regulation 1408/71, and one of the questions referred to the Court was whether the fact that refusal to pay the contributions was based solely on the grounds that the carers were not resident in Germany was compatible with Community law. The Court found that it was not necessary to establish whether the carers fell within the scope of Article 39 EC, since in any case they were Union citizens and as such they were covered by the general principle of non-discrimination. Given that the benefit fell within the scope of application of Regulation 1408/71, Articles 17 and 12 EC prohibited unjustified indirect discrimination. The residence requirement was therefore declared incompatible with Community law.

In *Commission v Austria*,[10] the Court relied also on the citizenship provisions where arguably there was no need to do so: in this case, Austria introduced indirectly discriminatory rules for admission to university in order to limit the influx of German students who, having failed to secure admission to a German university, registered in Austria. The rules established a different entrance regime for those students who had not studied in Austria. From previous case law, it was clear that the situation fell within the scope of the Treaty and that therefore any discrimination on grounds of nationality would be prohibited unless justified.[11] This notwithstanding, the Court referred also to the citizenship provisions to reinforce its finding that such discrimination was incompatible with the Treaty.

2. Similarities in Interpretation: The Hermeneutic Technique Adopted by the Court

Apart from the direct impact that Articles 17 and 18 EC have had on the case law, it should be noted that the Court has adopted a similar hermeneutic technique in the

---

[8] Joined Cases C-482/01 and C-493/01 *Orfanopoulos and Olivieri* [2004] ECR I-5257, para 65. This said the case is regrettably confused as to the possibility to apply Directive 64/221, and the narrow interpretation of the public policy proviso espoused by the Court to Article 18 EC; cf para 71. The Court seems also to suggest that in any event the claimant could be covered by Article 49 EC since receiving services in a State other than his own (para 54).

[9] Joined Cases C-502/01 and C-31/02 *Gaumain Cerri and Barth* [2004] ECR I-6483. See also Case C-135/99 *Elsen* [2000] ECR I-10409, where the Court relied *also* on Article 18 EC to find that a residence requirement in relation to child-rearing related benefits was incompatible with Community law.

[10] Case C-147/03 *Commission v Austria* (University admissions) [2005] ECR I-5969, para 45.

[11] Case 293/82 *Gravier* [1985] ECR 593; Case 24/86 *Blaizot* [1988] ECR 379; Case 42/87 *Commission v Belgium* [1988] ECR I-5445.

citizenship cases to that adopted in relation to the health care cases. In particular, and as we shall in detail below, in both strands of cases the Court has gone beyond the provisions of secondary legislation, so as to create additional rights by means of Treaty interpretation. Thus, as said in Chapter 2, in the health care cases the Court found that conditions imposed in order to obtain reimbursement for medical treatment obtained abroad fell within the scope of Article 49 EC. As a result, the prior authorization required for reimbursement constituted a barrier to the intra-Community provision of services.

This said, the Court did not question the compatibility with the Treaty of Article 22 Regulation 1408/71, which provides for a right to seek treatment abroad in given circumstances *conditional upon a prior authorization* granted by the competent national institution. Rather, the Court used the Treaty free movement provisions to go *beyond* the rights granted by secondary legislation, without calling the validity of such legislation into question. The Court took a similar approach in *Vanbraekel.*[12] In this case the national court enquired as to the level of reimbursement to be granted to a patient who had (or should have) been authorized to seek treatment in another Member State. Regulation 1408/71 provides that a patient authorized to receive treatment abroad should receive benefits in kind in the host institution as if she/he were insured with it. Thus, where prior authorization is unduly denied, the patient has, under Regulation 1408/71, a right to reimbursement according to the tariffs applied in the Member State where treatment is received. In the case at issue, Belgium, the State where the claimant was insured, provided for higher tariffs than France, the State where treatment had been administered. The question was whether reimbursement at the lower tariffs provided for by France was to be construed as a restriction on the freedom to receive services in another Member State. The Court found that – notwithstanding the provisions of Regulation 1408/71 – once authorization to seek treatment abroad has been (or should have been) given, Article 49 EC grants a right to be reimbursed at the tariffs of the State of origin if *those* are higher than the tariffs of the State where the treatment is received.

In *Müller-Fauré*,[13] the Court adopted the same hermeneutic technique. One of the issues for analysis in that case was whether the prior authorization requirement could be justified in the case of out-of-hospital treatment. As said above, it is Regulation 1408/71 which provides for such a requirement. The Court found that, in the case of out-of-hospital treatment, the authorization requirement was an *unjustified* barrier to the freedom to receive services. However, as in *Vanbraekel*, it did not question the validity of the provisions contained in the Regulation. Rather, lacking prior authorization, it imposed on the State a duty to reimburse patients who received treatment abroad at the tariffs applicable in their own

---

[12] Case C-368/98 *Abdon Vanbraekel and others v Alliance nationale des mutualités chrétiennes* [2001] ECR I-5363. See also Case C-326/00 *Idryma Koinonikon Asfaliseon (IKA) v Vasilios Ioannidis* [2003] ECR I-1703, for a generous interpretation of Article 31 Regulation 1408/71.
[13] Case C-385/99 *Müller-Fauré* and *van Riet* [2003] ECR I-4509.

territory rather than in the territory of the State where treatment is received as provided by the Regulation.[14]

In this way, the Court has used Article 49 EC to create additional rights than those granted by Regulation 1408/71 without however encroaching on the validity of that piece of legislation.[15] By using a binary approach whereby provisions of secondary legislation run parallel to those of primary law,[16] the Court increases citizen rights beyond the initial intention of the legislature. This approach thus creates a *tension* rather than a *breakage* between secondary legislation (decided at the political level) and the Treaty provisions (i.e. the Court's own view of the boundaries of Community law).[17]

This same approach is visible also in relation to the rights of family members of economically active citizens. In *Akrich*,[18] the Court held that Article 10 of Regulation 1612/68 (now subsumed in Directive 2004/38) did not apply to family members who were unlawfully present in the territory of a Member State.[19] For this reason, Mr Akrich, who was unlawfully present in the UK before moving with his British wife to Ireland, could not rely on the rights granted by the Regulation upon returning to the United Kingdom. Nonetheless, the Court also held that the national court was bound by Community law to take into account fundamental rights as general principles of Community law. One way of explaining this rather obscure ruling, as well as reconciling it with *Carpenter*,[20] which also concerned an unlawfully present third country national,[21] is to understand the ruling as recognizing that separation from a genuine spouse (and partner) is always a barrier to movement, since the Union citizen is less likely to move if the price to pay for migration is to be parted from loved ones. This is obviously the case regardless of the partner's migration status. Thus, secondary legislation grants an unconditional right to be followed by one's lawfully resident spouse; primary legislation (i.e. the Treaty free movement provisions), on the other hand, supplements this right by

[14] The Court also clarified that, should the Member State not have a system of tariffs in place, for instance because it provides directly also for out-of-hospital treatment, it would have to set them up.
[15] Cp also Case C-56/01 *Inizan* [2003] ECR I-12403, where the Court upheld the validity of Article 22 Regulation 1408/71.
[16] Cf AG Dámaso Ruiz-Jarabo Colomer Opinion in case C-56/01 *Inizan* [2003] ECR I-12403. On the fact that an expansion of the possibility of seeking health care abroad should be widened through legislation rather than judicial interpretation, see R Cornelissen 'The Principle of Territoriality and the Community Regulations on Social Security' (1996) 33 CMLRev 439, 466.
[17] This tension is now visible in Directive 2006/123 on services in the internal market [2006] OJ L 376/36, para 23 of the Preamble states that it does not affect the Court's case law on reimbursement, whilst Art. 2(f) excludes from the scope of the services directive healthcare services.
[18] Case C-109/01 *Akrich* [2003] ECR I-9607.
[19] The case seems to have overruled Case C-459/99 *Mouvement contre le racisme, l'antisémitisme et la xénophobie (MRAX) ASBL v Belgium* [2002] ECR I-6591, where the Court indicated that marriage to a Community economic migrant could rectify the status of a third country national illegal migrant. On the relationship between *MRAX and Akrich* see AG Geelhoed's Opinion in *Yunying Jia v Migrationsverket*, opinion delivered 27 April 2006, judgment of 9 January 2007, nyr.
[20] C-60/00 *Carpenter* [2002] ECR I-6279.
[21] See E Spaventa 'Annotation on *Akrich*' (2005) CMLRev 225.

requiring national authorities to take into account the Union citizen's right to family life, and of course, to apply any rule having due regard to the principle of proportionality and the individual circumstances of the claimant. It is in the space between secondary and primary legislation that the individual gains additional rights; those rights seem to have much more to do with recognizing her condition as a person, with recognizing a given level of fundamental rights protection, arguably more generous than those recognized by the European Court of Human Rights, than with protecting the citizen as an economic actor. As a result, the Member States see significantly reduced the possibility to control illegal immigration through 'exemplary' and perhaps draconian measures. Rather, Member States have to take into account – whenever there is a Community element, but even where such link is less evident – the personal situation of the persons concerned, both in assessing the applicability of the public policy derogation and in balancing immigration policies with the individual's fundamental rights.[22]

This binary technique is adopted also in relation to the citizenship cases. Thus the requirements of sufficient resources and comprehensive health insurance provided for by the residence directives first, and by Directive 2004/38 now, have not been called into question. At the same time, however, the Court has held that the blanket application of such requirements might be incompatible with the demands of Article 18 EC. In this way the Court creates a 'cleavage' between the provisions of primary and secondary legislation,[23] and in doing so it ensures the rights of the claimants without impacting upon the validity of secondary legislation and of the political compromise reached in such instruments. Even though it is too early to say, it is likely that such 'binary' approach will inform the Court's interpretation of Directive 2004/38. In particular, the rulings in *Collins* and in *Bidar* indicate that such might be the case. The ruling in *Collins* established that, in principle, and subject to justifications, work-seekers are entitled to equal treatment also in relation to welfare benefits. The ruling therefore appears to be inconsistent with Directive 2004/38, since the latter provides that Member States are not obliged to confer social assistance on work-seekers.[24] Admittedly the ruling in *Collins* predates the adoption of the Citizens' Rights Directive: however, such ruling has been confirmed in the later case of *Ioannidis*.[25] Even though the Directive had not yet entered into force at the time of the latter ruling, it is unlikely that the Court would be prepared to revisit its case law and exclude, once again, work-seekers from the scope of Article 39(2) EC. It is also unlikely that the Court would be prepared to invalidate Article 24(2) Directive 2004/38 to the extent to which it excludes work-seekers from entitlement to social assistance. Rather, it is

---

[22] For a much more restrictive approach however see Case C-257/00 *Givane* [2003] ECR I-345. Also restrictive, but in the writer's opinion justified, is the ruling in Cases C-356/98 *Kaba I* [2000] ECR I-2623 and C-466/00 *Kaba II* [2003] ECR I-2219.
[23] M Dougan and E Spaventa 'Educating Rudy and the (non-)English patient: A double-bill on residency rights under Article18 EC' (2003) 28 ELRev 699, 705.
[24] Article 24(2) Directive 2004/38.
[25] Case C-258/04 *Ioannidis* [2005] ECR I-8275.

to be expected that the Court will consider such exclusion as a limitation to Article 39 EC which needs to be applied in a proportionate way having due regard to the circumstances of the case. Thus, if the work-seeker has not established a sufficient link with the host-employment market, then the provision of the Directive applies and the work-seeker can be refused social assistance. But once the work-seeker has established such a link, then exclusion would not be possible because it would constitute a disproportionate limitation on Treaty rights, despite such exclusion having been in principle authorized by the Directive.

The same approach is likely to apply in relation to the ruling in *Bidar*,[26] again decided before the Directive entered into force, but after it was adopted. Directive 2004/38 provides that non-economically active Union citizens are not entitled to maintenance grants for studies before having acquired the right to permanent residence which matures after five years of continuous and lawful residence in the host State. Directive 93/96 (the students' directive) also excluded the right to maintenance grants for students. Notwithstanding this rather clear political will, the Court found that, since Mr Bidar was resident in the UK by virtue of the general residence directive,[27] rather than the students' directive,[28] the exclusion contained in the students' directive did not apply; and that Articles 18 and 12 EC conferred upon him a right to equal treatment (subject to justifications) also in relation to maintenance loans. Again, it is unlikely that the Court will be willing to reverse from the *Bidar* ruling. Rather, if the Union citizen has matured a right to permanent residence, then the entitlement to maintenance grant will follow as of right. If she/he has not matured such a right, it will be open to them to demonstrate that they have established a sufficient link with the host-State to justify posing a demand on its resources. That would be the case in the period between the three years, held by the Court to be reasonable, and the five years provided for by the Directive.

These links between Union citizenship and the free movement provisions, the similarity in the interpretative tools adopted by the Court as well as the direct impact of Union citizenship on the free movement provisions, is all but surprising given that the subject matter of these provisions is very closely linked. However, in the writer's opinion, Union citizenship might also serve to explain, retrospectively, the case law on non-discriminatory barriers to the economic free movement provisions.

3. Mr Gebhard Meets Mr Baumbast: Towards a Coherent Constitutional Framework

In the previous section we have highlighted the impact that Union citizenship has had on the persons' case law as well as how the Court is (naturally) adopting the

---

[26] Case C-209/03 *Bidar* [2005] ECR I-2119.
[27] Directive 90/364 now subsumed in Directive 2004/38.
[28] Directive 93/96 now subsumed in Directive 2004/38.

same means of interpretation in the two strands of case law, which are therefore producing similar constitutional effects. It is now time to take the analysis a step further to show how the citizenship case law might, with the benefit of hindsight, be of use in providing a stronger normative basis for the *Gebhard* line of cases.

In relation to Article 18 EC, the Court has held that *any* limitation and condition imposed on the right to move, on the right to reside in another Member State or on the right to equal treatment must comply with the general principles of Community law and in particular with the principle of proportionality and fundamental rights. This determines an *ad hoc* scrutiny whereby, even when the rules limiting the Community right are in themselves compatible with secondary Community law (*Baumbast*, *Bidar*, *Collins*), their application to a particular situation needs to be assessed for its conformity with the general principles of Community law. The application of the economic free movement provisions determines exactly the same effect – rules which are construed by the Court as barriers to movement are subject to the proportionality and fundamental rights scrutiny required by the mandatory requirements doctrine. The reason why the economic persons' case law is difficult to justify is because the notion of barrier to movement is stretched beyond any reasonable limit. However, once the right conferred by the Treaty is properly understood as granting a right to pursue an economic activity in another Member State, then any limitation on such a right would have to be justified and comply with the general principles of Community law. Since virtually any rule disciplining an economic activity can be understood as imposing a limitation on the possibility to engage in such economic activity, then the broad approach adopted by the Court could be explained. Viewed in this way, the *Gebhard* case law could be seen in a constitutionally satisfactory manner. However, before reaching this conclusion we need to be satisfied that the scope of the Treaty free movement provisions can indeed be construed as including also a right to exercise an economic activity in another Member State.

3.1. A Right to Exercise an Economic Activity in Another Member State

The economic free movement provisions confer upon Union citizens a right to move to another Member State *in order* to pursue an economic activity *and* to pursue an economic activity on the same footing as nationals of the host-State. Following the step beyond discrimination, both the scholarship and the Court have focused on the first limb of the equation, i.e. on the right to move. This has led to an artificial definition of barrier to movement on the part of the Court, and on the embracement of the notion of market access on the part of the scholarship. However, with the hindsight of the *Baumbast* ruling, the case law of the Court can be seen in another light.

The Treaty economic free movement provisions undoubtedly confer a right to move; the very substance of that right however lies in the right to exercise an economic activity in another Member State since, without it, the right to move would be devoid of any meaning and, of course, the willingness to exercise an economic activity is a precondition for the very enjoyment of the right to move, since without the former the Union citizen cannot rely on the economic free movement provisions.

Such right, the right to exercise an economic activity in any of the Member States, encompasses the right to do so on an equal footing with nationals of that Member State, but is not so limited. It could be argued that, even before the broadening of the scope of the Treaty which occurred in the 1990s, there was some indication that an absolute ban and/or conditions imposed on the exercise of an economic activity might fall within the scope of Article 49 EC, at least if they would deprive that provision of its useful effect, which is to say of the possibility for external providers to exercise the activity in the host State.

In fact, in its earlier case law, the Court adopts a reasoning similar to that later adopted in *Dassonville-Cassis*,[29] whereby the effect of national rules regulating economic activities on intra-Community service provision is presumed, unless the rules pursue a legitimate interest, are necessary and proportionate. Take for instance the ruling in *Van Binsbergen*[30] or the ruling in *Van Wesemael.*[31] In the former, the Court, faced with a residence requirement in order to provide services as lawyers, relied on the 'useful effect' of Article 49 EC in order to bring the rules within the scope of the Treaty. In *Van Wasemael*,[32] the issue was whether a licence requirement for fee-charging employment agencies for entertainers fell within the scope of the Treaty. In this case, the Court found that such a requirement was in principle 'justified', and therefore would fall outside the scope of the Treaty, unless it was not necessary, which was the case in the situation under consideration since the service provider, an employment agency, had already been subjected to similar requirements in the State of origin.

Whilst it is undeniably true that both rulings can be, and have been, conceptualized within the indirect discrimination/double burden framework, it is interesting to note the mode of analysis used by the Court. In this respect, we can distinguish between an earlier trend in the case law, where the discrimination discourse in relation to the freedom to provide services is less prominent,[33] and a 'middle' period in which the Court, maybe also thanks to the conceptualization offered by the scholarship, reasons predominantly in terms of discrimination.[34] On the other hand, and as we know, in relation to the other free movement

[29] It should be remembered that it is the *Cassis* reasoning, and especially the idea of mandatory requirements, that follows from *Van Binsbergen*, and not vice versa.

[30] Case 33/74 *Van Binsbergen* [1974] ECR 1299.

[31] Joined Cases 110 and 111/78 *Van Wesemael* [1979] ECR 35.

[32] Joined Cases 110 and 111/78 *Van Wesemael* [1979] ECR 35.

[33] E.g. Case 33/74 *Van Binsbergen* [1974] ECR 1299; Case 39/75 *Coenen* [1975] ECR 1574; Joined Cases 110 and 111/78 *Van Wesemael* [1979] ECR 35; Case 52/79 *Debauve* [1980] ECR 833; Case 279/80 *Webb* [1981] ECR 3305.

[34] The discriminatory approach becomes the standard approach: e.g. Case 15/78 *Koestler* [1978] ECR 1971; Joined Cases 62 and 63/81 *SECO v EVI* [1982] ECR 223.

provisions, until the 1990s, discrimination is very much the only framework informing the Court's discourse.[35]

Whatever our interpretation of the earlier case law, it later becomes clear that an absolute ban on an economic activity falls squarely within the scope of Article 49 EC. This is openly stated in *Schindler*,[36] where, it might be recalled, the Court held that the prohibition on the exercise of an economic activity constitutes a restriction on the freedom to provide services in need of justification regardless of discrimination. We have mentioned above that the ruling can be explained by adopting a traditional free movement/internal market rationale and by considering a service as a 'product' which, once lawfully produced, should be able to circulate freely within the Community unless there is a good reason to stop it. However, the ruling could also be seen in the context of a more general right to exercise an economic activity everywhere in the Community. The reason why a freedom to move is conferred in the first place is exactly so that Union citizens can exercise an economic activity in another Member State. But, if the exercise of the economic activity is forbidden, then the very *substance* of the right conferred by Article 49 EC is affected and, for this reason, the rule needs to be scrutinized for its conformity with Community law.

Furthermore, whilst, as said above, the traditional approach might well be used in relation to such cases, that approach might in some instances not be entirely satisfactory. In this respect, it should be considered that the analogy between goods and services is not necessarily accurate when the service is not 'cross-border' in nature, i.e. when the cross-border element arises from the fact that a person has moved to provide the service in the host-State. To impose the scrutiny of a non-discriminatory prohibition on the exercise of an economic activity even when all elements of such economic activity take place in the host-State is conceptually different from imposing such scrutiny where the client seeks to buy the service from an out-of-state provider, without either the provider or the client moving. In other words, there is a non-negligible difference between, say, the case of a client buying a financial product in another Member State's market place, when that financial product cannot be the subject of economic transactions at home, and the case where a person moves to offer a service (for sake of argument, prostitution or abortion) in the host-Member State where such a service is prohibited. In the latter case, it is more difficult to consider the person offering the service, or the service itself, as a product which has already been regulated and therefore should move unless there are good reasons to stop it. This conceptual difference between the two cases is fully played out in the assessment of the justifications; however, it seems that the notion of 'bar to an economic activity' better describes the rationale behind the Court's reasoning. Whatever the framework one wants to adopt to

---

[35] With the exception of Case 107/83 *Klopp* [1984] ECR 2971; however, it can be argued that the prohibition to have more than one establishment for lawyers went against the very wording of the Treaty which provides for the right to have secondary (and thus necessarily more than one) establishments.

[36] Case C-275/92 *Schindler* [1994] ECR I-1039.

explain the *Schindler* case, it is not only absolute barriers to the exercise of an economic activity that are perceived as affecting the right granted by the Treaty: any 'limitation or condition' imposed on such a right, which is to say virtually any market rule, is seen as a limitation to a fundamental Treaty right in need of justification. In this respect, consider the earlier case of *Gouda*, where the Court found that, in principle, rules relating to a ban on advertising on Sunday were caught by Article 49 EC,[37] and *De Agostini* where restrictions on advertising where also found to fall within the scope of Article 49 EC.[38]

3.2. The *Gebhard* Case Law

Once we accept that the very substance of the right to move lies in the right to exercise an economic activity in another Member State, there is no reason why the interpretation of Article 49 EC should differ, or develop, along different lines from the interpretation of Articles 39 and 43 EC. After all, market rules affect the right to exercise an economic activity in other Member States regardless of whether the migrant is established or not in the host Member State. The *Gebhard* expansion of the concept of barrier, and the move towards a global test for all persons provisions embraced in that case, is therefore consistent both with a teleological interpretation of the Treaty and with the earlier developments in the field of services. More importantly, once we redefine the scope of the free movement rights as granting a right to exercise an economic activity in another Member State, then the developments which have formed the focus of our critical analysis can be constitutionally justified.

Thus, consider the following. Market regulations inherently limit the possibility of pursuing an economic activity. We know from the ruling in *Baumbast* that any limitation or condition to a fundamental Community right must be justified and comply with the general principles of Community law. If we understand the right granted by the Treaty economic provisions as encompassing a right to pursue an economic activity in another Member State, then it is natural that any limitation or condition to such right should comply with the general principles of Community law, and especially with the principle of proportionality and fundamental rights. Thus, it is not that Mr Gebhard was hindered in his ability to move to Italy; he was hindered in his ability to exercise an economic activity when in Italy and it is for this reason that the rules had to be justified and comply with proportionality (and fundamental rights). It is in this sense that the *Baumbast* ruling sheds light on the case law of the past ten years, and it is the *Baumbast* ruling that affords us the tools to provide a consistent and uniform conceptual explanation for all of the free movement rights.

---

[37] Case C-288/89 *Gouda* [1991] ECR I-4007.

[38] Joined Cases C-34 to 36/95 *Konsumentombudsmannen (KO) v De Agostini (Svenska) Förlag AB and TV Shop I Sverige AB* [1997] ECR I-3843.

The rest of the case law can also be explained in this fashion. It is in fact undeniable that a professional requirement imposes a condition on the possibility to exercise that profession and as such needs to be justified. Therefore the rules which restricted eye examination tests to ophthalmologists in *McQuen*,[39] the rules that prohibited non-medical doctors to provide services as naturo-therapists in *Gräbner*,[40] and the rules that provided that only members of certain regulated professions could provide pay-slip calculation services in *Payroll*,[41] all restricted the exercise of an economic activity and therefore fell within the scope of the Treaty regardless of discrimination. But, if the rights granted by the Treaty are so widely construed then, of course, almost any market regulation falls within its scope. Thus, the rules in *CaixaBank*, by prohibiting the possibility of offering a given product, clearly also imposed a limitation on the exercise of the economic activity and, for this reason, they were scrutinized.[42]

The same can be said in relation to the case law on the free movement of workers, and in particular the *Bosman* and *Graf* rulings.[43] In the former, the rules, by imposing a fee payment requirement undoubtedly regulated (and restricted), the exercise of an economic activity. The rules in *Graf*, however, did not affect the exercise of the economic activity either in Austria or in any other Member State. Rules that provide for compensation for unfair or unjust dismissal, and do not provide for compensation in case of voluntary resignation of the worker, do not regulate, not even remotely, the exercise of an economic activity. Rather they provide a safety net in those circumstances where the economic activity is terminated through no fault of the worker.

This framework is also of use in relation to the case law on the free movement of capital, where, as said before, the Court has from the very beginning adopted a very wide notion of barrier to movement. Thus, it found that golden shares, shares held by the Government in privatized industries granting it special powers, were to be construed as barriers to the free movement of capital since they would affect access to the market by deterring (also) foreign investors from buying normal shares.[44] It has been remarked how the market access reasoning does not really explain such rulings: foreign investors were not prevented from buying shares; rather the shares they bought carried slightly less powers than ordinary shares. Leaving aside the discussion as to whether it should be for the Court to decide on the extent to which Member States can set up new mixed private/public ownership schemes, the case law seems to suggest that any limitation on ownership/property rights, the very reason why one would move and use capital, falls within the scope

[39] Case C-108/96 *McQuen* [2001] ECR I-837.
[40] Case C-294/00 *Gräbner* [2002] I-6515.
[41] Case C-79/01 *Payroll Data Services (Italy) et al* [2002] ECR I-8923.
[42] Case C-442/02 *Caixa-Bank* [2004] ECR I-8961.
[43] Case C-415/93 *Bosman* [1995] ECR I-4921; Case C-190/98 *Graf* [2000] ECR I-437.
[44] E.g. Case C-367/98 *Commission v Portugal* (Golden shares) [2002] ECR I-4732; Case C-483/99 *Commission v France* (Golden shares) [2002] ECR I-4781; Case C-503/99 *Commission v Belgium* (Golden shares) [2002] ECR I-4809; Case C-98/01 *Commission v UK* (BAA golden share) [2003] ECR I-4641; Joined Cases C-282 and 283/04 *Commission v Netherlands* (golden shares) [2006] ECR I-9141.

of the Treaty and needs to be justified. This is confirmed by the case of *Burtscher* mentioned above, where the Court indicated its willingness to carry out a substantive review of the penalties imposed for breach of the formalities required for the acquisition of property.[45]

3.3. The Different Approach Adopted in Relation to Tax Rules

If we describe the right granted by the Treaty as conferring upon individuals (and companies) a right to exercise an economic activity in another Member State, then the different interpretation adopted by the Court in relation to tax rules, including those rules governing social security contribution, can also be explained. As pointed out before, in relation to those rules the Court's assessment is, broadly speaking, limited to an assessment in terms of discrimination.[46] Tax rules are caught by the Treaty only insofar as directly or indirectly discriminatory.[47] Whilst those rules might well affect the choice to move, and especially corporate actors' choices, they do not affect the right to pursue an economic activity per se. There is only one caveat to this proviso: in the case of goods, the Court has indicated that non-discriminatory taxation (i.e. tax that does not fall within the scope of Article 90 EC) might fall within the scope of Article 28 EC if it is so high as to impede the free movement of goods, at least when there is no domestic production of the goods at issue.[48] The same seems to be true in the case of services: in *Viacom Outdoor*,[49] the Court examined a tax on billboard advertising. Having found that the tax was not discriminatory, the Court held that it fell outside the scope of the Treaty since the charge was modest in comparison to the value of the services provided, and was therefore not capable of impeding or hindering the free movement of services. Thus, it is possible that the Court has left the door open to the option of bringing non-discriminatory taxation within the scope of the Treaty free movement provisions in those cases in which the tax is so high as to virtually prohibit the exercise of the economic activity, by rendering the service which is subject to taxation so expensive as to be anti-economic. However, short of extreme cases, non-discriminatory taxation should fall outside the Treaty, since it does not affect the exercise of the economic activity.[50]

---

[45] Case C-213/04 *Burtscher* [2005] ECR I-10309; the notification procedure the breach of which was at stake in *Burtscher* had been declared compatible with Article 56 EC in Joined Cases C-515/99, C-519/99 to C-524/99 and C-526/99 to C-540/99 *Reisch and others* [2002] ECR I-2157.

[46] See Chapter 3 above.

[47] In the field of free movement of capital see e.g. Case C-513/03 *van Hilten-van der Heijden* [2006] ECR I-1957.

[48] Case C-383/01 *De Danske Billimportører* [2003] ECR I-6065, para 40; the Court clarified that the non applicability of Article 90 EC on discriminatory taxation, does not automatically trigger Article 28 EC, Joined Cases C-34/01 to C-38/01 *Enirisorse Spa* [2003] ECR I-14243.

[49] Case C-134/03 *Viacom Outdoor* [2005] ECR I-1167, para 38.

[50] As said in Chapter 3, in Case C-17/00 *De Coster* [2001] ECR I-9445, the Court indicated that non-discriminatory taxation might fall within the scope of the Treaty even when is not particularly high if it prevents or otherwise impede the free movement of services. However, and as remarked before, the

This said, even if the notion of exercise of economic activity might provide us with a useful conceptual framework, capable of affording a stronger normative basis for the Court's interpretation, not all case law can be explained in this way. In particular, a further step in our reasoning is necessary to justify the application of the Treaty to those cases in which the intra-Community element was weak at best, such as *Gourmet*,[51] where the issue was one of exercising an economic activity in the home-State; and *Freskot*,[52] where the issue was one of not being compelled to enter into an insurance contract with a State provider. But also a further step is necessary to justify those cases in which the intra-Community element for two otherwise domestic companies was established by the mere (arbitrary) fact of foreign ownership (*McQuen* and *Payroll*).

4. Seeking Consistency – the Case Law, the Treaty and the Cross-Border Element

It has been noted above how the Court has not only expanded its interpretation of what constitutes a barrier relevant for the purposes of the Treaty, but it has also considerably relaxed the cross-border requirement so that almost any economic operator can rely on the Treaty simply by claiming the existence of potential foreign clients/providers. It could be argued that the two developments are logically connected. Once we accept that the Treaty can be invoked to challenge rules that simply regulate an economic activity, that is to say, to challenge those rules that do not affect the out-of-State provider in any different way than the domestic provider, then there is no reason not to allow a domestic provider to challenge those same rules. Take by way of example the case of *Payroll*,[53] where a company was allowed to challenge successfully the Italian rules on the professional requirements needed for the calculation of pay-slips for employees. Payroll had been incorporated in Italy, and it was going to operate on the Italian market. The only connection with the Treaty was that it was owned by two French companies; a company owned by Italian corporate actors would have not been able to challenge the rule and would have had to comply with the qualification requirements. Now, it is clear that, since the rules at issue did not regulate ownership (the only element which had triggered the Treaty) they did not affect *Payroll* in any different way than they affected Italian-owned companies. Yet, according to the 'purely internal situation' rule,[54] the Italian owned companies would not be in a position to challenge the rule

case is not crystal clear in its significance since the Court then proceeded in what seemed to be a discriminatory assessment.

[51] Case C-405/98 *Gourmet International Products AB (GIP)*[2001] ECR I-1795.

[52] Case C-355/00 *Freskot* [2003] ECR I-5263.

[53] Case C-79/01 *Payroll Data Services (Italy) et al* [2002] ECR I-8923.

[54] One could wonder whether a minimum percentage of foreign ownership would be enough to trigger the Treaty, in which case the scope of purely internal situations for corporate actors would be further reduced.

and would have to await for a legislative amendment before being able to offer their services without having to have recourse to (more expensive) qualified professionals. This result would be clearly arbitrary and it is in this context that we should understand the development of the 'potential client/provider' doctrine according to which a provider might rely on the Treaty against its State of establishment in relation to its ability to offer a service in that State on the sole ground that its client might be foreign (*Gourmet*). Or a potential client might rely, again against his/her State of establishment, on the Treaty on the sole ground that a potential out-of-State provider might be willing to offer that service in the state where the client is established (*Freskot*). Through this rather artificial doctrine, the Court is able to dispose of the problems, and injustices, that would arise from a strict application of the purely internal situation rule, according to which the Treaty cannot be invoked when the intra-Community element is lacking.

Having said this, however, in order to be able to provide some normative force to this otherwise rational development we should consider the extent to which the 'purely internal situation' rule is still relevant in relation to cases involving non-discriminatory barriers to the exercise of economic activities; and whether the progressive reduction, if not altogether elimination, of the intra-Community element is justified.

4.1. The Cross-Border Element

The progressive erosion of the need for the claimant in the main proceedings to establish an intra-Community element occurred first in the field of the free movement of goods. In a series of rulings, the Court accepted jurisdiction in relation to cases referred by national courts where the main proceedings did not relate to the import of goods.[55] The references arose because of the national courts' need to assess the precise scope of Community law in order to be able to apply their own constitutional provisions guaranteeing a right to equal treatment. It is only more recently, however, that the need to establish an intra-Community credential in the field of free movement of persons has been relaxed. In this regard we can distinguish two trends.

First of all, there is a series of cases in which the Court either ignored whether the situation at stake in the main proceeding actually involved an intra-Community element,[56] or reasoned in a way similar to the goods cases indicating that it is not going to refuse jurisdiction when the national court is seeking assistance as to the interpretation of Community law in order to apply its own constitutional guarantees of equality to eliminate reverse discrimination.[57] In the latter cases, the Court

[55] Case 298/87 *Smanor* [1988] ECR 4489; Joined Cases C-321/94 to C-324/94 *Pistre and Others* [1997] ECR 2343 and Case C-254/98 *TK-Heimdienst Sass GmbH* [2000] ECR I-151; Case C-448/98 *Guimont* [2000] ECR I-10663; Case C-71/02 *Karner* [2004] ECR I-3025. On these issues see further E. Spaventa, 'Annotation on *TK-Heimdienst*' (2000) *Common Market Law Review* 1265.

[56] E.g. Case C-398/95 *SETTG v Ypourgos Egasias* [1997] ECR I-3091.

[57] E.g. Joined Cases C-515/99, C-519/99 to C-524/99 and C-526/99 to C-540/99 *Reisch and others* [2002] ECR I-2157, paras 24 and ff.; Case C-300/01 *Salzmann* [2003] ECR I-4899 esp. para 32;

clarified that it is for the national courts to determine the relevance and the need for a preliminary ruling: for this reason, it is only in the most extreme circumstances that the Court will refuse to provide the national court with the requested ruling, i.e. in those cases in which it is 'quite obvious' that the interpretation of Community law bears no relation to the case, or is purely hypothetical.[58]

Secondly, there is a line of cases in which, despite the fact that the factual situation was confined to the territory of one Member State, the Court accepted jurisdiction and declared the Treaty provisions to be in principle relevant. In those cases, it is the fact that the situation might (or might have been) potentially of intra-Community relevance that triggered the scrutiny of the Court. We have mentioned in the course of the book those cases in which the Court relied on foreign ownership (*McQuen* and *Payroll*) and on the existence of a potential out-of-State provider/client (*Freskot* and *Gourmet*) in order to trigger the Treaty. However, there is also another line of cases, relating to the procedure for the award of public service concessions, where the Court relied on the existence of a purely potential intra-Community element in order to justify the application of Articles 49 and 43 EC. According to this case law, when the public procurement directives do not apply,[59] Articles 43 and 49 EC require in any event the awarding body to comply with the principles of transparency and non-discrimination.[60] This is so even when the situation which gave rise to the case is internal to the Member State, i.e. where the complainant is a domestic company. In order to justify this finding, the Court adopted teleological reasoning and stressed how lack of transparency and publicity might lead to *de facto* discriminatory effects and foreclosure of the market since, lacking transparency, it is impossible to determine whether a non-domestic undertaking could/would have expressed an interest in the contract. Furthermore, in *Parking Brixen*,[61] the Court also added that, in those cases, the more general principle of non-discrimination, rather than just non-discrimination on grounds of nationality, applies. Therefore the principle of equal treatment of tenderers has to be applied even when there is no discrimination on grounds of nationality, i.e. when the tenderers are all domestic companies.

The public awards cases are entirely consistent with the principles enshrined in the Treaty; this said, they also offer fertile grounds for reflection for those cases

---

Case C-6/01 *Anomar and others* [2003] ECR I-8621, paras 39 and ff; Joined Cases C-94/04 and 224/04 *Cipolla v Fazari*, and *Macrino and Capodarte v Meloni*, judgment of 5/12/06, nyr, para 30.

[58] Cf Case 244/80 *Foglia v Novello* (No 2) [1981] ECR I-3045.

[59] Now Directive 2004/17 coordinating the procurement procedures of entities operating in the water, energy, transport and postal services sectors OJ L 134/1 and Directive 2004/18 on the coordination of procedures for the award of public works contracts, public supply contracts and public service contracts OJ L 134/114.

[60] Case C-324/98 *Telaustria and Telefonadress* [2000] ECR I-10745 where however the purely internal issue had not been explicitly examined by the Court; Case C-231/03 *Coname* [2005] ECR I-7287; Case C-458/03 *Parking Brixen* [2005] ECR I-8612, esp. para 55.

[61] Case C-458/03 *Parking Brixen* [2005] ECR I-8612; see also Case C-410/04 *ANAV* [2006] ECR I-3303. See also Commission interpretative communication on the Community law applicable to contract awards not or not fully subject to the provisions of the Public Procurement directives, (2006) OJ C 179/2.

in which the Court, without elaborating on its reasoning, found the situation concerning a non-discriminatory barrier to fall within the scope of the Treaty by relying on the fact that there was a potential intra-Community dimension, since the company was owned by foreigners or might have wanted to contract with out-of-State clients or providers. Once we accept that truly non discriminatory obstacles fall within the scope of the Treaty, then the foreclosure of the market/potential intra-Community reasoning adopted in relation to the award of public concessions can be extended to those cases so as to establish an inherent Community dimension.

Here, in order to justify the reasoning of the Court, and the application of the Treaty rules to situations which in all respects appeared to be purely internal, it is necessary to take a step back and consider the nature of the internal market, once the Treaty is pushed to require the elimination of non-discriminatory obstacles to the exercise of an economic activity. We have highlighted above how, in the case of non-discriminatory rules, once a rule is found to be incompatible with the Treaty then it has to be amended, or disposed of, in relation to *all* economic operators. In other words, whilst when the rule has a *specific effect* on an intra-Community situation, then the Member State must amend the rule so as just to eliminate *that* effect, this is not possible in relation to truly non-discriminatory obstacles: once there is no requirement to prove a specific effect on movement, then any situation is potentially of Community relevance. This is the case for three different, and interrelated, reasons.

First, rules which are defined as obstacles might have a foreclosing effect whereby a market which would otherwise develop does not develop because of the very existence of the contested rules. In this respect, it is irrelevant whether the person/company mounting the challenge is a domestic or out-of-State company. If the rule constitutes a disproportionate limitation on the right to exercise an economic activity, despite it not specifically affecting movement, then it needs to be removed because its very existence limits the possibility for out-of-State providers to exercise that economic activity. In other words, this is nothing more than another step in the private enforcement of Community law and in enhancing the useful effect of the Treaty.

Secondly, the very notion of wholly internal situation does not seem to hold. Once it is decided that mere foreign ownership of an otherwise domestic company, as in *Payroll*,[62] or mere belonging to a holding comprising companies in more than one Member State, as in *McQuen*,[63] is sufficient to trigger the Treaty, then it has to be recognized that in an internal market, at least potentially, any company might acquire intra-Community credentials through, for instance, change in ownership, merger etc. The same can be said for individuals who might well decide to change their place of residence.[64] Not to allow challenges because the situation at that

---

[62] Case C-79/01 *Payroll Data Services (Italy) et al* [2002] ECR I-8923.
[63] Case C-108/96 *McQuen* [2001] ECR I-837.
[64] Cf Case C-470/04 *N v Inspecteur van de Belastingdienst Oost/kantoor Almelo* [2006] ECR I-6409. There the Court, against the advice of AG Kokott, accepted that a mere change in the Member State of

particular point in time is confined to a single Member State leads to entirely arbitrary results. After all, in an internal market the existence of a 'potential' intra-Community element is inherent.[65]

Thirdly, and in relation to the above mentioned considerations, once we step outside intra-Community *specificity*, not to allow a challenge in internal situations is economically inefficient. Take the case of *CaixaBank*: the rules prohibiting remuneration of sight accounts did not affect *CaixaBank*,[66] the subsidiary of a Spanish bank, in any different way than they would have affected any new market entrant not having access to an established branch network. Now either those rules are in principle excluded from the scope of the Treaty, and do not require justification, or they fall within the scope of the Treaty and, if considered unjustified, need to be amended. Whilst the writer is firmly convinced that it should not be for the Court of Justice to make such an assessment, once we accept that such an assessment can be made in relation to a subsidiary of a foreign company, there is no reason why it should not also be made when the claimant is a domestic company/individual.

Therefore, once it is accepted (as a matter of fact) that the Treaty can be interpreted as prohibiting unjustified restrictions to the exercise of an economic activity in another Member State, then the scope of the purely internal situation should be reduced to the minimum; in fact it should be reserved to those cases where the effect of the rules under scrutiny is 'too uncertain and indirect' to warrant any scrutiny even under a broad interpretation of the Treaty free movement provisions, i.e. in those cases in which there is no connection between the rule and the ability to exercise an economic activity.

5. Conclusions

In the last two chapters, an attempt has been made to bring together different strands of case law to show both the impact that the introduction of Union citizenship has had on the free movement provisions and the similarities in the hermeneutic techniques adopted by the Court. But those similarities go far beyond a mere formalistic approach. The constitutional impact that those provisions have is also the same – and both free movement and Union citizenship rights are a vehicle to assert individual rights which do not necessarily have a clear connection with market integration. In this way, they concur in creating a new constitutional dimension.

One of the effects of Union citizenship is to reshape the notion of social solidarity, and to redefine the traditional link of belonging which justifies the

residence was enough to trigger Article 43 EC against the State of previous residence regardless of the fact that the person concerned was not engaging in an economic activity in his new state of residence.

[65] Cf also Case C-148/02 *Garcia Avello* [2003] ECR I-11613, where the Court relied on the potential willingness of the claimants' children to exercise their free movement rights in order to establish the intra-Community element necessary to trigger the Treaty.

[66] Case C-442/02 *Caixa-Bank* [2004] ECR I-8961.

imposition of mutual responsibilities between State and individual. This determines the emergence of 'new models of social solidarity – whose terms of reference are partly national, partly *communautaire*'.[67] Thus, Union citizens who traditionally would not be seen as sufficiently belonging to the host society to rely on its welfare might now become active claimants – albeit to a limited extent. The budgetary worries of the Member Sates, which clearly inspired the Residency Directives and – even though to a lesser degree – Directive 2004/38, need therefore partially to give way to the emergence of a new constitutional dimension.

Similarly, the consequence of the health care cases is partially to redefine, in the light of the general principles of Community law, the responsibilities that the Member States bear towards their citizens. Thus, the effect of the expansion of the scope of Article 49 EC is to impose upon the Member State substantive duties in ensuring effective health care provision, not only by allowing more choice to the citizen in the case of out-of-hospital treatment, but also by super-imposing conditions on the assessment of the criteria which need to be fulfilled to gain a right to be treated in a foreign hospital at the expense of the Member State of provenance. In this respect, for instance, Member States will not be able anymore to have recourse to waiting lists as an indirect means to control health expenditure. Again, the budgetary worries which inspired the system of prior authorization contained in Regulation 1408/71 need to evolve to accommodate the new constitutional developments.

But more fundamentally, the effect of Union citizenship and free movement is to afford an enhanced right to diffuse judicial scrutiny. As we have seen in the previous chapters, it is difficult to conceptualize even the 'economic' rights case law having regard to a market access model. Rather, starting in the 1990s there is a perceptible evolution of the free movement provisions. Thus, all constituent elements of the free movement provisions loosen up to the point of explosion; within a comparatively short amount of time, we witness the relaxation of the intra-Community element necessary to trigger the Treaty (*Sodemare*, *Gourmet*, *Freskot*, but also *McQuen* and *Payroll*); the relaxation of what is to be defined as barrier (the *Gebhard* case law as well as *Carpenter*); the relaxation of the economic element (*Peerobooms*). As a result, it becomes significantly easier for individuals to seek protection under Community law: this protection comes first and foremost by the obligation imposed on the national courts to assess not only the proportionality of the rules at issue in an abstract way, but also to assess whether the application of those rules to the particular circumstances of the case, to *that* particular individual, is proportionate.

The same is true in relation to the citizenship provisions: Articles 17 and 18 EC naturally make it easier for Union citizens to bring themselves within the personal scope of the Treaty. But also those provisions can be used not only to attack rules which might discriminate on grounds of nationality or residence, but

---

[67] M Dougan and E Spaventa 'Educating Rudy and the (non-)English patient: A double-bill on residency rights under Article18 EC' (2003) 28 ELRev 699, at 704.

also to attack rules which, whilst in themselves legitimate, might be inconsistent with the Treaty when applied to *that particular* individual, in those particular circumstances (e.g. *Baumbast* and *Avello*, but also *Bidar*).

Overall then, this case law not only impacts on the Member States' regulatory autonomy, but also on the Member States' regulatory practices, i.e. on the way the rules are applied to the particular circumstances of the case. And this development signals possibly the most important shift in the effect of the Court's assessment, no doubt due to the desire to maximize the effect of, and protection afforded by, Community law. Whilst in the case of indirect discrimination, the assessment is characterized by its *abstractness*, so that the potentiality of the rule to act at the disadvantage of migrants (even though not of *that* particular migrant) is enough to trigger the Treaty, once the discrimination line is crossed, the assessment becomes rooted in the particular facts of the case. Thus, the effect of this case law is to introduce the possibility of a sort of diffuse judicial review very similar in kind to that available in administrative law against acts of public authorities, where the scrutiny is usually on the facts of the particular case. In a way, then, the effect of this case law is to impact on the principle of general application of legislation: even in those cases in which the legislation is, in principle, compatible with the demands of Community law, its application to a particular individual might still be contrary to it. This is so even when the legislature has not left any discretion to the authority implementing the legislation. If such discretion is not conferred by national law, it is conferred by Community law, which not only *allows* the authority to assess the particular situation, but it *requires* it to do so.

This trend, the expansion of Community law to assess not only the compatibility of national rules with the principle of free movement in the abstract, but also on the *way* those rules impact on individual lives (with the consequent increase in protection), is visible also in other areas. Thus in the field of goods,[68] the Court has held that rules which in principle might be justified according to the mandatory requirements doctrine, might still fall foul of the Treaty because of the way they have been adopted.

The fundamental question that this book has attempted to answer is then how such pervasive constitutional effects of the Treaty free movement provisions can be normatively justified. Whilst the author is not entirely persuaded that the *Gebhard* turn was a sensible (or politically defensible) one, it seems that that case law is there to stay, since in the past ten years it has been confirmed by a number of full Court rulings. For this reason, it is crucial that a stronger normative basis is provided for the Court's interpretation and such basis can indeed be provided once we step beyond free movement orthodox thinking and we look at the broader picture. If we want to explain the case law on the free movement of persons then we have to look at all the hermeneutic tools adopted by the Court: the *Baumbast* stance that any limitation to a right granted by the Treaty needs to be justified, even when at first sight such limitation is consistent with secondary

[68] Case C-463/01 *Commission v Germany* (reusable packaging) [2004] ECR I-11705, esp. para 75; Case C-320/03 *Commission v Austria* (ban on heavy lorries) [2005] ECR I-9871, esp. para 90.

Community law; the notion of 'potentiality' in assessing a cross-border element; and the effect of Article 12 EC which should not be seen as protecting only those who have left their country of origin.

Thus, if we redefine the right granted by the Treaty free movement provisions as granting also a right to pursue an economic activity in another Member State, then any limitation to such a right, which is to say virtually any market regulation must comply with the general principles of Community law. Such interpretation is in line with (accepted) interpretation of Community law, according to which the very substance of a right granted by Community law, the reason why a right is granted in the first place, must be protected. In this respect, it is sufficient to recall the pervasive effect that Community law has had on national procedural autonomy, and once we understand the right granted by the Treaty as encompassing a right to exercise an economic activity, then virtually any market rule bears an intra-Community potential. And finally, if we understand the *Carpenter* ruling as belonging to the citizenship cases, then the combined effect of Articles 17 and 12 EC provide a satisfactory normative basis to justify that case.

Table of Cases

26/62 *Van Gend en Loos* [1963] ECR 1 – p. 1
13/63 *Italy v Commission* (French duties) [1963] ECR 337 – p. 17
75/63 *Hoekstra* [1964] ECR 1771 – p. 2
15/69 *Ugliola* [1969] ECR 363 – p. 6, 26

76/72 *Michel S* [1973] ECR 457 – p. 32
2/73 *Geddo* [1973] ECR 865 – p. 36
152/73 *Sotgiu* [1974] ECR 153 – p. 6, 16, 20
167/73 *Commission v France* (Code maritime) [1974] ECR 359 – p. 2
2/74 *Reyners* [1974] ECR 631 – p. 2, 7, 16, 18
8/74 *Procureur du Roi v Dassonville* [1974] ECR 837 – p. 36, 81
9/74 *Casagrande* [1974] ECR 773 – p. 32
33/74 *J H Van Bisbergen Bestuur van der Berdifsvereniging voor de Metaalnijverheid* [1974] ECR 1299 – p. 2, 11, 27, 28, 41, 80, 144
36/74 *Walrave and Koch* [1974] ECR 1405 – p. 6, 11, 66
39/75 *Coenen* [1975] ECR 1574 – p. 144
41/74 *Van Duyn* [1974] ECR 1337 – p. 18
67/74 *Bonsignore* [1975] ECR 297 – p. 13, 18
32/75 *Cristini* [1975] ECR 1085 – p. 28
36/75 *Rutili* [1975] ECR 1219 – p. 13, 14
39/75 *Coenen* [1975] ECR 1575 – p. 25
48/75 *Royer* [1976] ECR 497 – p. 4, 6
118/75 *L Watson and A Belmann* [1976] ECR 1185 – p. 117
13/76 *G Doná v M Mantero* [1976] ECR 1333 – p. 8, 66
63/76 *Inzirillo* [1976] ECR 2057 – p. 28
71/76 *Thieffry* [1977] ECR 765 – p. 25
90/76 *Henry van Ameyde* [1977] ECR 1091 – p. 16, 27
8/77 *C Sagulo, G Brenca et A Bakhouche* [1977] ECR 1495 – p. 117
11/77 *Patrick* [1977] ECR 1199 – p. 25

30/77 *Bouchereau* [1977] ECR 1999 – p. 13, 18
15/78 *Koestler* [1978] ECR 1971 – p. 27, 144
16/78 *Criminal proceedings against M Choquet* [1978] ECR 2293 – p. 103
110 and 111/78 *van Wesemael* [1979] ECR 35 – p. 27, 144
115/78 *Knoors* [1979] ECR 399 – p. 22
120/78 *Rewe-Zentrale AG v Bundesmonopolverwaltung für Branntwein* (Cassis de Dijon) [1979] ECR 649 – p. 36, 81
207/78 *Even* [1979] ECR 2019 – p. 29
15/79 *Groenveld* [1979] ECR 3409 – p. 45
34/79 *Henn and Darby* [1979] ECR 3795 – p. 19, 94, 105
52/79 *Debauve* [1980] ECR 833 – p. 27, 144
157/79 *Pieck* [1980] ECR 2171 – p. 15, 117

97/80 *Jenkins* [1981] ECR 911 – p. 20
113/80 *Commission v Ireland* (Irish souvenirs) [1981] ECR 1625 – p. 36
155/80 *Oebel* [1981] ECR 1993; Case 75/81 *JHT Blegsen v Belgium* [1982] ECR 1211 – p. 38
244/80 *Foglia v Novello* (No 2) [1981] ECR I-3045 – p. 151
279/80 *Webb* [1981] ECR 3305 – p. 27, 144
53/81 *Levin* [1982] ECR 1035 – p. 2, 3
62 and 63/81 *Seco SA and Desquenne & Giral SA* [1982] ECR 223 – p. 25, 144
65/81 *Reina* [1982] ECR 33 – p. 28
115 and 116/81 *Adoui and Cornuaille* [1982] ECR 1665 – p. 13, 18
240/81 *Senta Einberger v Hauptzollamt Freiburg* [1982] ECR 3699 – p. 11
286/81 *Criminal Proceedings against Oosthoek's Uitgeversmaatschappij Bv* [1982] ECR 4575 – p. 38
35 and 36/82 *Morson and Jhanjan* [1982] ECR 3723 – p. 6
59/82 *Schutzverband Gegen Unwesen I D Wirtschaft v Weinvertriebs-GMBH* [1983] ECR 1224 – p. 36
237/82 *J Kaas BV et al v Dutch Government Central Organ Zuivelkontrole* [1984] ECR 483 – p. 45, 97
286/82 and 26/83 *Luisi and Carbone* [1984] ECR 377 – p. 11, 22
293/82 *Gravier* [1985] ECR 593 – p. 22, 138
294/82 *Senta Einberger v Hauptzollamt Freiburg* [1984] ECR 1177 – p. 11
107/83 *Ordre des Avocats au Barreau de Paris v O Klopp* [1984] ECR 2971 – p. 20, 103, 145
182/83 *Fearon & Co.* [1984] ECR 3677 – p. 16
229/83 *Association de Centres Distributeurs Edouard Leclerc and others v Sàrl 'Au Blé vert' and Others* [1985] ECR 1 – p. 36
267/83 *Diatta* [1985] ECR 567 – p. 31
270/83 *Commission v France* (Shareholders' tax credits) [1986] ECR 273 – p. 17, 25
293/83 *Gravier v City of Liège* [1985] ECR 379 – p. 8, 138
60 and 61/84 *Cinéthèque SA and others v Fédération Nationale des Cinéma Français* [1985] ECR 2605 – p. 38
197/84 *P Steinhauser v City of Biarritz* [1985] ECR 1819 – p. 9
205/84 *Commission v Germany* (Insurance) [1986] ECR 3755 – p. 19, 42

300/84 *A J M van Roosmalen v Bestuur van de Bedrijfsvereniging voor de Gezondheid, Geestelijke en Maatschappelijke Belangen* [1986] ECR 3097 – p. 8

59/85 *Reed* [1986] ECR 1283 – p. 29, 30
66/85 *Lawrie-Blum* [1986] ECR 2121 – p. 3
79/85 *Segers* [1986] ECR 2375 – p. 7
139/85 *Kempf* [1986] ECR 1741 – p. 3
221/85 *Commission v Belgium* (Clinical biology laboratories) [1987] ECR 719 – p. 24
225/85 *Commission v Italy* (CNR) [1987] ECR 2625 – p. 18
316/85 *Lebon* [1987] ECR 2811 – p. 28
352/85 *Bond van Adverteenders and others v The Netherlands* [1988] ECR 2085 – p. 8, 11, 18, 52, 56
427/85 *Commission v Germany* (Restrictions on lawyers) [1988] ECR 1123 – p. 27

24/86 *Blaizot* [1988] ECR 379 – p. 8, 138
63/86 *Commission v Italy* (Social housing) [1988] ECR I-29 – p. 9
196/86 *Steymann v Staatssecretaris van Justitie* [1988] ECR 2085 – p. 8
197/86 *Brown* [1988] ECR 3205 – p. 3, 117
198/86 *Conradi* [1987] ECR 4469 – p. 24
222/86 *Heylens* [1987] ECR 4097 – p. 25
263/86 *Belgium v Humbel and M T Edel* [1988] ECR 5365 – p. 8, 50
292/86 *Gullung* [1988] ECR 111 – p. 24

42/87 *Commission v Belgium* [1988] ECR I-5445 – p. 138
81/87 *Daily Mail* [1988] ECR 593 – p. 22
143/87 *Stanton v INASTI* [1988] ECR 3877 – p. 23, 25
186/87 *Cowan v Trésor Public* [1989] ECR 195 – p. 9, 29,114
196/87 *Steymann* [1988] ECR 6159 – p. 3
298/87 *Smanor* [1988] ECR 4489 – p. 150
344/87 *Bettray* [1989] ECR 1621 – p. 3
379/87 *Groener* [1989] ECR 3967 – p. 26, 28
382/87 *R Buet and Educational Business Services v Ministère Public* [1989] ECR 1235 – p. 38, 107
389 and 390/87 *Echternach and Moritz* [1989] ECR 723 – p. 32

C-21/88 *Du Pont de Nemours Italiana* [1990] ECR I-889 – p. 19
C-33/88 *Allué and Coonan* [1989] ECR I-1591 – p. 26
C-47/88 *Commission v Denmark* [1990] ECR I-4509 – p. 91
C-145/88 *Torfaen Borough Council v B & Q plc* [1989] ECR I-3851 – p. 38, 39
C-177/88 *Dekker* [1990] ECR I-3941 – p. 18
C-265/88 *Messner* [1989] ECR 4209 – p. 18, 117
C-306/88 *Rochdale Borough Council v Steward John Anders* [1992] ECR I-6458 – p. 38
C-362/88 *GB-INNO-BM v Confédération du Commerce Luxembourgois* [1990] ECR I-667 – p. 38, 47

C-23/89 *Quietlynn Ltd and B J Richards v Southend Borough Council* [1990] ECR I-3059 – p. 38
C-61/89 *Bouchoucha* [1990] ECR I-3551 – p. 22, 69
C-149/89 *Commission v France* (Tourist guides) [1991] ECR I-659 – p. 11
C-260/89 *ERT* [1991] ECR I-2925 – p. 13
C-279/89 *Commission v UK* (Factortame 2) [1992] ECR I-5785 – p. 17
C-288/89 *Stichting Collectieve Antennevoorziening Gouda and Others v Comissariaat voor de Media* [1991] ECR I-4007 – p. 26, 42, 78, 146
C-292/89 ex parte *Antonissen* [1991] ECR-745 – p. 4, 5, 137
C-312/89 *Union départementale des syndicats CGT de l'Aisne v SIDEF Conforama and others* [1991] ECR I-997 – p. 38
C-332/89 *Criminal Proceedings against A Merchandise et al* [1991] I-1027 – p. 38
C-340/89 *Vlassopoulou* [1991] ECR I-2357 – p. 25, 28, 64, 103
C-350/89 *Sheptonhurst Ltd v Newnham Borough Council* [1991] ECR I-2387 – p. 38
C-357/89 *Raulin* [1992] ECR I-1027 – p. 3
C-360/89 *Commission v Italy* (Award of public works contracts) [1992] ECR I-340 – p. 19
C-76/90 *M Säger v Dennemeyer & Co. Ltd* [1991] ECR I-4221 – p. 26, 42, 78
C-159/90 *Society for the Protection of Unborn Children v Grogan* [1991] ECR I-4685 – p. 8, 10
C-204/90 *Bachmann* [1992] ECR I-249 – p. 19
C-239/90 *SCP Boscher, Studer and Fromentin v Sa British Motors Wright and others* [1991] ECR I-2023 – p. 38
C-370/90 *The Queen v Immigration Appeal Tribunal et Surinder Singh,* ex parte *Secretary of State for Home Department* [1992] ECR I-4265 – p. 6, 22, 23, 24, 49
C-106/91 *Ramrath* [1992] ECR I-3351 – p. 20
C-111/91 *Commission v Luxembourg* (childbirth and maternity allowances) [1993] ECR I-817 – p. 24
C-126/91 *Schutzverband gegen Unwesen in der Wirtschaft e.V. v Yves Rocher GmbH* [1993] ECR I-2361 – p. 38
C-159 and 160/91 *Poucet v Assurances Generales de France (AGF) and Caisse Mutuelle Regionale du Languedoc-Roussillon* and *Pistre v Caisse Autonome Nationale de Compensation de l'Assurance Vieillesse des Artisans* [1993] ECR I-637 – p. 8, 10, 55
C-165/91 *Van Munster* [1994] ECR I-4661 – p. 23, 72
C-168/91 *Konstantinidis v Stadt Altensteig, Standesamt und Landratsamt Calw, Ordnungsamt* [1993] ECR I-1191 – p. 28, 49, 124, 127
C-169/91 *Council of the City of Stoke-on-Trent and Norwich City Council v B & Q plc* [1992] ECR I-6635 – p. 38
C-211/91 *Commission v Belgium* (Access to cable television networks) [1992] ECR I-6757 – p. 18 – 19
C-264/91 *ICI v Colmer* [1998] ECR I-4695 – p. 18
C-267/91 and C-268/91 *Keck and Mithouard* [1993] ECR I-6097 – p. 40, 81, 94
C-330/91 ex parte *Commerzbank* [1993] ECR I-4017 – p. 17, 25
C-19/92 *Dieter Kraus v Land Baden-Württemberg* [1993] ECR I-1663 – p. 99, 103
C-17/92 *Fedecine* [1993] ECR I-2239 – p. 18
C-19/92 *Kraus* [1993] ECR I-1663 – p. 7, 22, 64

C-102/92 *Wirth v Landeshauptstadt Hannover* [1993] ECR I-6447 – p. 8, 50
C-275/92 *HM Customs Excise v Schindler* [1994]
ECR I-1039 – p. 10, 19, 43, 47, 92, 105, 145
C-292/92 *R Hünnermund and others v Landesapothekerkammer Baden-Wurttemberg*
[1993] ECR I-6787 – p. 82, 96, 102
C-319/92 *Haim I* [1994] ECR I-425 – p. 7
C-379/92 *Peralta* [1994] ECR I-3453 – p. 44, 46
C-391/92 *Commission v Greece* (processed milk for infants) [1995]
ECR I-1621 – p. 7
C-401 and 402/92 *Tankstation't' Heukske and Boermans* [1994] ECR I-2199 – p. 82
C-419/92 *Scholz* [1994] ECR I-505 – p. 26

C-1/93 *Halliburton* [1994] ECR I-1137 – p. 25
C-18/93 *Corsica Ferries* [1994] ECR I-1783 – p. 46
C-45/93 *Commission v Spain* (Museum admission) [1994] ECR I-911 – p. 9, 29, 114
C-55/93 *Van Schaik* [1994] ECR I-4837 – p. 19
C-279/93 *Schumaker* [1995] ECR I-225 – p. 25
C-384/93 *Alpine Investments BV v Minister van Financiën* [1995]
ECR I-1141 – p. 11, 44, 46, 81, 91
C-412/93 *Société d'importation Éduard Leclerc-Siplec v TF1 Publicité SA* [1995] ECR
I-179 – p. 40, 75, 89, 94, 95
C-415/93 *Union Royal Belge des Sociétés de Football Association ASBL v Jean-Marc Bosman* [1995] ECR I-4921 – p. 12, 64, 66, 80, 83, 91, 97, 147
C-418/93 et al. *Semeraro Casa Uno* [1996] ECR I-2975 – p. 82
C-443/93 *Ioannis Vougioukas v Idryma Koinonikon Asfalisseon (IKA)* [1995]
ECR I-4033 – p. 26
C-470/93 *Mars* [1995] ECR I-1923 – p. 85
C-484/93 *Svensson and Gustavsson* [1995] ECR I-3955 – p. 19

C-5/94 *Hedley Lomas* [1996] ECR I-2553 – p. 45
C-7/94 *Gaal* [1996] ECR I-1031 – p. 32
C-55/94 *Gebhard v Consiglio dell'Ordine degli Avvocati e Procuratori di Milano* [1995]
ECR I-4165 – p. 7, 63, 64, 65, 78, 80, 83, 92, 99, 101
C-80/94 *Wielockx* [1995] ECR I-2493 – p. 25
C-101/94 *Commission v Italy* (Dealing in transferable securities) [1996]
ECR I-2691 – p. 20, 103
C-107/94 *Asscher* [1996] ECR I-3089 – p. 25
C-173/94 *Commission v Belgium* (Employment in the public sector) [1996]
ECR I-3265 – p. 18
C-193/94 *Skanavi* [1996] ECR I-929 – p. 29, 117
C-237/94 *O'Flynn* [1996] ECR I-2617 – p. 22, 23, 24
C-278/94 *Commission v Belgium* [1996] ECR I-4307 – p. 5, 137
C-315/94 *de Vos* [1996] ECR I-1417 – p. 29
C-321 to 324/94 *Pistre and others* [1997] ECR I-2343 – p. 150
C-336/94 *Dafeki* [1997] ECR I-6761 – p. 29

C-18/95 *Terhoeve* [1999] ECR I-345 – p. 22, 72
C-34 to 36/95 *Konsumentombudsmannen (KO) v De Agostini (Svenska) Förlag AB and TV Shop I Sverige AB* [1997] ECR I-3843 – p. 92, 146
C-70/95 *Sodemare Sa and others v Regione Lombardia* [1997] ECR I-3395 – p. 10, 45, 50, 83
C-120/95 *Decker* [1998] ECR I-1831 – p. 10, 45, 50, 83
C-189/95 *Franzén* [1997] ECR I-5909 – p. 40, 41, 77
C-344/95 *Commission v Belgium* [1997] ECR I-1035 – p. 4
C-388/95 *Belgium v Spain* (Rioja) [2000] ECR I-3123 – p. 45, 97
C-398/95 *SETTG v Ypurgos Ergasias* [1997] ECR I-3091 – p. 19, 150
C-15/96 *Kalliope Schöning* [1998] ECR I-47 – p. 26
C-51/96 and C-191/97 *C Deliège v Ligue Francophone de Judo et Disciplines Associées ASBL et al* [2000] ECR I-2549 – p. 67, 68, 104
C-85/96 *M M Martínez Sala v Freistaat Bayern* [1998] ECR I-2691 – p. 115, 116, 137
C-108/96 *D McQuen et al v Grandivision Belgium SA* [2001] ECR I-837 – p. 69, 83, 92, 100, 101, 106, 147, 152
C-118/96 *Safir* [1998] ECR I-1897 – p. 19
C-122/96 *Saldanha* [1997] ECR I-5323 – p. 29
C-158/96 *R Kohll v Union des Caisses de Maladie* [1998] ECR I-1931 – p. 10, 19, 42, 50, 51
C-176/96 *Jiry Lehtonen, Castors Canada Dry Namur-Braine ASBL v Fédération Royale Belge des Sociétés de Basket-ball ASBL* [2000] ECR I-2681 – p. 66, 67, 68, 80, 104
C-184/96 *Commission v France* (Foie gras) [1998] ECR I-6197 – p. 81
C-274/96 *Bickel and Franz* [1998] ECR I-1121 – p. 29, 114, 116, 131
C-336/96 *Gilly* [1998] ECR I-2793 – p. 21
C-348/96 *D Calfa* [1999] ECR I-11 – p. 13, 14, 18
C-350/96 *Clean Car* [1998] ECR I-2521 – p. 3
C-124/97 *Läärä* [1999] ECR I-6067 – p. 43
C-167/97 *Seymour-Smith* [1999] ECR I-623 – p. 22
C-224/97 *E Ciola v Land Voralberg* [1999] ECR-I2517 – p. 11, 19, 46, 100
C-255/97 *Pfeiffer Groβhandel GmbH v Löwa Warenhandel GmbH* [1999] ECR I-2835
C-262/97 *Engelbrecht* [2000] ECR I-732 – p. 66, 68
C-307/97 *Compagnie de Saint-Gobain* [1999] ECR I-6161 – p. 25
C-337/97 *Meussen* [1999] ECR I-3289 – p. 28
C-378/97 *F A Wijsenbeek* [1999] ECR I-6207 – p. 115, 117
C-391/97 *Gschwind* [1999] ECR I-5451 – p. 25
C-424/97 *S Haim v Kassenzahnärztliche Vereinigung Nordrhein* (Haim I) [2000] ECR I-5123 – p. 26, 68

C-55/98 *Skatteministeriet* [1999] ECR I-7641 – p. 19
C-58/98 *Corsten* [2000] ECR I-7919 – p. 66, 101
C-67/98 *Zenatti* [1999] ECR I-7289 – p. 43
C-190/98 *V Graf v Filzmoser Maschinenbau GmbH* [2000] ECR I-437 – p. 23, 66, 67, 92, 102, 131, 147
C-195/98 *Österreichischer Gewerkschaftsbund* [2000] ECR I-10497 – p. 26
C-200/98 *X AB, X AC v Riksskatteverket* [1999] ECR I-8261 – p. 25

C-203/98 *Commission v Belgium* (Registration for aircrafts) [1999] ECR I-4899 – p. 29
C-220/98 *Estée Lauder v Lancaster* [2000] ECR I-117 – p. 85
C-224/98 *M N D'Hoop v Office national d'emploi* [2002] ECR I-6191 – p. 23, 119, 129
C-254/98 *TK-Heimdienst* [2000] ECR I-2487 – p. 82, 128, 150
C-281/98 *Angonese* [2000] ECR I-4139 – p. 6, 7, 11
C-302/98 *Sehrer* [2000] ECR I-4585 – p. 23
C-324/98 *Telaustria and Telefonadress* [2000] ECR I-10745 – p. 151
C-356/98 *Kaba* (No. 1) [2000] ECR I-2623 – p. 17, 21, 141
C-367/98 *Commission v Portugal* (Golden shares) [2002] ECR I-4732 – p. 70, 101, 147
C-368/98 *Abdon Vanbraekel and others v Alliance nationale des mutualités chrétiennes* [2001] ECR I-5363 – p. 10, 19, 50, 139
C-397/98 and C-410/98 *Metallgesellchaft Ltd and Others* [2001] ECR I-1727 – p. 25
C-376/98 *Germany v Parliament and Council* (Tobacco Advertising) [2000] ECR I-8419 – p. 87, 110
C-405/98 *Konsumentombudsmannen (KO) v Gourmet International Products AB (GIP)* [2001] ECR I-1795 – p. 8, 11, 41, 46, 83, 92, 94, 100, 149
C-411/98 *A Ferlini v Centre Hospitalier de Luxembourg* [2000] ECR I-8081 – p. 29, 113
C-448/98 *Guimont* [2000] ECR I-10663 – p. 150

C-23/99 *Commission v France* (Spare parts for motor vehicles) [2000] ECR I-7653 – p. 36
C-87/99 *Zurstrassen* [2000] ECR I-3337 – p. 25
C-124/99 *Borawitz* [2000] ECR I-7293 – p. 23, 72
C-135/99 *U Elsen v Bundesversicherungsanstalt für Angestellte* [2000] ECR I-10409 – p. 72, 117, 138
C-157/99 *B S M Geraets-Smits v Stichting Ziekenfonds VGZ* and *Peerbooms v Stichting CZ Groep Zorgverzekeringen* [2001] ECR I-5473 – p. 10, 19, 50, 51, 52
C-184/99 *R Grzelczyk v Centre public d'aide social d'Ottignies-Louvain-la-Neuve* [2001] ECR I-6193 – p. 115, 117, 118, 131, 137
C-205/99 *Asociación Profesional de Empresas Navieras de Líneas Regulares (Analir) and Others v Administración General del Estado* [2001] ECR I-1271 – p. 59
C-264/99 *Commission v Italy* (Haulage) [2000] ECR I-4417 – p. 101
C-268/99 *Jany* [2001] ECRI-8615 – p. 7
C-451/99 *Cura Anlagen GmbH* [2002] ECR I-3193 – p. 108
C-459/99 *Mouvement contre le racisme, l'antisémitisme et la xénophobie (MRAX) ASBL v Belgium* [2002] ECR I-6591 – p. 12, 31, 140
C-385/99 *Müller-Fauré v Onderlinge Waarborgmaatschappij OZ Zorgverzekeringen UA*, and *van Riet v Onderlinge Waarborgmaatschappi ZAO Zorgverzekeringen* [2003] ECR I-4509 – p. 10, 19, 50, 53, 57, 59, 139
Case C-413/99 *Baumbast and R v Secretary of State for the Home Department* [2002] ECR I-7091 – p. 15, 31, 32, 120, 122
C-430 and 431/99 *Sea-Land Service Inc and Nedlloyd Lijnen BV* [2002] ECR I-5235 – p. 21
C-459/99 *MRAX* [2002] ECR I-6591 – p. 12, 31, 140
C-483/99 *Commission v France* (Golden shares) [2002] ECR I-4781 – p. 70, 101, 147
C-493/99 *Commission v Germany* (Restrictions on the construction industry) [2001] ECR I-8163 – p. 19

C-503/99 *Commission v Belgium* (Golden shares) [2002] ECR I-4809 – p. 70, 101, 147
C-515/99, C-519/99 to C-524/99 and C-526/99 to C-540/99 *Reisch and others* [2002] ECR I-2157 – p. 148, 150

C-17/00 *De Coster* [2001] ECR I-9445 – p. 73, 148
C-50/00 *Unión de Pequeños Agricultores v Counci* [2002] ECR I-6677 – p. 130
C-60/00 *Carpenter v Secretary of State for the Home Department* [2002] ECR I-6279 – p. 11, 13, 48, 49, 80, 83, 86, 93, 126–128, 135, 140
C-112/00 *Schmidberger* [2003] ECR I-5659 – p. 1, 41, 85
C-134/00 *Viacom Outdoor* Srl [2005] ECR I-1167 – p. 73
C-218/00 *Cisal di Battistello Venanzio & C. Sas v Istituto Nazionale per l'assicurazione contro gli infortuni sul lavoro (INAIL)* [2002] ECR 691 – p. 10, 55
C-224/00 *Commission v Italy* (Fines for road offences) [2002] ECR I-2965 – p. 29
C-257/00 *Givane* [2003] ECR I-345 – p. 141
C-294/00 *Deutsche Paracelsus Schulen für Naturheilverfaharen GmbH v K Gräbner* [2002] I-6515 – p. 65, 69, 100, 101, 107, 147
C-324/00 *Lankhorst-Hohorst GmbH* [2002] ECR I-11779 – p. 25
C-326/00 *Idryma Koinonikon Asfaliseon (IKA) v Vasilios Ioannidis* [2003] ECR I-1703 – p. 139
C-355/00 *Freskot* [2003] ECR I-5263 – p. 47, 80, 83, 93, 101, 149
C-385/00 *de Groot* [2002] ECR I-4517 – p. 25
C-466/00 *Kaba* (No. 2) [2003] ECR I-2219 – p. 141

C-6/01 *Anomar and others* [2003] ECR I-8621 – p. 43, 151
C-34/01 to C-38/01 *Enirisorse Spa* [2003] ECR I-14243 – p. 148
C-56/01 *Patricia Inizan* [2003] ECR I-12403 – p. 10, 50, 60, 140
C-79/01 *Payroll Data Services (Italy) et al* [2002] ECR I-8923 – p. 65, 69, 83, 86, 100, 101, 106, 147, 149, 152
C-98/01 *Commission v UK* (BAA golden share) [2003] ECR I-4641 – p. 70, 71, 83, 93, 101, 107, 147
C-100/01 *Olazabal* [2002] ECR I-10981 – p. 13, 14
C-109/01 *Akrich* [2003] ECR I-9607 – p. 3, 31, 48, 128, 132, 140
C-234/01 *Gerritse* [2003] ECR I-5933 – p. 25, 72
C-264/01, C-306/01, C-354/01 and C-355/01 *AOK Bundesverband and others v Ichthyol-Gesellschaft Cordes and others*, [2004] ECR I-2493 – p. 10, 55
C-243/01 *Gambelli and others* [2003] ECR I-13031 – p. 43
C-300/01 *Salzmann* [2003] ECR I-4899 – p. 150
C-322/01 *Deutscher Apothekerverband eV v 0800 DocMorris NV* [2003] ECR I-14887 – p. 90
C-383/01 *De Danske Billimportører* [2003] ECR I-6065 – p. 148
C-387/01 *Weigel* [2004] ECR I-9445 – p. 72
C-388/01 *Commission v Italy* (Italian museums) [2003] ECR I-721 – p. 9, 29, 114
C-405/01 *Colegio de Oficiales de la Marina Mercante Española* [2003] ECR I-10391 – p. 18
C-413/01 *Ninni-Orasche* [2003] ECR I-13187 – p. 3

C-463/01 *Commission v Germany* (reusable packaging) [2004] ECR I-11705 – p. 135, 155
C-482/01 and 493/01 *Orfanopoulos and Olivieri* [2004] ECR I-5257 – p. 13, 138
C-502/01 and C-31/02 *Gaumain Cerri and Barth* [2004] ECR I-6483 – p. 130, 138

C-8/02 *Leichte* ECR I-2641 – p. 19, 56
C-36/02 *Omega* [2004] ECR I-9609 – p. 43
C-47/02 *Anker and others* [2003] ECR I-10447 – p. 18
C-71/02 *Karner* [2004] ECR I-3025 – p. 150
C-138/02 *Collins* [2004] ECR I-2703 – p. 4, 5, 121, 122, 137
C-148/02 *Garcia Avello* [2003] ECR I-11613 – p. 17, 124, 130, 131, 153
C-200/02 *Chen* [2004] ECR I-9925 – p. 122, 123
C-224/02 *Pusa* [2004] ECR I-5763 – p. 72, 119, 125
C-365/02 *Lindfords* [2004] ECR I-7183 – p. 25, 72
C-386/02 *Baldinger* [2004] ECR I-8411 – p. 29, 121
C-442/02 *Caixa-Bank* [2004] ECR I-8961 – p. 65, 69, 83, 86, 92, 93, 101, 102, 147, 153
C-456/02 *Trojani* [2004] ECR I-7573 – p. 3, 118, 121, 122
C-464/02 *Commission v Denmark* [2005] ECR I-7929 – p. 24

C-20/03 *Burmanjer and others* [2005] ECR I-4133 – p. 82, 90
C-104/03 *Commission v Greece* (opticians) [2005] ECR I-3177 – p. 103
C-134/03 *Viacom Outdoor* [2005] ECR I-1167 – p. 43, 148
C-145/03 *Keller* [2005] ECR I-2529 – p. 58
C-147/03 *Commission v Austria* (University admissions) [2005] ECR I-5969 – p. 138
C-169/03 *Wallentin* [2004] ECR I-6443 – p. 17, 25
C-209/03 *Bidar* [2005] ECR I-2119 – p. 119, 131, 142
C-227/03 *A. J. van Pommeren-Bourgondiën* [2005] ECR I-6101 – p. 72
C-278/03 *Commission v Italy* (teaching staff) [2005] ECR I-3747 – p. 26
C-231/03 *Coname* [2005] ECR I-7287 – p. 151
C-320/03 *Commission v Austria* (ban on heavy lorries) [2005] ECR I-9871 – p. 153, 155
C-403/03 *Schempp* [2005] ECR I-6421 – p. 25, 72, 125
C-446/03 *Marks and Spencer* [2005] ECR I-10837 – p. 25
C-458/03 *Parking Brixen* [2005] ECR I-8612 – p. 151
C-513/03 *van Hilten-van der Heijden* [2006] ECR I-1957 – p. 148
C-544 and C-545/03 *Mobistar* [2005] ECR I-7723 – p. 73

C-8/04 *Leichtle* [2004] ECR I-2641 – p. 10, 50
C-39/04 *Laboratoires Fournier SA* [2005] ECR I-2057 – p. 19
C-94/04 and 224/04 *Cipolla v Fazari*, and *Macrino and Capodarte v Meloni*, judgment of 5/12/06, nyr – p. 151
C-96/04 *Standesamt Stadt Niebüll* [2006] ECR I-3561 – p. 125
C-109/04 *Kranemann* [2005] ECR I-2421 – p. 24
C-174/04 *Commission v Italy* (gas and electricity) [2005] ECR I-4933 – p. 71
C-213/04 *Burtscher* [2005] ECR I-10309 – p. 71, 93, 101, 107, 148
C-258/04 *Ioannidis* [2005] ECR I-8275 – p. 5, 137, 141

C-282 and 283/04 *Commission v Netherlands* (Golden shares in the telecommunication sector) [2006] ECR I-9141 – p. 70, 147
C-300/04 *Eman and Sevinger* [2006] ECR I-8055 – p. 130
C-372/04 *Watts* [2006] ECR I-4325 – p. 10, 19, 50, 53
C-338/04, C-359/04 and 360/04 *Placanica, Palazzese, e Sorrichio*, judgment 06/03/07, nyr – p. 43
C-386/04 *Centro di Musicologia Walter Stauffer v Finanzamt München für Körperschaften*, judgment of 14/09/06, nyr – p. 4, 7
C-406/04 *De Cuyper* [2006] ECR I-6947 – p. 72, 119, 125
C-410/04 *ANAV* [2006] ECR I-3303 – p. 151
C-441/04 *A-Punkt Schmuckhandel v Schmidt* [2006] ECR I-2043 – p. 82
C-470/04 *N v Inspecteur van de Belastingdienst Oost/kantoor Almelo*, judgment of 07/09/06, nyr – p. 152
C-520/04 *Turpeinen* [2006] ECR I-10685 – p. 125

C-1/05 *Yunying Jia v Migrationsverket*, judgment of 09/01/07, nyr – p. 31, 132
C-76/05 *Schwarz*, case pending, opinion delivered 21/09/06 – p. 57
C-112/05 *Commission v Germany* (Volkswagen), case pending – p. 70
C-170/05 *Denkavit International BV* [2006] ECR I-11949 – p. 25
C-318/05 *Commission v Germany*, opinion delivered 21/09/06, case pending – p. 57, 125
C-438/05 *The International Transport Workers' Federation et al v Viking Line APB et al.*, case pending – p. 1
C-444/05 *Aikaterini Stamatelaki v Organismos Asfaliseos Eleftheron Epangelmation (O.A.E.E.)*, opinion delivered 11/01/07, case pending – p. 53
C-466/05 *Damonte*, case pending – p. 44
C-192/05 *Tas-Hagen and Tas* [2006] ECR I-10451 – p. 29, 30, 72, 119, 121, 125, 131
C-11 and 12/06 *Morgan and Bucher*, Opinion delivered 20 March 2007, case pending – p. 50, 151

Pending Cases

Commission v UK, Commission's case reference number 2005/2281, Press Release IP/06/864 of 10/07/2006 – p. 4

Non EC Cases

Griggs v Duke Power 401 US 424 (1971) – p. 20
Italian Constitutional Court 30 December 1997, n. 443 – p. 128

Selected Bibliography

A Acierno 'The *Carpenter* judgement: fundamental rights and the limits of the Community legal order' (2003) 28 ELRev 398.

P Alston (ed) *The EU and Human* Rights, OUP, Oxford, 1999.

M Andenas and W H Roth *Services and Free Movement in EU Law*, OUP, Oxford, 2002.

K Armstrong 'Mutual Recognition' in C Barnard and J Scott (eds) *The Law of the Single European Market. Unpacking the premises* (Hart, Oxford, 2002), 225–267.

A Arnull 'What shall we do on Sunday?' (1991) 16 ELRev 112.

A Arnull, A A Dashwood, M Dougan, M Ross, E Spaventa and D Wyatt *Wyatt and Dashwood's EU Law*, 5th ed., Sweet and Maxwell, London, 2006.

Y Art 'Legislative Lacunae, the Court of Justice and Freedom to Provide Services'.

C Barnard 'Fitting the remaining pieces into the goods and persons jigsaw?' (2001) 26 ELRev 34.

C Barnard and J Scott (eds) *The Law of the Single European Market. Unpacking the premises.*, Hart Publishing, Oxford, 2002.

C Barnard and S Deakin 'Market Access and Regulatory Competition' in C Barnard and J Scott (eds) *The Law of the Single European Market. Unpacking the premises.* (Hart, Oxford, 2002), 197.

C Barnard *The Substantive Law of the EU – The Four Freedoms* (OUP, Oxford, 2004).

C Barnard 'EU Citizenship and the Principle of Solidarity' in M Dougan and E Spaventa *Social Welfare and EU Law* (Hart Publishing, Oxford, 2005), Ch. 8.

C Barnard 'Annotation on *Bidar*' (2005) 42 CMLRev 1465.

R C Béraud 'Les mesures d'effet équivalent au sens des articles 30 et suivants du Traité de Rome' (1968) 3 RTDE 265.

N Bernard 'Discrimination and Free movement in EC Law' (1996) 45 ICLQ 82.

N Bernard 'La libre circulation des marchandises, des personnes et des services dans le Traité CE sous l'angle de la compétence' (1998) 33 CDE 11.

N Bernard *Multi Level Governance*, Kluwer Law International, The Hague, 2002.

A Biondi 'Advertising alcohol and the free movement principle: the *Gourmet* decision' (2001) 26 ELRev 616.

A Biondi 'Recurring Cycles in the Internal Market: Some Reflections on the Free Movement of Services' in A Arnull, P Eeckhout and T Tridimas, *Liber Amicorum Jacobs* (Oxford, OUP, Forthcoming).

J Black *Oxford Dictionary of Economics*, OUP Oxford, 2nd ed., 2002.

P Cabral 'Cross-Border Medical Care in Europe: Bringing Down a First Wall' (1999) 24 ELRev 387.

R Cornelissen 'The Principle of Territoriality and the Community Regulations on Social Security' (1996) 33 CMLRev 439.

P Craig and G de Búrca *EU Law*, OUP, Oxford 3rd ed., 2002.

P Craig 'The Evolution of the Single Market' in C Barnard and J Scott (eds) *The Law of the Single European Market. Unpacking the premises.* (Hart, Oxford, 2002), 1.

D Curtin and D O'Keeffe (eds) *Constitutional Adjudication in European Community and National Law* (Butterworths, Dublin, 1992), 121.

L Daniele 'Non-discriminatory restrictions to the free movement of persons' (1997) 22 ELRev 191.

A A Dashwood and S O'Leary (eds) *The Principle of Equal Treatment in EC Law*, Sweet & Maxwell London, 1997.

G Davies 'Welfare as a Service' (2002) 29 LIEI 27.

G Davies *Nationality Discrimination in the European Internal Marker,* Kluwer Law International, the Hague, 2003.

G Davies 'Can selling arrangements be harmonised' (2005) ELRev 370.

G Davies ' "Any place I hang my hat?" or: residence is the new nationality' (2005) 11 ELJ 43.

G Davies 'Competition, Free Movement and Consumers of Public Services' (2006) 17 EBL Rev 95.

R W Davis 'Citizenship of the Union ... Rights for All' (2002) 27 ELRev 121.

A Dawes ' "Bonjour Herr Doctor": national health care systems, the internal market and cross-border medical care within the European Union' (2006) 33 LIEI 167.

T M de Boer (ed) *Forty years on: the Evolution of Postwar Private International Law in Europe*, Kluwer Law International, Amsterdam, 1990.

G de Búrca 'The Principle of Proportionality and its Application in EC Law' (1993) YEL 105.

G de Búrca 'The Role of Equal Treatment in European Community Law' in A A Dashwood and S O'Leary (eds) *The Principle of Equal Treatment in EC Law* (Sweet & Maxwell, London, 1997), 13.

G de Búrca 'Unpacking the Concept of Discrimination in EC and International Trade Law' in C Barnard and J Scott (eds) *The Law of the Single European Market. Unpacking the premises.* (Hart, Oxford, 2002), 181.

G de Búrca (ed) *EU Law and the Welfare State. In Search of* Solidarity, OUP, Oxford, 2005.

L de Novellis *L'unificazione economica dell'Europa* (Fratelli Treves Editori Milano 1931).

U Djuberg 'Historic decision lifts restrictions on commercial advertising in Sweden' (2003) 27 *European Lawyer* 13.

H U J D'Oliveira 'The Community Case – Is Reverse Discrimination Still Permissible Under the Single European Act?' in T M de Boer (ed) *Forty years on: the Evolution of Postwar Private International Law in Europe*, Kluwer Law International, Amsterdam, 1990, 71.

M Dougan and E Spaventa 'Educating Rudy and the (non-)English patient: A double-bill on residency rights under Article18 EC' (2003) 28 ELRev 699.

M Dougan and E Spaventa ' "Wish You Weren't Here . . . " New Models of Social Solidarity in the European Union' in M Dougan and E Spaventa *Social Welfare and EU Law* (Hart publishing, Oxford, 2005), 181.

M Dougan and E Spaventa *Social Welfare and EU Law*, Hart Publishing, Oxford, 2005.

M Dougan 'Fees, grants, loans and dole cheques: who covers the costs of migrant education within the EU?' (2005) 42 CMLRev 943.

M Dougan 'The Constitutional Dimension to the case law on Union citizenship' (2006) 31 ELRev 613.

S Douglas-Scott 'In Search of Union Citizenship' (1998) 18 YEL 29.

E Edward 'Establishment and Services: an Analysis of the Insurance Cases' (1987) 12 ELRev 231.

D Esty and D Geradin (eds), *Regulatory Competition and Economic Integration: Comparative Perspectives* (OUP, Oxford, 2001).

U Everling 'Sur la jurisprudence récente de la Cour de Justice en matière de libre prestation des services rendues dans d'autres Etats membres' (1984) 19 CDE 3.

M Everson 'The Legacy of the Market Citizen' in J Shaw and G More (ed) *New Legal Dynamics of the European Union* (Clarendon Press, Oxford, 1995), 73.

J Feenstra 'Annotation of *Gouda*' (1993) 30 CMLRev 425.

F E Foldovary *Dictionary of free market economics*, Edward Elgar Publishing Inc, Northampton Massachusetts USA, 1998.

S Fredman 'Combating Racism with Human Rights: the Right to Equality' in Fredman S (ed) *Discrimination and Human Rights. The Case of Racism* (Oxford, OUP, 2001), 9.

S Fredman (ed) *Discrimination and Human Rights. The Case of Racism*, Oxford, OUP, 2001.

M Fuchs 'Free Movement of Services and Social Services: Quo Vadis?' (2002) 8 ELJ 536.

L Goffin 'Liberté d'établissement et égalité de traitement ou un avocat peut-il 's'établir' sans être inscrit à l'ordre professionnel? (A propos de l'arrêt *Gebhard*)' (1996) 31 CDE 723.

O Golynker 'Jobseekers' rights in the European Union: challenges of changing the paradigm of social solidarity' (2005) 30 ELRev 111.

O Golynker 'Student Loans: the European concept of social justice according to *Bidar*' (2006) 31 ELRev 390.

L Gormley 'Recent Case Law on the Free Movement of Goods: Some Hot Potatoes' (1990) 27 CMLRev 825.

E Guild *The Legal Elements of EU Identity: EU Citizenship and Migration Law*, Kluwer Law International, The Hague, 2004.

K Hailbronner 'Union citizenship and access to social benefits' (2005) 42 CMLRev 1245.

J L Hansen 'Full Circle: Is there a Difference between the Freedom of Establishment and the Freedom to Provide Services?' in M Andenas and W H Roth (eds) *Services and Free Movement in EU Law* (OUP, Oxford, 2002), 197.

V Hatzopoulos 'Killing the National Health Systems but Healing the Patients? The European market for health care after the judgement of the ECJ in *Vanbraekel* and *Peerbooms*' (2002) 39 CMLRev 683.

T Hervey 'Mapping the Contours of European Union Health Law and Policy' (2002) 8 EPL 69.

C Hilson 'Discrimination in Community free movement law' (1999) 24 ELRev 445.

A Illiopoulou and H Toner 'A new approach to discrimination against free movers? *D'Hoop v Office National de l'Emploi*' (2003) 28 ELRev 389.

C Jacqueson 'Union citizenship and the Court of Justice: something new under the sun? Towards social citizenship' (2002) 27 ELRev 260.

E Johnson and D O'Keeffe 'From discrimination to obstacles to free movement: Recent developments concerning the free movement of workers 1989–1994' (1994) 31 CMLRev 1313.

R Joliet 'The Free Circulation of Goods: the *Keck and Mithouard* decision and the new directions in the case law' (1995) 1 Columbia J Eur L 436.

E I Kaldellis 'Freedom of Establishment versus Freedom to Provide Services: An Evaluation of Case-Law Developments in the area of Indistinctly Applicable Rules' (2001) 28 LIEI 23.

P Koutrakos 'On Groceries, Alcohol and Olive Oil: More on the Free Movement of Goods after *Keck*' (2001) 26 ELRev 391.

P Koutrakos 'Healthcare as an economic service' in M Dougan and E Spaventa (eds) *Social Welfare and EU Law* (Hart Publishing, Oxford, 2005), Ch. 5.

R Lane and N Shuibhne 'Annotation on *Angonese*' (2000) 37 CMLRev 1237.

K Lenaerts 'L'égalité de traitement en droit communautaire' (1991) 26 CDE 3.

J Lombay 'Annotation on *Gebhard*' (1996) 33 CMLRev 1073.

G Marenco 'Pour une interprétation traditionnelle de la notion de mesure d'effet équivalant à une restriction quantitative' (1984) CDE 291.

D Martin '«Discriminations», «Entraves» et «Raisons Impérieuses» dans le Traité CE: Trois Concepts en Quête D'Indentité', (1998) 33 CDE 261 and 561.

E Meehan *Citizenship and the European* Community, Sage Publications, 1993.

J Meulman and H de Waele 'A Retreat from *Säger*? Servicing or Fine-Tuning the Application of Article 49 EC' (2006) 33 LIEI 207.

J Montgomery 'Impact of European Union Law on English Healthcare Law' in M Dougan and E Spaventa (eds) *Social Welfare and EU Law* (Hart Publishing, Oxford, 2005), Ch. 7.

K Mortelmans 'Article 30 of the EEC Treaty and Legislation Relating to Market Circumstances: Time to Consider a New Definition?' (1991) 28 CMLRev 115.

K Mortelmans 'The Relationship between the Treaty Rules and Community Measures for the Establishment and Functioning of the Internal Market – Towards a Concordance Rule' (2002) 39 CMLRev 1303.

D O'Keeffe 'Union Citizenship' in D O'Keeffe and P M Twomey (eds) *Legal Issues of the Maastricht Treaty* (Chancery Law, London, 1994), Ch. 6.

D O'Keeffe and P M Twomey (eds) *Legal Issues of the Maastricht Treaty* (Chancery Law, London, 1994).

D O'Keeffe and M Horspool 'European Citizenship and the Free Movement of Persons' (1996) 31 The Irish Jurist 145.

S O'Leary 'The Relationship between Community Citizenship and the Protection of Fundamental Rights in Community Law' (1995) 32 CMLRev 519.

S O'Leary *The Evolving Concept of Community Citizenship,* Kluwer Law International, The Hague 1996.

S O'Leary 'Putting flesh on the bones of European Union citizenship' (1999) 24 ELRev 68.

P Oliver and W H Roth 'The internal market and the four freedoms' (2004) 41 CMLRev 407.

H Oosterom-Staples (2005) 42 'Annotation on *Collins*' (2005) 42 CMLRev 205.

M Poiares Maduro *We, the Court,* Hart Publishing, Oxford, 1998.

M Poiares Maduro 'The Saga of Article 30 of the Treaty: To Be Continued' (1998) 5 MJ 298.

M Poiares Maduro 'Striking the Elusive Balance Between Economic Freedom and Fundamental Rights' in P Alston (ed) *The EU and Human Rights* (OUP, Oxford, 1999).

U K Preuß 'Problems of a Concept of European Citizenship' (1995) 1 ELJ 267.

A Rosas and E Antola (eds) *A Citizens' Europe: in search of a new order* (Sage Publications, London, 1995).

W H Roth 'Annotation of *Kraus*' (1993) 30 CMLRev 1251.

W H Roth 'The European Court of Justice's Case Law on Freedom to Provide Services: Is *Keck* Relevant?' in M Andenas and W H Roth *Services and Free Movement in EU Law* (OUP, Oxford, 2002), 1.

J Shaw and G More (ed) *New Legal Dynamics of the European Union*, Clarendon Press, Oxford, 1995.

J Shaw 'The Many Past and Futures of Citizenship in the European Union' (1997) 22 ELRev 554.

J Snell *Goods and Services in EC Law*, OUP, Oxford, 2002.

J Snell 'Who's Got the Power: Free Movement and Allocation of Competences in EC Law' (2003) YEL 323.

E Spaventa 'Annotation on *TK-Heimdienst*' (2000) 37 CMLRev 1265.

E Spaventa 'On Discrimination and the Theory of Mandatory Requirements' (2000) 3 CYELS 457.

E Spaventa 'Public Services and European Law: Looking for Boundaries' (2002–3) 5 CYELS 271.

E Spaventa 'From *Gebhard* to *Carpenter*: towards a (non-)Economic European Constitution' (2004) 41 CMLRev 743.

E Spaventa 'Annotation on *Akrich*' (2005) 42 CMLRev 225.

E Spaventa 'Annotation on *Caixa-Bank*' (2005) 42 CMLRev 1151.

J Steiner 'Drawing the line: Uses and Abuses of Article 30 EEC' (1992) 29 CMLRev 749.

E Steyger 'National Health Care Systems Under Fire (but not too heavily)' (1999) 29 LIEI 97.

G Straetmans 'Annotation on *Gourmet*' (2002) 39 CMLRev 1407.

N Shuibhne 'Free movement of persons and the wholly internal rule: time to move on?' (2002) 39 CMLRev 731.

S van den Bogaert 'The Court of Justice on the Tatami: Ippon, Waza-Ari or Koka' (2000) 25 ELRev 554.

A P van der Mei 'Cross-border access to medical care in the European Union – some reflections on the judgments in *Decker* and *Kohll*' (1998) 5 MJ 277.

A P van der Mei 'Cross-border access to medical care in the European Union – some reflections on *Garaets-Smits* and *Peerbooms* and *Vanbraekel*' (2002) 9 MJ 189.

A P van der Mei 'EU Law and Education: Promotion of Student Mobility versus Protection of Education Systems' in M Dougan and E Spaventa (eds) *Social Welfare and EU Law* (Hart Publishing, Oxford, 2005), Ch. 10.

W van Gerven 'The Right of Establishment and free Supply of Services within the Common Market' (1965–66) 2 CMLRev 344.

S Weatherill 'After *Keck*: some thoughts on how to clarify the clarification' (1996) 33 CMLRev 885.

S Weatherill 'Annotation on *Bosman*' (1996) 33 CMLRev 991.

S Weatherill 'Recent case law concerning the free movement of goods: mapping the frontiers of market deregulation' (1999) 36 CMLRev 51.

S Weatherill 'Pre-emption, Harmonisation and the Distribution of Competence to Regulate the Market' in C Barnard and J Scott (eds) *The Law of the Single European Market. Unpacking the premises.* (Hart, Oxford, 2002), 41.

E L White 'In Search of the Limits to Article 30 of the EEC Treaty' (1989) CMLRev 235.

R C A White 'Free Movement, Equal Treatment and Citizenship of the Union' 54 (2005) ICLQ 885.

R C A White *Workers, Establishment and Services in the European Union* (OUP, Oxford, 2004).

B Wilkinson 'Towards European Citizenship? Nationality, Discrimination and Free Movement of Workers in the European Union' (1995) 1 EPL 417.

W P J Wils 'The Search for the rule in Article 30 EEC: much ado about nothing?' (1993) ELRev 475.

D Wyatt 'Constitutional Significance of the Tobacco Advertising Judgment of the European Court of Justice' in *The ECJ's Tobacco Advertising Judgment* (CELS Occasional Paper No. 5, Cambridge, 2001).

D Wyatt 'Community Competence to Regulate Medical Services' in M Dougan and E Spaventa *Social Welfare and EU Law* (Hart Publishing, 2005), 131.

LEGISLATION

Regulation 1612/68 on freedom of movement for workers within the Community OJ Sp. Ed. 1968 L257/2, p. 475.

Directive 68/360 on the abolition of restrictions on movement and residence within the Community for workers of Member States and their families [1968(I)] OJ Sp. Ed. 485.

Commission Directive 70/50/EEC on the abolition of measures which have an effect equivalent to restriction on imports and are not covered by other provisions adopted in pursuance of the EEC Treaty, OJ Sp. Ed. 1970, I no. L13/29, p. 17.

Council Regulation (EEC) 1408/71 on the application of social security schemes to employed persons, to self-employed persons ad to members of their families moving within the Community, as amended. Consolidated version [1997] OJ L28/1, and <http://www.europa.eu.int/eur-lex/en/consleg/pdf/1971/en_1971R1408_do_001.pdf?>.

Directive 73/148 on the abolition of restrictions on movement and residence within the Community for nationals of Member States with regard to establishment and the provision of services [1973] OJ L 172/14.

Directive 76/207 on the implementation of the principle of equal treatment for men and women as regards access to employment, vocational training and promotion and working conditions [1976] OJ L 39/40 (the Directive has been amended by Directive 2002/73 [2002] OJ L 269/15).

Directive 77/249 to facilitate the effective exercise by lawyers of freedom to provide services [1977] OJ L 78/17.

Directive 90/364 on the right of residence [1990] OJ L 180/26.

Directive 90/365 on the right of residence for employees and self-employed persons who have ceased their occupational activity [1990] OJ L 180/28.

Directive 93/96 on the right of residence for students [1993] OJ L 317/59.

Directive 2000/43 implementing the principle of equal treatment between persons irrespective of racial and ethnic origin [2000] OJ L 180/22.

Directive 2000/78 establishing a general framework for equal treatment in employment and occupation [2000] OJ L 303/16.

Regulation 539/2001 listing the third countries whose nationals must be in possession of visas when crossing the external borders of Member States and those whose nationals are exempt from that requirement [2001] OJ L 81/1.

Treaty concerning the Accession of the Czech Republic, Estonia, Cyprus, Latvia, Lithuania, Hungary, Malta, Poland, Slovenia and Slovakia, [2003] OJ 236/803.

Directive 2004/17 coordinating the procurement procedures of entities operating in the water, energy, transport and postal services sectors OJ L 134/1.

Directive 2004/18 on the coordination of procedures for the award of public works contracts, public supply contracts and public service contracts OJ L 134/114.

Directive 2004/38 on the right of citizens of the Union and their family members to move and reside freely within the territory of the Member States amending Regulation (EEC) No 1612/68 and repealing Directives 64/221/EEC, 68/360/EEC, 72/194/EEC, 73/148/EEC, 75/34/EEC, 75/35/EEC, 90/364/EEC, 90/365/EEC and 93/96/EEC [2004] OJ L 229/35.

Regulation (EC) 883/2004 on the co-ordination of social security systems [2004] OJ L 166/1.

Treaty concerning the accession of the Republic of Bulgaria and Romania to the European Union [2005] OJ L 157/1.

Directive 2005/36 on the recognition of professional qualifications [2005] OJ L 255/22.

Directive 2006/123 on services in the internal market [2006] OJ L 376/36.

LEGISLATIVE PROPOSALS

Proposal for a directive on services in the internal market COM(2006) 160 final.

Proposal for a Council Regulation amending Regulation 539/2001 (2006) COM 84 final Commission's Proposal for a Regulation of the European Parliament and the

Council laying down the procedure for implementing Regulation (EC) 883/2004 on the co-ordination of social security systems, COM(2006)16 final.

OTHER DOCUMENTS

Communication from the Commission concerning the consequences of the judgement given by the Court of Justice on 20 February in case 120/78 ('Cassis de Dijon'), [1980] OJ C 256/2.

Commission's Communication on certain aspects concerning intra-EU investments [1997] OJ C 220/15.

Commission interpretative communication on the Community law applicable to contract awards not or not fully subject to the provisions of the Public Procurement directives, (2006) OJ C 179/2.

Employment, Social Policy, Health and Consumer Affairs Council Conclusions *Council Conclusions on Common values and principles in EU Health systems*, Luxembourg 1 and 2 June.

European Parliament Press Release *Services of General Interest: Legal Clarity the Key*, 12 September 2006.

Index

A

Advertisement 8, 46, 47, 79, 92–94, 96, 97
Advocate General 9, 52, 94, 102–105
Akrich 3, 31, 48, 128, 132, 133, 140
Alpine 44, 45, 47, 79, 82, 91, 97
Anti-discrimination provision 22
Application, scope of 2, 8–10, 21, 29, 68, 90, 100, 103, 116, 129, 131, 137, 138
Approach
  broad 67, 68, 70, 71, 75, 143
  narrow 75–77, 84, 86, 88, 89
Arrangements, selling 40, 45, 66, 77, 79, 82, 86, 89, 90, 94–96, 110
Authorities, national 59, 141
Authorization requirement 53, 54, 58, 59, 139
  prior 50–53, 58, 59, 139

B

Ban
  absolute 19, 105, 144, 145
  total 46, 76, 77, 84, 92, 96, 97
Bar, local 64, 65, 99
Barrier
  absolute 18, 105, 146
  frontier 76
  potential 38, 94
Baumbast 15, 31, 32, 115, 117, 120–123, 135, 136, 142, 143, 146, 155
Belgium 4, 5, 8, 13, 18, 24, 29, 38, 45, 70, 97, 101, 117–119, 122, 124, 137–140
Benefits, welfare 29, 118, 119, 121, 137, 141
Bernard 21, 23, 41, 75, 77, 79–83, 85, 111
Bernard Multi Level Governance 75, 80–82
Bidar 119, 120, 131, 141–143, 155
Bilateral Treaty 116
Bosman 6, 12, 64, 66, 67, 80, 83, 91, 97, 104, 108, 109, 147
Bouchereau 13, 18
Boundaries 35, 39, 40, 50, 57, 67, 84, 90, 108, 140
British immigration rules 23, 48, 49, 126, 128, 129
Burtscher 71, 93, 101, 107, 108, 148

C

Caixa-Bank 65, 69, 70, 83, 86, 87, 92, 93, 101, 102, 106, 108, 109, 111, 147, 153
Capital, free movement of 70, 71, 101, 147, 148
Carpenter
  case 87, 115, 126
  exercises 49, 126
  ruling 127, 156
  situation 132

Case law
  citizenship 143
  consistent 16–18, 22, 24, 66
  existing 60
  explicit 11
  post-Keck 79
  strands of 142, 153
Cassis 36, 37, 81
Chen 122, 123
Citizenship provisions 115, 116, 124, 132, 136, 138, 154
Coherent Theory of free movement 135, 137, 139, 141, 143, 145, 147, 149, 151, 153, 155
Collins 4, 5, 121, 122, 137, 141, 143
Commission interpretative communication 151
Commission's Communication 70
Community
  competence 71, 87, 131
  economic migrant 140
  free movement law 77
  law
    general principles of 13, 32, 49, 120–122, 127, 130, 133, 136, 140, 143, 146, 154, 156
    purposes 3, 30, 32
    scope of 49, 121, 125, 127, 128, 133, 150
  legislature 85, 88, 111
  market 92, 95, 107
  migrant workers 9
Company, domestic 149, 151–153
Consumer protection grounds 38, 43, 45
Court
  adopted teleological reasoning 151
  of Justice 37, 42, 68, 84, 116, 153
Court's
  analysis 54, 98
  approach 83, 96, 105, 110
  assessment 9, 43, 85, 148, 155
  case law 74, 76, 81, 111, 135, 140
  considerations 102
  decision 73, 77
  discourse 145
  hermeneutic 61
  interpretation 1, 35, 58, 64, 88, 100, 101, 110, 136, 137, 141, 149, 155
  reasoning 7, 9, 23, 51, 56, 67, 68, 84, 94, 107, 124, 145
  ruling 49, 87, 127
  scrutiny 45, 106, 107
Cowan 9, 29, 114

D

Davies Nationality Discrimination 16, 20, 75, 79
De Agostini 8, 43, 92, 146
Deliège 67, 68, 104, 107, 108
Discrimination
  approach 80, 90, 91
  direct 16–18
  material 25, 77
  matérielle 77
  prohibiting 21
  prohibition of 21, 23, 30, 124, 129
Discriminatory
  approach 39, 76, 78, 80, 88, 94, 110, 144
  measures 76, 77
  provisions 20, 27
  restrictions 26, 27, 39, 64, 69, 78, 90, 107
    prohibited 77
  rules 18, 24, 29, 76, 77, 84, 88, 90, 95, 97, 100, 102, 109, 138
    applying 100
  taxation 21, 24, 25, 148
  test 73, 85, 95
  treatment 23
Double burden theory 25, 42, 78, 79, 100
Dougan 5, 10, 12, 18, 54, 58, 88, 110, 114–116, 119, 121, 141, 154

E

EC Law 16, 21, 23, 37, 75, 77–79, 85–87, 91, 111
EC rules 7
EC Treaty 46, 87, 122
Economic
  activity
    exercise of 107, 149, 150
    regulating 144
  migrants 1–3, 5, 7, 9, 11, 13–15, 17, 19, 21, 23, 25, 27–33, 63, 135, 137
    status of 15

EEC Treaty 36, 39, 40
Elements
  cross-border 6, 7, 11, 46, 124, 127, 130, 145, 149, 150, 156
  redistributive 54, 55
Equal treatment
  of non-comparable situations 17, 77
  obligation 30, 115, 123, 132
  rights 120
Establishment
  case law 63
  country of 82
  freedom of 2, 6, 16, 28, 46, 63–65, 69–71, 80, 84, 88, 96, 98, 101, 102, 105, 109
  provisions 26, 98, 100
  requirement 18, 19
  rules 82
  state of 78–80, 82
EU Citizenship 116
EU Law 10, 54, 58, 84, 85, 109, 110, 115, 116, 119
European Court of Justice 84, 85, 110, 131
European Union 10, 11, 50, 109, 111, 115, 116, 121
Exercise
  of Community competence 71, 131
  of fundamental freedoms 65, 99

F

Filzmoser Maschinenbau GmbH 92, 102, 103, 131
Football Association 66, 80, 83, 91, 97
Foreigners 17, 18, 22, 23, 26, 29, 46, 65, 72, 77, 78, 83, 85, 99, 100, 128, 152
Framework 20, 25, 50, 75, 77–79, 81–83, 85, 87, 91, 92, 114, 127, 134, 145, 147
France 2, 9–11, 14, 17, 25, 36, 53–55, 69, 70, 81, 82, 87, 92, 101, 117, 119, 139
Free movement
  law 2, 17, 22
    comparability 21
  orthodox thinking 155
  orthodoxy, traditional 136
  of persons provisions 2, 7, 11, 36, 111
  provisions 1, 2, 8, 12, 29, 30, 32, 35, 36, 67, 68, 71, 72, 74–77, 79–81, 83–88, 90, 91, 104, 105, 108–111, 134, 135
  rights 22, 101, 119, 123, 125, 129, 134, 146, 153
  rules 66, 90
Freedom of movement 6, 16, 68, 117
Freskot 47–49, 80, 83, 93, 101, 106, 109, 111, 149–151, 154

G

Garcia Avello 17, 124, 125, 130, 131, 153
Gebhard
  approach 66, 68, 69, 80, 88, 101, 102, 109
  case law 92, 98, 100, 104, 143, 154
  formula 65, 66, 71
  ruling 69, 80, 102
Geraets-Smits 10, 50–52
Germany 13, 19, 23, 24, 27, 42, 51, 57, 64, 70, 78, 87, 102, 116, 117, 125, 138
GIP 8, 11, 41, 46–49, 79, 83, 92, 94, 98, 100, 101, 106, 108, 109, 111, 149–151, 154
Goods, free movement of 19, 27, 35, 36, 40, 41, 81, 85, 92, 135, 148, 150
Grant, maintenance 118–120, 132, 142
Grzelczyk 115, 117–120, 131, 137

H

Health
  effective 57, 154
  provider 50, 55, 56
  services 52, 55, 56
  systems 51
  treatment 54, 120
Home Department 80, 83, 93, 120, 122, 126, 127
Hospitals 51, 52, 55, 58, 60, 61
Host State 15, 16, 27, 30, 60, 66, 78, 86, 99, 101, 102, 105, 113, 118, 132, 142, 144
Human Rights 20, 127, 133, 137, 141

I

Immigration rules 23, 123
  harsher 24
Imperative requirements doctrine 10, 18–20, 65, 66, 69, 76, 78, 81, 94

Imported products 37, 40, 41, 79, 81, 90, 91, 94, 96
Indirect discrimination 16–18, 20, 22, 24, 26, 32, 35, 43, 72, 76, 78, 116, 144, 155
  interpretation of 24, 42, 78
Insurance
  fund 52, 54, 55
  services 48
    social 45
Interpretation of Community law 150, 151, 156
Intra-Community
  element 7, 35, 49, 60, 149, 150, 153, 154
  trade 36–40, 49, 60, 74, 81, 83–85, 87, 89, 95–97

J

Justifications
  normative 75, 76, 88, 111, 135, 136
  objective 20, 21, 120, 126

K

Keck 40, 41, 66, 75, 79, 81, 82, 88, 94–98, 107, 110
  ruling 35, 36, 40, 41, 45, 77, 81, 86, 94
Kohll 10, 19, 42, 50–52, 54–56
Kraus 7, 22, 64, 99, 103

L

Labour market 3, 11, 67, 92, 93, 137
Luxembourg 10, 19, 24, 54, 55, 113

M

Maastricht Treaty 115
Market
  deregulation 85
  domestic 12, 92, 93, 101
  foreign 90–92, 101
  internal 6, 10, 17, 23, 26, 36, 41, 43, 50, 60, 76, 86, 87, 100, 101, 105, 106, 152, 153
  regulation 1, 70, 74, 85, 109, 135, 146, 147, 156
  rules 63, 146, 156
Market access
  approach 88, 90–92, 104, 108
  test 41, 67, 73, 76, 88–92, 94, 96, 98, 102, 107, 108, 110, 135
Market Circumstances 39
McQuen 83, 92, 100, 106, 108, 147, 149, 151, 152, 154
Member States
  of destination 41, 79, 81, 106
  of establishment 11, 26, 27, 43–48, 60, 63, 65, 79, 83, 86, 100, 101, 106
  host 15, 26, 42, 45, 100, 146
  importing 79
  recipient 26, 27, 44, 45, 79
  request 105
  result 101
  single 115, 153
Movement, intra-Community 49, 58, 71, 102, 104, 107
Movement-neutral 99
Movement provisions 92
  economic free 72, 123, 136, 137, 142–144
Movement-related barrier, free 96
Movement rights 4, 125
  economic free 134
Mutual recognition 26, 27, 37, 69, 75, 77, 80, 81, 83, 84, 106, 109
  approach 44, 77, 79–81, 83, 86, 106

N

National
  courts 13, 32, 38, 42, 43, 48, 53, 59, 64, 69, 84, 92, 116, 133, 139, 140, 150, 151
  rules 37, 38, 42, 76, 84, 87, 107, 109, 119, 123, 131, 144
    challenged 102
    compatibility of 37, 155
    disputed 39
  territory 25, 28, 29, 50, 55, 57
NHS
  treatment 53, 54
NHS-type systems 52–55
Non-discrimination 17, 21, 27, 29, 58, 116, 129–131, 151
  obligation 8, 9, 131
Non-discriminatory 16, 21, 42, 43, 45, 65, 66, 69, 71, 79, 82, 89, 94, 97, 105

assessment 91, 100, 101
barriers 1, 6, 23, 35, 42, 63, 64, 73, 85, 94, 98, 103, 135, 142, 150, 152
cases 84
obstacles 73, 152
restrictions 24, 26, 37, 45, 60, 64, 65, 76, 79, 83, 90, 97, 102
court scrutinized 103
path 64
rules 38, 60, 65, 67, 71, 73, 74, 86, 92, 96, 152
tax 73
taxation 148

O

Operators, economic 18, 28, 43, 80, 82, 83, 94, 135, 149, 152

P

Payroll Data Services 65, 69, 83, 86, 100, 101, 106, 147, 149, 152
Post-Gebhard Case Law 68
Proportionality assessment 26, 41, 48, 67, 74, 84, 87, 99, 101, 107, 110
Providers
domestic 26, 27, 54, 86, 149
foreign 27, 47, 54, 56
out-of-state 145

R

Regulatory competences 77, 81, 82, 85, 87, 88, 96, 105
Residence
permanent 120, 142
requirement 16–19, 24, 27, 72, 78, 116, 138, 144
rights 132
Residence Directives 114, 118, 120, 121, 131, 141
Restrictions
abolition of 5–7, 15, 16
formal 102–104
territorial 13, 14
Reverse discrimination 6, 24, 97, 126–128, 130, 150
abolition of 133
elimination of 115, 129, 132, 133
Rights
citizenship 2, 15, 136
of economic migrants 3, 5, 7, 9, 11, 13, 15, 17, 19, 21, 23, 25, 27, 29, 31
fundamental 1, 13, 32, 35, 49, 85, 116, 122, 126–128, 133, 136, 137, 140, 141, 143, 146
residency 116, 121, 141, 154
voting 71, 130

S

Schempp 25, 72, 125
Schindler 10, 19, 43, 44, 47, 92, 97, 105, 145
Scholarship 37, 40, 50, 74, 77, 85, 88, 89, 96, 130, 143, 144
Scope rationae materiae 116, 119, 121, 125
Secondary legislation 25, 30, 72, 118, 120–122, 139–141
provisions of 139, 140
Service
providers 15, 27, 42–44, 47–49, 66, 78, 99, 100, 106, 126, 127, 144
prevented 92
domestic 100
temporary 101
provisions 47, 52, 127
intra-Community 144
recipients 15, 30, 114
Services
cross-border provision of 48, 49, 100
economic 9, 10, 54–56
free movement of 13, 18, 26, 33, 35, 37, 39, 41–43, 45, 47, 49–51, 53–55, 57, 59–61, 148
intra-Community 35, 92
patent renewal 42, 78
provisions of 9, 15, 41, 44, 45, 47, 49, 52, 53, 63, 73, 76, 79, 105, 106
public 10, 12, 18, 32, 50, 51, 57
Shares 28, 70, 71, 90, 93, 103, 147
Situation
comparable 17, 21, 25, 72, 77, 124, 132
internal 11, 127–129, 131, 149, 150, 152, 153
intra-Community 47, 60, 98, 99, 102, 109, 152

State of establishment 11, 19, 42, 44, 101, 102, 150
Students 15, 114, 118, 120, 132, 138, 142
Subsidiaries 7, 69, 70, 106, 153
Support 9, 76, 77, 80, 88–91, 94, 105, 108, 122
Sweden 43, 46, 79, 84, 92, 93
System of compulsory insurance 47, 48, 93, 101

T

Tas-Hagen 29, 30, 72, 119, 121, 125, 131
Tax rules 4, 17, 25, 73, 108, 148
  national 73
Taxation 11, 28, 43, 53, 71, 72, 99, 125, 148
Territory 4, 9, 12, 14, 24, 31, 46, 55, 81, 82, 86, 99, 120, 121, 130, 132, 140
Test 18, 36, 39, 65, 84, 89–91, 94, 95, 97, 102, 104, 107, 108, 110
Tourists 9, 113, 114
Traders 69, 82, 90, 95, 96
Treatment
  effective 57
  emergency 120
  equal 5, 8, 9, 16–18, 20, 25, 28, 32, 105, 113, 114, 116, 118–123, 129, 130, 137, 141–143, 150, 151
  holistic 51
  hospital 53, 58, 59
  out-of-hospital 139, 140, 154
  received 139
  reimburse 51, 57
Treaty
  derogations 4, 10, 13, 18, 32, 76
  free movement provisions 16, 22, 32, 41, 76, 86, 89, 109, 114, 127, 129, 131, 135, 139, 140, 155, 156
  freedoms 27–29, 49, 60, 90, 102, 119, 127
  provisions 2, 23, 27, 29, 36, 47, 57, 72, 77, 78, 87, 104, 140, 151

U

Union citizens 3, 4, 6, 10, 12–16, 29–32, 114–118, 121–125, 129–133, 137, 138, 140–145, 154
  active 120, 121, 142
Union Citizenship 113, 115–117, 119, 121, 123, 125, 127, 129, 131, 133, 137
Union citizenship, effect of 117, 131, 153, 154
United Kingdom 4, 23, 24, 70, 87, 120, 122, 128, 140

V

Vanbraekel 10, 19, 50, 139

W

Watts 10, 19, 50, 53, 54, 57, 59
Weatherill 12, 40, 75, 85, 94, 96–98
Welfare provision 3, 5, 28, 118, 121
Welfare State 114, 115
Work-seekers 4, 5, 28, 121, 122, 137, 141, 142
Workers
  free movement of 2, 61, 63–65, 67, 69, 71, 73, 96, 98, 115, 129, 137, 147
  migrant 6, 23, 30, 117, 119
Wyatt 5, 12, 18, 110